INFORMATION BROKERING ACROSS HETEROGENEOUS DIGITAL DATA

A Metadata-based Approach

The Kluwer International Series on
ADVANCES IN DATABASE SYSTEMS

Series Editor
Ahmed K. Elmagarmid

Purdue University
West Lafayette, IN 47907

Other books in the Series:

DATA DISSEMINATION IN WIRELESS COMPUTING ENVIRONMENTS, *Kian-Lee Tan and Beng Chin Ooi*; ISBN: 0-7923-7866-0

MIDDLEWARE NETWORKS: Concept, Design and Deployment of Internet Infrastructure, *Michah Lerner, George Vanecek, Nino Vidovic, Dad Vrsalovic;* ISBN: 0-7923-7840-7

ADVANCED DATABASE INDEXING, *Yannis Manolopoulos, Yannis Theodoridis, Vassilis J. Tsotras;* ISBN: 0-7923-7716-8

MULTILEVEL SECURE TRANSACTION PROCESSING, *Vijay Atluri, Sushil Jajodia, Binto George* ISBN: 0-7923-7702-8

FUZZY LOGIC IN DATA MODELING, *Guoqing Chen* ISBN: 0-7923-8253-6

INTERCONNECTING HETEROGENEOUS INFORMATION SYSTEMS, *Athman Bouguettaya, Boualem Benatallah, Ahmed Elmagarmid* ISBN: 0-7923-8216-1

FOUNDATIONS OF KNOWLEDGE SYSTEMS: With Applications to Databases and Agents, *Gerd Wagner* ISBN: 0-7923-8212-9

DATABASE RECOVERY, *Vijay Kumar, Sang H. Son* ISBN: 0-7923-8192-0

PARALLEL, OBJECT-ORIENTED, AND ACTIVE KNOWLEDGE BASE SYSTEMS, *Ioannis Vlahavas, Nick Bassiliades* ISBN: 0-7923-8117-3

DATA MANAGEMENT FOR MOBILE COMPUTING, *Evaggelia Pitoura, George Samaras* ISBN: 0-7923-8053-3

MINING VERY LARGE DATABASES WITH PARALLEL PROCESSING, *Alex A. Freitas, Simon H. Lavington* ISBN: 0-7923-8048-7

INDEXING TECHNIQUES FOR ADVANCED DATABASE SYSTEMS, *Elisa Bertino, Beng Chin Ooi, Ron Sacks-Davis, Kian-Lee Tan, Justin Zobel, Boris Shidlovsky, Barbara Catania* ISBN: 0-7923-9985-4

INDEX DATA STRUCTURES IN OBJECT-ORIENTED DATABASES, *Thomas A. Mueck, Martin L. Polaschek* ISBN: 0-7923-9971-4

DATABASE ISSUES IN GEOGRAPHIC INFORMATION SYSTEMS, *Nabil R. Adam, Aryya Gangopadhyay* ISBN: 0-7923-9924-2

VIDEO DATABASE SYSTEMS: Issues, Products, and Applications, *Ahmed K. Elmagarmid, Haitao Jiang, Abdelsalam A. Helal, Anupam Joshi, Magdy Ahmed* ISBN: 0-7923-9872-6

REPLICATION TECHNIQUES IN DISTRIBUTED SYSTEMS, *Abdelsalam A. Helal, Abdelsalam A. Heddaya, Bharat B. Bhargava* ISBN: 0-7923-9800-9

INFORMATION BROKERING ACROSS HETEROGENEOUS DIGITAL DATA
A Metadata-based Approach

by

VIPUL KASHYAP
Member of Technical Staff
Micro-electronics and Computer Technology Corporation (MCC)
3500, W. Balcones Center Drive
Austin, TX 78759

Current address:
Research Scientist
Applied Research, Telcordia Technologies
MCC-1G332R, 445 South Street
Morristown, NJ 07960

AMIT SHETH
Director, Large Scale Distributed Information Systems Laboratory
Department of Computer Science
The University of Georgia
Athens, GA 30602

KLUWER ACADEMIC PUBLISHERS
Boston / Dordrecht / London

Distributors for North, Central and South America:
Kluwer Academic Publishers
101 Philip Drive
Assinippi Park
Norwell, Massachusetts 02061 USA
Telephone (781) 871-6600
Fax (781) 681-9045
E-Mail <kluwer@wkap.com>

Distributors for all other countries:
Kluwer Academic Publishers Group
Distribution Centre
Post Office Box 322
3300 AH Dordrecht, THE NETHERLANDS
Telephone 31 78 6392 392
Fax 31 78 6546 474
E-Mail <services@wkap.nl>

Electronic Services <http://www.wkap.nl>

Library of Congress Cataloging-in-Publication Data

Information brokering over heterogeneous digital data / Vipul Kashyap, Amit Sheth.
p. cm. -- (The Kluwer international series on advances in database systems)
Includes bibliographical references and index.

1. Heterogeneous computing. I. Kashyap, Vipul. II. Sheth, A. (Amit), 1959 - III. Series.

QA76.88. I52 2000 ISBN 978-1-4419-4987-5
004'.35--dc21 e-ISBN 978-0-306-47028-8

00-034934

Printed on acid-free paper.

Printed in the United States of America

To my parents, Yogendra and Vibha, whose blessings and encouragement have played an active life-long role in my work, and my wife Nitu for being patient with me.

-Vipul

To the members of the InfoHarness and InfoQuilt team at the LSDIS Lab, who helped us in thinking about metadata and semantics.

-Amit and Vipul

Contents

List of Figures

List of Tables

Preface

Information intermediation is the foundation stone of some of the most successful Internet companies, and is perhaps second only to the Internet Infrastructure companies. On the heels of information integration and interoperability, this book on information brokering discusses the next step in information interoperability and integration.

The emerging internet economy based on burgeoning B2B and B2C trading, will soon demand semantics-based information intermediation for its feasibility and success. Even as we speak, new B2B ventures are involved in the "rationalization" of new vertical markets and construction of domain specific product catalogs. In this book we provide approaches for re-use of existing vocabularies and domain ontologies as a basis for this rationalization and provide a framework based on inter-ontology interoperation. Infrastructural trade-offs that identify optimizations in performance and scalability of web sites will soon give way to information based trade-offs as alternate rationalization schemes come into play, and the necessity of interoperating across these schemes is realized.

The complex issues of intermediation as conceived by information brokering involve the following:

- Construction of information content descriptions that resolve information "impedance" or mismatch between what is required by the information consumer and presented by the information provider.

- Using "information brokering" to provide intermediation to resolve impedance at multiple levels. Architectures for brokering/intermediation should provide a framework for resolution of impedance at different levels, and may be multi-level in nature. New paradigms such as agent based architectures need to be evaluated for their applicability to information intermediation.

- Exploration of the critical role of Metadata. Information content descriptions may be at different levels, such as content-independent, representation dependent, representation independent or domain specific. The descriptions enable resolution of impedances at various levels. Domain specific metadata descriptions are crucial for intermediation based on the semantics (meaning and use) of the information content.

- Using ontology or vocabulary to construct metadata descriptions for aligning the "world views" of consumers and providers. Techniques for re-using existing vocabularies/ontologies and interoperation across them need to be developed to perform this type of intermediation.

- Characterizing loss of information that inevitably arises in semantics-based intermediation due to differences in world views between the consumers and providers. Information-based trade-offs need to be characterized and computed to provide effective semantics-based intermediation.

This book's intended readers are researchers, software architects and CTOs, and advanced product developers dealing with information intermediation issues in the context of e-commerce (B2B and B2C), information technology professionals in various vertical markets (e.g., geo-spatial information, medicine, auto), and practically all librarians at higher-education, technical institutions and universities.

VIPUL KASHYAP AND AMIT SHETH

Acknowledgments

Amit Sheth and I have thoroughly enjoyed intense discussion sessions with each other which we often had in the course of working on this book. Many new research directions and possibilities emerged from those discussions and have played a critical role in enhancing and adding value to this book. This was supplemented by our interactions with members of the InfoHarness and InfoQuilt projects, that helped us in our thinking about metadata and semantics.

Special thanks goes to Eduardo Mena, the heated discussions with whom resulted in the OBSERVER system. Mention needs to be made of the members of the InfoSleuth project team that I worked with. Dr. Marek Rusinkiewicz officially my manager at Micro-electronics and Computer Technology Corporation (MCC), has been a great source of inspiration and help in my research endeavors. I am also indebted to my managers at Telcordia, Sid Dalal and Gardner Patton for their encouragement and advice. Gardner's comments on the draft manuscript were very useful and helped in improving the readability and presentation of content in this book.

Finally, I am grateful to my wife, Nitu, who was gracious enough to donate her time (which we would have otherwise spent together) towards the editing and proof reading of this book.

Foreword

Computing is fast becoming ubiquitous and pervasive. It is *ubiquitous* because computing power and access to the Internet is being made available everywhere; it is pervasive because computing is being embedded in the very fabric of our environment. Xerox Corp. has recently coined the phrase "smart matter" to capture the idea of computations occurring within formerly passive objects and substances. For example, our houses, our furniture, and our clothes will contain computers that will enable our surroundings to adapt to our preferences and needs. New visions of interactivity portend that scientific, commercial, educational, and industrial enterprises will be linked, and human spheres previously untouched by computing and information technology, such as our personal, recreational, and community life, will be affected.

However, when there is information everywhere and all manner of things are interconnected, there arise the problems of information overload and misunderstandings. Dogbert, from Scott Adams' Dilbert, describes the situation as "Information is gushing toward your brain like a fire hose aimed at a teacup". This book analyzes the problems of information overload and misunderstandings and provides a solution: a way for all of the different devices, components, and computers to understand each other, so that they will be able to work together effectively and efficiently. This is a powerful and important advance.

Dr. Vipul Kashyap and Professor Amit Sheth have long been leaders in the area of information system semantics and are widely known as two of the area's most dedicated, productive, and insightful researchers. Together in this book they have crafted a coherent vision of the single most important element of a distributed heterogeneous information system: the information broker. Previously, Kashyap has been the architect of a broker-based multiagent system for cooperative information access. Sheth has been an innovator of metadata-based approaches to the integration of heterogeneous semantics for database systems and workflow systems. Together, their expertise is complementary and forms the unique perspective of this book.

The essential agent-based architecture that they describe and analyze is becoming canonical. Agents are used to represent users, resources, middleware, security, execution engines, ontologies, and brokering. As the technology advances, we can expect such specialized agents to be used as standardized building blocks for information systems. Two trends lend credence to such a prediction.

First, software systems in general are being constructed with larger components, such as ActiveX and JavaBeans, which are becoming closer to being agents themselves. They have more functionality than simple objects, respond to events autonomously, and, most importantly, respond to system builders at development-time, as well as to events at run-time.

Second, there is a move toward more cooperative information systems, in which the architecture itself plays an important role in the effectiveness of the system, as opposed to traditional software systems where effectiveness depends on the quality of the individual components. These are the architectures of standardized agents that Kashyap and Sheth elucidate. Architectures based on standardized agent types should be easier to develop, understand, and use. Perhaps most important of all, these architectures will make it easier for separately developed information systems to interoperate.

Among the reasons why agents are attractive, there are two main ones of interest here. One, agents enable the construction of modular systems from heterogeneous pieces, potentially created by any number of vendors. Two, the agents themselves embody diverse knowledge, reasoning approaches, and perspectives. This diversity is sometimes essential, because the agents represent people or business interests that have different goals and motivations. Diversity can sometimes be added in by design: it can make an agent system more robust by enabling a variety of viewpoints to be represented and exploited.

However, agents are typically complex pieces of software, so the question arises whether a set of different agents would unnecessarily add to a system's complexity. The more kinds of agents there are, the harder it might be to build and maintain them. Fortunately, this turns out to be a false concern. The agents have to be diverse in content, e.g., knowledge, reasoning techniques, and interaction protocols, but not in the form in which that content is realized, e.g., the language or toolkit with which they are constructed. Problems arise through unnecessary heterogeneity in construction; the cost of necessary heterogeneity in content is more than recovered through the flexibility it offers.

In summary, the results in this book are applicable not only to the huge amount of information available globally over the World-Wide Web, but also to the diverse information soon to be available locally over household, automobile, and environment networks. I am excited by the possibilities for new applications and uses for information that are engendered by this book, as well as by the challenges that remain. This book provides a solid foundation for advances in distributed heterogeneous information systems.

Professor Michael N. Huhns,
Director, Center for Information Technology,
University of South Carolina, Columbus, SC

Chapter 1

INTRODUCTION

We are witnessing today an explosive growth in the creation of digital data, facilitated by affordable multimedia systems and capture devices. The data is managed in autonomous repositories (often seen as parts of Web sites), and varies in format and representation from structured (e.g., relational databases) to semi-structured (e.g., e-mail, newsgroups, HTML pages) and unstructured (e.g., image data) formats, enabled by the Global Information Infrastructure (GII). Excellent and near-ubiquitous connectivity afforded by the Internet, the web, and distributed computing infrastructures, resulting in a computing and information systems infrastructure, has allowed easy access to a large number of autonomous and heterogeneous information sources. Unfortunately, easy access has not necessarily translated into effective use or user productivity. The key reasons for this include the large amount and variety of data, use of the data beyond the original intent of those creating or capturing it, and the use of relatively low precision access techniques. This has led to the well recognized problem of *information overload*.

For over two decades, interoperability has been crucial for modern information systems. Starting from earlier research in federated systems (Heimbigner and McLeod, 1985) and multidatabase systems (Litwin and Abdellatif, 1986), the need to consider the three dimensions of distribution, heterogeneity and autonomy has been well-recognized (Sheth and Larson, 1990). The scale and variety of the issues involved has made it necessary to develop a better understanding of interoperability concerns. One perspective, in the form of the types of heterogeneity we need to deal with, and the corresponding interoperability issues, is presented in Figure 1.1 (Sheth, 1999). With the benefit of past and current research, into the increasing complexity and issues involved in dealing with information overload, the focus on interoperability is decidedly shifting from system, syntax, and structure to semantics (Sheth, 1999). As we move from managing data to managing information, and in the future, managing knowledge (along with supporting increased specialization of work performed by knowledge workers), the need for achieving semantic interoperability will become more crucial than ever.

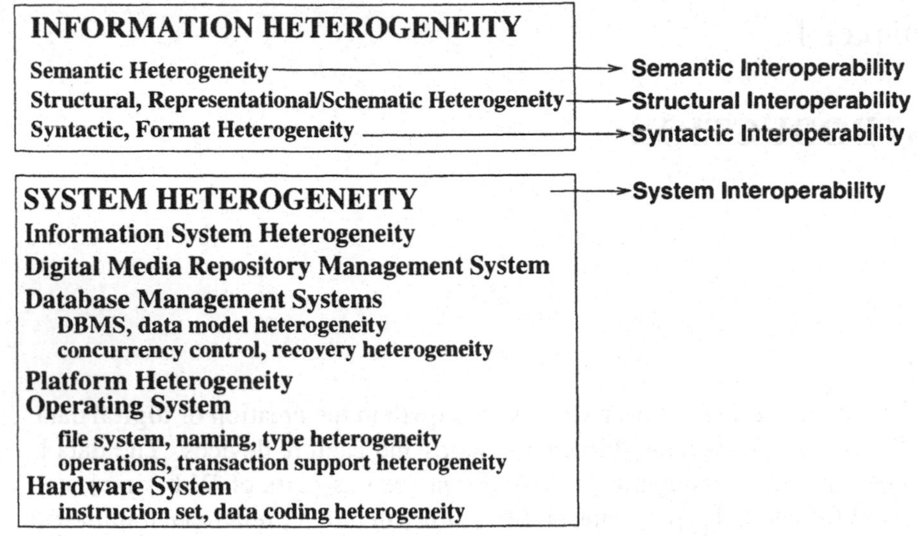

Figure 1.1. A Taxonomy of Heterogeneity and Interoperability

The increasing specialization of work, and at the same time, an increasing need to share data, information, and knowledge in a form that would be useful for a particular work specialty, makes semantic interoperability a crucial issue for information systems of the future. Information heterogeneity, and an increasing trend towards globalization, are crucial factors behind information overload on the GII. The *information brokering* architecture discussed here is geared toward supporting interoperability at various levels. Our discussion focuses on strategies for achieving semantic interoperability. Techniques for representational and structural interoperability, are discussed to the extent they form the building blocks for semantic interoperability.

1. INFORMATION OVERLOAD: IMPACT OF HETEROGENEITY AND GLOBALIZATION

The information overload created by the necessity of keeping track of various data types, representation formats, and query languages, is further compounded by the trend to globalization in current and future information systems. Globalization leads to the participation of a broad variety of users - both naive and specialized - with data being used in ways not anticipated by the original data collectors. This section provides a brief overview of the sources of information overload, and key techniques and capabilities that can help alleviate the problem.

1.1 HETEROGENEITY

Many types of heterogeneity are due to technological differences; for example, differences in hardware and operating system platforms. Researchers and developers have been working on resolving such heterogeneities for years. We refer to these as *system heterogeneities*. Differences in the machine readable aspects of data representation, formats, and storage for digital media may be referred to as *syntactic heterogeneity*. We consider representational heterogeneity involving schematic mismatches, and differences in data modeling constructs as *structural heterogeneity*. Differences in meaning are dependent on the vocabulary and terminology used to express information, and the contexts in which it is interpreted. They are referred to as *semantic heterogeneity*. Interoperability issues that deal with semantic heterogeneity are receiving increasing importance lately [e.g., see (Ouksel and Sheth, 1999)]. We now discuss common types of structural and semantic heterogeneities, and how they contribute to information overload.

Differences in Structure Different data models provide different structural primitives. For example, object oriented data models support inheritance while relational data models do not (data model heterogeneity). Even if the data model is the same, similar information content may be represented differently in different schemas (schematic heterogeneity). For example, an address may be stored as an entity, or as a composite attribute in different schemas based on the E-R data model. When retrieving information from systems using different structures to represent and store data, an *information overhead* related to keeping track of these differences and reconciling them is imposed on the user.

Differences in Query Languages Different languages are used to manipulate data represented in different data models. Even when two Database Management Systems (DBMSs) support the same data model, differences in their query languages (e.g., different versions of Structured Query Language (SQL) or support for specialized primitives) contribute to the heterogeneity. In this case, the information overhead imposed on the user is related to keeping track of appropriate languages and operations to be used when retrieving information from a given information system.

Semi-structured or Unstructured Data Increasingly, data available on the GII is unstructured or in some cases semi-structured. Examples of unstructured data are images, free text, and video data. Some textual data such as an Hypertext Markup Language (HTML) page or a bibliographic entry comes in a semi-structured format. Data guides and document type definitions (DTDs) expressed as grammar rules have been proposed to model semi-structured data. This type of data is typically handled by defining and using wrappers and translators. In this case, the information overhead is related to keeping track of, and defining appropriate wrappers and translators to retrieve information from a semi-structured or unstructured data source.

Media Heterogeneity Quite often, information sources store data corresponding to different media (e.g., text, image). Very often, a response to an information request requires correlation of information stored in different media. For example, it may be necessary to correlate area and population characteristics of a region (textual data), with its land cover and relief characteristics (image data). In this case, the information overhead is related to extraction of relevant information (i.e., keeping track of relevant text and image processing methods to perform the extraction), and the actual correlation of various characteristics of the region.

Terminology (and Language) Heterogeneity A user has to choose the vocabulary or ontology to express his or her information request. Different information sources may have used different ontologies to describe their information content. Some of these ontologies may be closely tied to a metamodel, such as those specified by the Federal Geographic Data Committee (FGDC), Dewey Decimal Classification (DDC), and Environmental Data Catalog (UDK) metadata standards in geographical and environmental information domains. There is an information overhead related to keeping track of the appropriate vocabulary and (re-)formulation of the information request to access information stored in a given source.

Contextual Heterogeneity Contexts are an implicit, yet integral, part of any information request. Though two information requests may appear to be the same syntactically, they can return different results when interpreted under different contexts. In current information systems, results are retrieved under all possible interpretations of a given request. A large proportion of the result returned is based on contextual interpretations that are completely irrelevant to the information request, thus leading to an information overload on the user.

1.2 GLOBALIZATION

The trend of globalization in information systems has increased the complexity of information overload introduced by the structural and semantic heterogeneity of various forms of digital data. The scope of the problem has increased from tens/hundreds of databases, to millions of information sources on the GII. The impact of globalization on information overload is discussed below.

Information Resource Discovery Due to the presence of millions of information sources on the GII, it is no longer feasible to expect the user to determine, and keep track of, repositories relevant to his or her information request. An information request may not be completely satisfied at an information source, or one or more sources may contain information similar to, though not exactly the same as, that required by the request. This is the information resource discovery problem.

Modeling of Information Content Information from different sources may be modeled at different levels of abstraction, e.g., information about a student from one information source may be modeled in more detail (say as a graduate student) in another. Also, information modeled in one source may not be modeled in another. This introduces an information overhead related to keeping track of the level of abstraction at which the results are returned. The user has also to keep track of the level at which information is modeled at each source. With millions of information sources, the number of possibilities related to an information request on the GII may be overwhelmingly large.

Querying of Information Content Typically on the GII, information required to satisfy a request is likely to be distributed across a wide variety of sources. In this scenario, it is crucial to be able to identify the subset of relevant information at a source, and to combine partially relevant information across different sources.

Information Focusing This is the process of identification and retrieval of the required subset of information from an information source. In a typical scenario on the GII, different information sources would provide relevant information to a different extent. The most obvious choice of the source from which information should be retrieved, is the one that returns most (or all) of the relevant information. In that case, the user will have to keep track of which source has the most relevant information.

Information Correlation This is the process of combining partially relevant information from different repositories to return a precise and complete answer to an information request. In a typical scenario on the GII, there will be a combinatorial number of possibilities to be considered for determining the most precise and complete combination of partial information. Given the huge number of information sources, there will be an exponential number of possibilities, leading to an enormous information overhead.

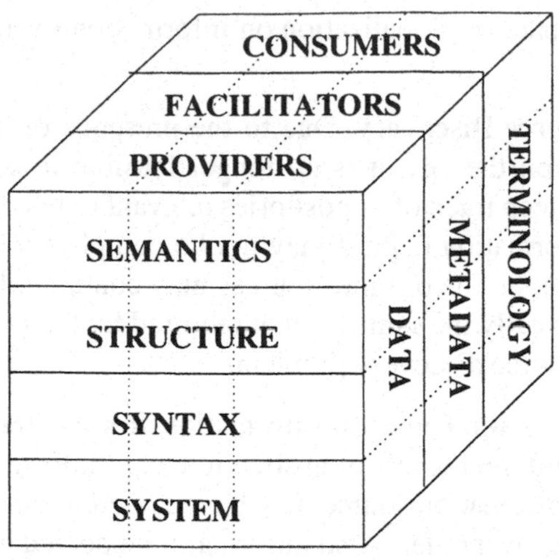

Figure 1.2. Dimensions of Information Brokering

2. INFORMATION BROKERING: HANDLING THE INFORMATION OVERLOAD

An *information brokering* architecture helps in reducing information overload, by supporting techniques that match information requests to data exported by various information sources on the GII. This involves identification and use of existing research and technologies that provide building blocks for addressing syntactic, schematic, and structural issues, while proposing novel techniques to tackle the difficult problem of semantic heterogeneity.

Information brokering can be viewed as an interplay across the three dimensions illustrated in Figure 1.2. This representation facilitates a pedagogical discussion of the information brokering architecture. A minimal definition of an information brokering architecture on the GII is **an architecture that guides creation and management (brokering) of systems and solutions to serve the information and business needs of a variety of information stakeholders, including *providers, facilitators*, and *consumers*.** Semantics is an important aspect of this architecture, which is reflected in the explicit attention to understand and exploit the meaning and use of data, as well as in understanding participants' needs, intentions, and perception of information (not data). To a certain extent, this architecture borrows from, and builds upon, the federated database and information systems architecture (Heimbigner and McLeod, 1985; Litwin and Abdellatif, 1986; Sheth and Larson, 1990), and the mediator architecture (Wiederhold, 1992).

We first discuss and identify the key players on the GII, and define information brokering based on the interchange of information between them.

Different levels of brokering that should be enabled by an information brokering architecture are then presented, and the critical role of *facilitators* is discussed.

2.1 INFORMATION BROKERING: STAKEHOLDER AND BENEFICIARIES

The key players on the GII are *information providers* which export information, *information consumers* which use information, and *information facilitators* which help match a consumer's requests with information exported by various providers (Figure 1.3)[1]

Information Providers The GII consists of millions of data/information repositories made available through information systems provided by various information providers. Examples of data/information repositories are newswires, corporate statistics, satellite images, broadcast videos archived over a long period of time, and audio and video themes on the web. They may be represented as structured (e.g., databases), semi-structured (e.g., HTML pages), or unstructured data (e.g., text and bitmap files).

Information Consumers Millions of consumers utilize services and information made available by numerous information providers on the GII. These consumers might be individual users (or their agents) on workstations, or application programs running on many machines at the same time.

Information Facilitators The information consumer on the GII is deluged by a variety of information (information overload) from thousands of information providers. Information facilitators enable **brokering** between the information consumer and provider, that may be defined as follows.

- Arbitration between information consumers and providers for resolving *information impedance* i.e., their differing world views on information.
- Dynamic re-interpretation of information requests for determination of relevant *information services* and *products*.
- Dynamic creation and composition of *information products* after suitable assembly or correlation of *information components* available from various providers, or other value added activities.

[1]Organizational (including ownership), financial and business, legal, and other issues are relevant but are beyond the scope of this book.

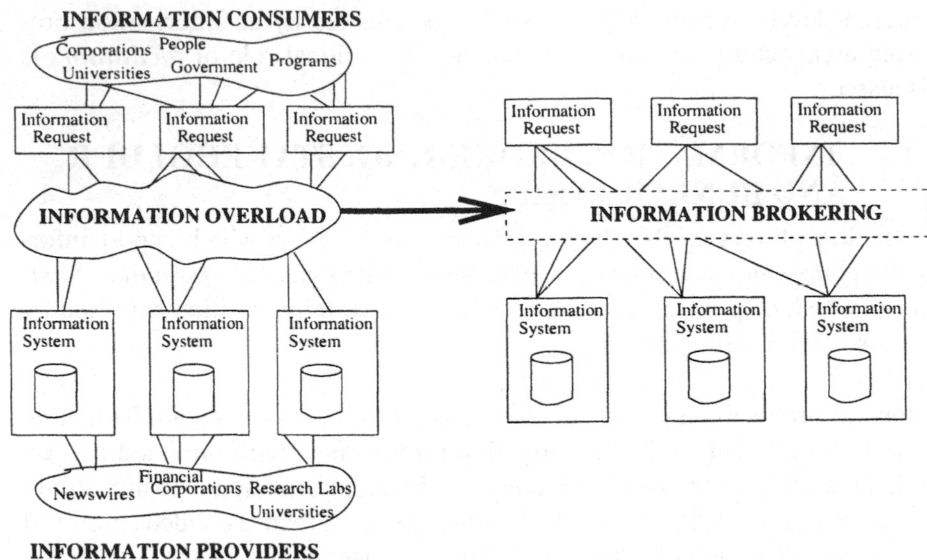

Figure 1.3. Information Brokering: A Stakeholder Perspective

2.2 LEVELS OF INFORMATION BROKERING

We view information on the GII at three levels - *data*, which comprises the data stored in a variety of representations (formats, media structures) in information sources on the GII; *metadata*, which may be thought of as information/data about the data and used to capture information content; and *semantics*, the use of standard terminologies and domain ontologies to specify intensional metadata descriptions, describing information content, application and user needs (Figure 1.2). Brokering at the data level, and partially at the metadata level has made excellent progress primarily due to the development and use of widespread standards (Paepcke et al., 1998). However, current R&D challenges involve investigating issues in semantic brokering using domain specific metadata, terminologies, and context.

2.2.1 DATA BROKERING: STANDARDS-BASED INTEROPERABILITY

One of the oldest approaches to achieving interoperability among heterogeneous components is to agree on a standard that achieves a limited amount of homogeneity among them. The key reason for the success of these standards has been that they were compelling and easy to use, and fulfilled an important need at the right time. Some examples are:

- The Transmission Control Protocol/Internet Protocol (TCP/IP) and HyperText Transfer Protocol (HTTP) protocols, that have become the de-facto standard for transmission of data (in the form of packets), over a network.
- Other protocols like Common Request Broker Architecture (CORBA) and Java/RMI, that support the transmission of data objects, and are fast gaining acceptance in the Internet community.
- HTML, which is a de-facto standard; and Extensible Markup Language (XML), which is fast gaining acceptance as a standard for markup of textual and digital content, and semi-structured data.
- The Lightweight Directory Access Protocol (LDAP) has become a popular standard for accessing information stored in specialized directories or databases. The Java Database Connectivity (JDBC) protocol, on the other hand, is a standard for accessing information from more general relational databases.
- Protocols such as Open Knowledge Base Connectivity (OKBC), and standards such as Knowledge Query Manipulation Language (KQML)/Knowledge Interchange Format (KIF) are being proposed for knowledge interchange and communication among processes and agents, but have not yet reached sufficient levels of acceptance.
- Languages such as Unified Modeling Language (UML) are being proposed for modeling software systems and processes, and are rapidly gaining acceptance.

2.2.2 METADATA-BASED BROKERING

Metadata may be distinguished based on the amount of information content they are able to capture (a classification of metadata based on this criteria appears later in this book). Significant progress has been made in enabling interoperability based on metadata that capture limited or no information content, and those that capture the structural characteristics of data. A lot of work has been done on issues relating to the use of schema metadata for resolving schematic and structural heterogeneity (Batini et al., 1986; Kim et al., 1993) in the context of databases storing structured data. These techniques have however, focused on structured data and have not adequately dealt with the issues of semantics. Data formats, representations, and media are typically domain independent, and can be automatically characterized by structural and media-specific metadata.

Further progress in achieving interoperability at the metadata level has been achieved through the use of models (also called meta-models), standards, or specifications for metadata. Some well-accepted metadata standards or specifications for domain independent metadata are the Dublin Core and Warwick frameworks. They capture rather limited information and consequently provide limited value in achieving interoperability. However, domain specific standards, such as geo-spatial standards and specifications (e.g., FGDC, Open Geospatial Interoperability Standard (OGIS), and Spatial Data Transfer Standard (SDTS)) provide a more meaningful level of interoperability at the metadata level, when multiple information providers subscribe to the same metadata standard or specification.

On the GII, however, it is not only possible, but likely, that different providers in the same domain subscribe to different metadata standards or specifications, once again giving rise to complex interoperability challenges. As domain specific metadata bring more semantics to the information they help model, we need to achieve semantic interoperability to address the challenges. It is unlikely that we can devise a fully automatic approach for achieving such interoperability that avoids the involvement of domain experts. Techniques for interoperation should however, be designed to minimize the participation of, and to optimally utilize, the knowledge of domain or subject matter experts.

2.2.3 SEMANTIC ASPECTS OF INFORMATION BROKERING

The critical issue in capturing information content necessary to perform semantic information brokering, is the terminology used to characterize information content. It may be noted that domain specific metadata needs to be mapped into structural and media specific metadata, and is necessarily constructed by using terms specific to an information domain. These domain specific terms are provided by domain experts responsible for the construction and mapping of metadata descriptions. This gives rise to the issue of semantic heterogeneity, where the heterogeneity may stem from the following factors:

- The use of different terms to describe similar information (synonymy) and the use of similar terms to describe dissimilar information (homonymy). For example, the concepts *doctor* and *physician* are synonyms of each other, and the concept *instrument* as interpreted by lawyers and doctors are homonyms.

- The use of different modeling choices for describing similar information. For example, describing a student using the concept *student* as opposed to the concept *graduate student*.

- The use of different metadata expressions describing similar information. For example, a *rich person* may alternatively be described as a *person making* $\geq$ *\$100,000* per year.

- Different contexts are relevant to the interpretation of data and information requests. For example, when a doctor asks for information about *instruments*, the request needs to be evaluated in a context that is different from the case where a lawyer asks for the same information.

Whereas the first three factors are the focus of terminological representation systems (also known as the KL-ONE family of systems), the last factor is an example of a semantic issue that goes beyond terminological issues. The problem of representation and reasoning within a context is both crucial and difficult, and has engaged the attention of researchers across various disciplines. In this book, we focus on the terminological aspects of semantics and use domain specific ontologies as one tool to handle this aspect. An attractive approach is based on the re-use of standardized terminologies captured as domain specific ontologies (Mena et al., 1998; Mena et al., 1996b; Mena et al., 1996a). A domain specific ontology may be defined as the specification of a representational vocabulary for a shared domain of discourse, which may include definitions of classes, relations, functions, and other objects (Gruber, 1993). Metadata descriptions can then be constructed from ontological concepts. Some well-known ontologies/thesauri that attempt to capture and represent a global collection of knowledge are Cyc (Lenat and Guha, 1990) and WordNet (Miller, 1995a). Attempts have also been made to use a common domain ontology for information gathering within the context of an information domain (Arens et al., 1993; Levy et al., 1995).

However, we recognize that it is not practical to design a common ontology that satisfies the needs of various user communities on the GII, who may be interested in different information domains. Concepts in these ontologies may differ in the ways enumerated above, and may participate in multiple contexts within an ontology (Ouksel and Ahmed, 1999), or across different ontologies. True semantic interoperability requires interoperation across multiple ontologies and contexts. Inter-ontology interoperation requires characterization of overlaps across different ontologies and techniques for merging ontologies. Reformulations of metadata expressions across ontologies change the semantics of the query. This change needs to be measured in a meaningful manner. In this book, we discuss novel solutions to the above mentioned difficult problems that arise in semantic information brokering.

2.2.4 LEVELS OF INFORMATION BROKERING

We discussed above how brokering can be implemented at various levels. Information was viewed at three levels, viz., *data* with its *heterogeneous representations*, *metadata* as a means to capture *information content* to some degree, and *semantics*, which is crucially dependent on the *terminology* used to characterize information content.

The first step in handling information overload on the GII deals with data and its multiple digital heterogeneous *representations*. The key to brokering is the ability to capture *information content* in a manner independent of its underlying representations. Information consumers are primarily concerned with the information though they may also desire to see its different manifestations. A critical problem in specifying information content is the issue of the *terminology* used to characterize information. Typically, different terminologies are used by information providers and consumers, for specifying and requesting the same piece of information. A crucial issue in handling information overload involves the ability to deal with multiple *terminologies* expressing similar information. Hence, the two basic components of brokering can be characterized as:

1. Use of metadata descriptions to abstract from representational heterogeneities and capture information content (the **metadata brokering** component); and

2. Use of domain specific ontologies as standard terminologies to characterize metadata descriptions, and terminological relationships between them, to enable transformation of information across heterogeneous terminologies (the **vocabulary brokering** component).

The association of symbolic metadata descriptions with digital data (maintained by the metadata brokering component) helps insulate the user from data and media specific heterogeneity. The user can retrieve information from heterogeneous media using these metadata descriptions, which can also be used to define multimedia views. Also, information is captured at an intensional level (e.g., classes) as opposed to the extensional level (e.g., instances), and helps reduce by an order of magnitude, the volume of data to be processed when determining relevance of information.

Domain specific ontologies are used to characterize vocabularies and terminological relationships between them for interoperation. This helps reduce information overload by: (a) precise specification of the information domain of the information request; and (b) efficient and precise semantic interoperation, as the number of terminological relationships between terms across ontologies is typically an order of magnitude smaller than the number of terms in all ontologies (Mena et al., 1996b).

The key objective of our approach is to reduce the problem of knowing the structure and semantics of data in the huge number of information sources on the GII to the significantly smaller problem of knowing terminological relationships between terms across domain ontologies.

2.3 THE ROLE OF FACILITATORS ON THE GII

Information facilitators can support various brokering functions and capabilities. There are two ways to organize them, viz., the metadata and vocabulary components. Capabilities in the metadata brokering component that a facilitator may support are:

- Design and construction of multimedia views using metadata descriptions from consumer specified standardized terminologies. This may be done either manually as a part of a consultation, or by providing tools that specify views in a high level definition language that enables a consumer to specify and customize his own multimedia views. These descriptions enable search and retrieval for relevant information with greater precision.

- Storage and maintenance of associations between digital data exported by the providers, and metadata descriptions designed by the facilitators. These associations help providers increase the likelihood of consumers *discovering* the information exported by them. They also help broker between the differing world views of providers and consumers.

  - As in the case of multimedia views, the associations may be specified manually, or specialized tools may be provided to enable users to specify their own associations or mappings.
  - Tools may also be designed to apply statistical data mining and machine learning techniques to "learn" associations between digital data and the specified metadata descriptions.

The facilitator thus acts as a bridge between providers and consumers, and enables a transition from the structural aspects of information to the semantic aspects of information. A facilitator may also support capabilities that involve semantic aspects of information, especially those based on terminological management and reasoning. Some capabilities that involve the vocabulary brokering component are:

- Providing a collection of standard terminologies and domain specific ontologies to the consumer, who can choose and align himself to the ontology closest to his world view. This collection can also be used by providers to construct appropriate metadata descriptions.

- Providing support for interoperation across multiple domain specific ontologies. A facilitator maintains inter-ontological terminological relationships across different ontologies, and provides services to both, the consumers and providers, to help introduce new ontologies into the system. The facilitator is responsible for "incorporating" the new ontology by maintaining terminological relationships between the new and existing ontologies on the GII.

- Providing support for transformation of information requests across different ontologies in a manner that minimizes loss of information. The consumer's specification of an information request using ontologies of his choice is reformulated by a facilitator across ontologies used by the information sources, thus retrieving more relevant information.

An information facilitator thus helps enable *semantic interoperability* across different world views/ontologies supported by consumers and providers.

2.4 INFORMATION BROKERING: RELATION TO OTHER APPROACHES

Approaches for interoperability across information systems were proposed in the context of database management systems in the 1980s. They focused on issues related to the distribution, heterogeneity, and autonomy of information, in the context of providing integrated access to databases. A federated architecture was proposed for interoperation across a set of databases. An extensive review of this architecture is presented in (Heimbigner and McLeod, 1985; Litwin and Abdellatif, 1986; Sheth and Larson, 1990). A federated schema designed after integration of component database schemas, is used to interoperate across different systems. A drawback with this approach has been the relatively static nature of integration, and the inability of the approach to scale beyond tens of information systems.

Mediator approaches propose a more dynamic approach for the integration of information. Wiederhold (Wiederhold, 1992) defines a mediator as "a software module that exploits encoded knowledge about some sets or subsets of data to create information about a higher layer of applications". One interesting class of mediators has been those used to encapsulate and fuse information in semi-structured data sources using (multimedia) views and object templates [see (Wiederhold, 1996) and (Sheth, 1999) for examples]. While the federated database architecture distinctly focused on data representation through different types of schemas, the focus of the mediator architecture has been on software modules that perform value added activities. Most implemented mediator systems such as SIMS (Arens et al., 1993), TSIMMIS (Garcia-Molina et al., 1995) and InfoSleuth (Bayardo et al., 1997) consider scenarios with one central mediator module collaborating with a collection of wrapper modules within the context of a given information or domain model.

Given a large number of user communities on the GII, there is an urgent need to make explicit the information model, and support multiple information models belonging to different user communities. Just as autonomy was critical to federated databases, explicit identification of the various stakeholders (providers, consumers) is a crucial component of the brokering perspective. We identify the need to support the respective information models chosen by a user community, and use metadata descriptions to broker between them by bridging the provider-consumer mismatch. The mediator concept is a viable component of information brokering, but the latter recognizes additional dimensions of the problem space, and presents a multi-layer approach. This enables a more comprehensive solution to challenges on the GII and covers both data/information/knowledge (as emphasized in the federated database architecture), and software perspectives (as emphasized in the mediator architecture).

Approaches using agents have been proposed for information discovery and management on the internet (Klusch, 1999). Various features of multi-agent systems make them an appropriate architectural choice for implementing information brokering techniques. We discuss the InfoSleuth system (Bayardo et al., 1997) as an illustrative multi-agent system in this book. However, in order to implement semantic interoperability and brokering, we need to extend the functionalities of agents to: (a) capture, view and interrogate the semantics of the underlying data (metadata component); (b) request information in a manner independent of data type, structure, format, location, and even knowledge of existence (metadata component); and (c) support for interoperation across multiple terminologies or domain specific ontologies (vocabulary component). In this book, we discuss and illustrate, with the help of a succession of prototype systems, the design and implementation of architectures to support the above functionalities, and enable semantic information brokering.

3. BOOK ORGANIZATION

The overall organization of the book is as follows:

- Metadata descriptions constructed from domain specific ontologies form a critical component of our brokering approach. Chapter 2 discusses issues related to different types of metadata used by various researchers. A metadata classification is presented, and roles played by different types of metadata in capturing information content is discussed. The role played by ontologies in constructing metadata descriptions is also discussed.

- In the Introduction, we discussed a multi level architecture for information brokering. Chapter 3 presents a metadata-based architecture induced by the multi-level approach. A set of qualitative evaluation criteria called the "SEA" properties are defined, and the conditions under which the above architecture satisfies these properties are discussed. The evolution of earlier architectures designed for interoperability is traced, and their relation to the metadata-based architecture is discussed.

- Chapter 4 discusses metadata-based brokering across different types of digital data. In particular, domain specific correlation of information across structured, text, and image databases is illustrated with the help of an example. The InfoHarness and MIDAS brokering systems are discussed in this context. One piece of the InfoSleuth system (Chapter 6), the text agent, is presented as an example of brokering over textual data.

- Chapter 5 discusses issues specific to structured databases in the context of information brokering. Schematic conflicts across databases are identified, and metadata expressions constructed from ontological terms are used to: (a) capture information content after abstracting from schematic details, and (b) enable determination of relevant information without accessing data in the underlying databases.

- Chapter 6 discusses the InfoSleuth system being developed at the Microelectronics and Computer Technology Corporation (MCC). This system primarily performs metadata brokering implemented by a community of distributed cooperating agents. The agent architecture is expressed as an instantiation of the brokering architecture discussed in Chapter 3 and the "SEA" properties it satisfies, are identified. The use of this architecture to support data mining, information integration and event detection is also discussed.

- Chapter 7 discusses the OBSERVER system, the final prototype discussed in this book. The use of domain specific ontologies and interoperation across them enabling vocabulary brokering is demonstrated. The OBSERVER system architecture is expressed as the instantiation of the brokering architecture discussed in Chapter 3, and the "SEA" properties it satisfies are discussed.

- Chapter 8 illustrates domain specific brokering techniques discussed in this book with the help of an example.

- Chapter 9 presents a survey of systems and prototypes designed for information brokering on the GII. Approaches and techniques used for brokering in various systems are compared and contrasted, and features in our approach not offered by these systems are discussed.

- Chapter 10 presents conclusions, where contributions of this work and future research directions are discussed.

Chapter 2

METADATA AND ONTOLOGIES

In Chapter 1, we discussed a multi-level view of information on the GII, and presented a brokering approach spanning these levels. The approach consists of two main brokering components (metadata and vocabulary), both of which depend on the pivotal idea of metadata descriptions, that fulfill a two-fold purpose in the context of our approach:

- They enable abstraction of representational details, such as the format and organization of data, and capture information content of the underlying data independent of representational details. This represents the first step in the reduction of information overload, as intensional metadata descriptions are, in general, an order of magnitude smaller in size than the underlying data.

- They enable representation of domain knowledge describing the information domain to which the underlying data belongs. This knowledge may be used to make inferences about the underlying data. The knowledge helps in reducing the information overload as inferences may be used to determine *relevance* of the underlying data, without accessing it.

In this chapter, we discuss issues related to the management of metadata from two different perspectives (Boll et al., 1998), and discuss how information brokering is an important component in each of these perspectives. We identify the types of metadata that are crucial to support semantic interoperability. Also discussed are issues related to the use of domain specific ontologies and knowledge bases, to provide the language and vocabulary for construction of the metadata descriptions.

1. PERSPECTIVES ON METADATA MANAGEMENT

Issues related to the management of metadata can be viewed from two different perspectives: (a) a perspective based on application scenarios involving multimedia data; and (b) a perspective based on information content captured in the different types of metadata used.

1.1 THE APPLICATION SCENARIOS PERSPECTIVE

Information brokering is an integral component of new and emerging applications due to the need for handling the heterogeneity of multimedia data. The components of our approach and associated issues that are relevant in these scenarios, are discussed below.

Navigation, Browsing and Retrieval from Image Collections An increasing number of applications, such as those in healthcare, maintain large collections of images. There is a need for semantic content based navigation, browsing, and retrieval of images. An important issue is to associate a user's semantic impression with the images, e.g., image of a brain tumor. This requires knowledge of spatial content of the image, and its evolutionary behavior which can be represented as metadata. Issues of constructing metadata expressions and associating them with various images belong to the metadata brokering component in our approach.

Video In many applications relevant to news agencies, there exist collections of video footage which need to be searched based on semantic content, e.g., videos containing field goals in a soccer game. This gives rise to the same set of issues as described above (spatial evolution), except that there is a temporal aspect to videos which was not captured above. These issues belong to the metadata brokering component in our approach.

Audio and Speech Radio stations collect many, if not all of their important and informative programs, such as radio news, in archives. Parts of such programs are often reused in other radio broadcasts. However, to efficiently retrieve parts of radio programs, it is necessary to have the right metadata generated from, and associated with, the audio recordings. This issue belongs to the metadata brokering component in our approach. An important issue here is capturing in text, the essence of the audio, i.e., speech recognition in which vocabulary plays a central role. Domain specific vocabularies can drive the metadata extraction process making it more efficient. Issues relating to domain specific vocabularies belong to the vocabulary brokering component in our approach.

Structured Document Management As the publishing paradigm is shifting from popular desktop publishing to database-driven publishing, processing of structured documents becomes more and more important. Particular document information models, such as SGML and XML, introduce structure and content-based metadata. Efficient retrieval is achieved by exploiting document structure, as the metadata can be used for indexing, which is essential for quick response times. Thus, queries asking for documents with a title containing "Computer Science" can be easily optimized. Issues of metadata-based indexing belong to the metadata brokering component in our approach.

Geographic and Environmental Information Systems These systems have a wide variety of users that have very specific information needs. Information integration is a key requirement, which is supported by provision of descriptive information to end users and information systems. This involves issues of capturing descriptions as metadata (metadata brokering component), and reconciling the different vocabularies used by the different information systems in interpreting the descriptions (vocabulary brokering component).

Digital Libraries Digital libraries offer a wide range of services and collections of digital documents, and constitute a challenging application area for the development and implementation of metadata frameworks. These frameworks are geared towards description of collections of digital materials such as text documents, spatially referenced data sets, audio, and video. Issues related to metadata frameworks belong to the metadata brokering component in our approach. Some frameworks follow the traditional library paradigm with metadata like subject headings and thesauri. Issues related to these types of frameworks belong to the vocabulary brokering component in our approach.

Mixed Media Access This is an approach which allows queries to be specified independent of the underlying media types. Data corresponding to the query may be retrieved from different media such as text and images, and "fused" appropriately before being presented to the user. Symbolic metadata descriptions may be used to describe information from different media types in a uniform manner. Issues related to mixed media access belong to the metadata brokering component in our approach.

1.2 THE INFORMATION CONTENT PERSPECTIVE

In the previous section, we discussed how metadata can be used to provide a semantic description, and improve retrieval efficiency by providing the basis for indexing underlying data. We now characterize various types of metadata based on the amount of information content they capture, and present a classification of various types of metadata used by researchers (Table 2.1). The types of metadata that play a key role in enabling semantic interoperability are also identified.

Content Independent Metadata This type of metadata captures information that does not depend on the content of the document with which it is associated. Examples of this type of metadata are location, modification-date of a document and type-of-sensor used to record a photographic image. There is no information content captured by these metadata but these might still be useful for retrieval of documents from their actual physical locations, and for checking whether the information is current or not. This type of metadata also helps to encapsulate information into units of interest, and organizes their representation in an object model.

Content Dependent Metadata This type of metadata depends on the content of the document it is associated with. Examples of content dependent metadata are size of a document, max-colors, number-of-rows, and number-of-columns of an image. They typically capture representational and structural information, and enable interoperability through support for browsing and navigation of the underlying data. Content dependent metadata can be further sub-divided as follows:

Direct Content-based Metadata This type of metadata is based directly on the contents of a document. A popular example of this is full-text indices based on the document text. Inverted tree and document vectors are examples of this type of metadata. Media specific metadata such as color, shape, and texture are typically direct content-based metadata.

Content-descriptive Metadata This type of metadata describes information in a document without directly utilizing its contents. An example of this metadata is textual annotations describing the contents of an image. This metadata comes in two flavors:

Domain Independent Metadata These metadata capture information present in the document independent of the application or subject domain of the information, and are primarily structural in nature. They often form the basis of indexing the document collection to enable faster retrieval. Examples of these are C/C++ parse trees and HTML/SGML document type definitions. Indexing a document collection based on domain independent metadata may be used to improve retrieval efficiency.

Domain Specific Metadata Metadata of this type is described in a manner specific to the application or subject domain of the information. Issues of vocabulary become very important in this case, as the metadata terms have to be chosen in a domain specific manner. This type of metadata, that helps abstract out representational details and capture information meaningful to a particular application or subject domain, is Domain Specific Metadata. Examples of such metadata are relief, land-cover from the geographical information domain, and area, population from the Census domain. In the case of structured data, the database schema is an example of such metadata.

Vocabulary for Information Content Characterization Domain Specific Metadata can be constructed from terms in a domain specific ontology, or terms in concept libraries describing information in an application or subject domain. Thus, we view ontologies as metadata, which themselves can be viewed as a vocabulary of terms for construction of more domain specific metadata descriptions. Semantic interoperability at the vocabulary level is achieved with the help of terminological relationships.

Metadata	Media/Metadata Type
Q-Features	Image, Video/Domain Specific
R-Features	Image, Video/Domain Independent
Impression Vector	Image/Content Descriptive
NDVI, Spatial Registration	Image/Domain Specific
Speech feature index	Audio/Direct Content-based
Topic change indices	Audio/Direct Content-based
Document Vectors	Text/Direct Content-based
Inverted Indices	Text/Direct Content-based
Content Classification Metadata	MultiMedia/Domain Specific
Document Composition Metadata	MultiMedia/Domain Independent
Metadata Templates	Media Independent/Domain Specific
Land-Cover, Relief	Media Independent/Domain Specific
Parent-Child Relationships	Text/Domain Independent
Contexts	Structured Databases/Domain Specific
Concepts from Cyc	Structured Databases/Domain Specific
User's Data Attributes	Text, Structured Databases/Domain Specific
Domain Specific Ontologies	Media-Independent/Domain Specific

Table 2.1. Metadata for Digital Media

In the above table we have surveyed different types of metadata used by various researchers. Q-Features and R-Features were used for modeling image and video data (Jain and Hampapuram,). Impression vectors were generated from text descriptions of images (Kiyoki et al.,). NDVI and spatial registration metadata were used to model geo-spatial maps, primarily of different types of vegetation (Anderson and Stonebraker,). Interesting examples of mixed media access are the speech feature index (Glavitsch et al.,) and topic change indices (Chen et al.,). Metadata capturing information about documents are document vectors (Deerwester et al., 1990), inverted indices (Kahle and Medlar, 1991), document classification and composition metadata (Bohm and Rakow,) and parent-child relationships (based on document structure) (Shklar et al., 1995c). Metadata Templates (Ordille and Miller, 1993) have been used for information resource discovery. Semantic metadata such as contexts (Sciore et al., 1992; Kashyap and Sheth, 1994), land-cover, relief (Sheth and Kashyap, 1996), Cyc concepts (Collet et al., 1991), concepts from domain ontologies (Mena et al., 1996b) have been constructed from well defined and standardized vocabularies and ontologies. An attempt at modeling user attributes is presented in (Shoens et al., 1993). The above discussion suggests that domain specific metadata capture information which is more meaningful with respect to a specific application or a domain. The information captured by other types of metadata primarily reflect the format and organization of underlying data. Thus, domain specific metadata is the most appropriate among others, for dealing with issues related to semantic heterogeneity.

2. LANGUAGE AND VOCABULARY ISSUES FOR METADATA CONSTRUCTION

In this section, we discuss issues related to the construction of semantic metadata expressions. These involve requirements that a language and vocabulary used for creating metadata expressions must satisfy.

2.1 LANGUAGE FOR METADATA REPRESENTATION

The properties desired in a language used to represent expressions constructed from domain specific metadata are as follows.

- The language should be declarative in nature as the metadata expression will typically, be used to express constraints on objects in an intensional manner. Besides, the declarative nature of the language will make it easier to perform inferences on the metadata.

- The language should be able to represent the metadata expression as a collection of properties and values, each describing a specific aspect of information present in the database, or requested by a query.

- The language should have primitives in the model world (for determining the subtype of two types, pattern matching, etc.). These can be used in comparing and manipulating metadata expressions.

- The language should have primitives to perform navigation in the ontology, and to identify abstractions related to ontological objects in the query.

The Extensible Markup Language (XML) (Bray et al.,) and Resource Description Format (RDF) (Lassila and Swick,) have been proposed to describe documents on the Web. These are complementary languages and fulfill a different purpose. XML provides a set of "semantic" tags to describe underlying data, and can be used to express metadata descriptions. The focus of RDF is to describe underlying data at a semantic level.

2.2 VOCABULARY FOR METADATA EXPRESSIONS

The choice of properties and values assigned to them is very important when constructing metadata expressions. There should be *ontological commitments*, that imply agreements about the terms used by both, users and information system designers. In our case, this corresponds to an agreement on the terms and values used by both a user in formulating query metadata, and a system/data administrator for formulating metadata expressions that capture information content in the underlying data.

Each information resource is expected to design or select an associated ontology, and ensure that metadata expressions take their terms and values from this ontology. Some issues that arise in constructing metadata expressions are given below, and discussed later in this section.

- The methodology for choosing terms for metadata expressions from the ontology depends on the richness of relationships represented in the ontology, and whether these relationships are exploited to improve information content captured in the metadata expression.

- It is not feasible for all information resources on the GII to use a common global ontology or knowledge base to construct the metadata. If different ontologies are used by different users and system managers to design metadata and query expressions, the feasibility of transforming them to a common ontology needs to be investigated.

- The possibility of re-using existing ontologies and classifications, in an attempt to construct a suitable ontology for a particular information domain also needs to be investigated.

RDF (Lassila and Swick,) deals with some of the issues discussed above. RDF expressions define a schema from which semantic XML tags can be chosen to describe data on the web. RDF helps standardize the vocabulary for construction of the XML expressions and provides a mechanism for expressing ontological commitments. It also enables interoperability across systems using XML expressions. However, RDF doesn't handle issues related to inferences such as subsumption and rule processing that might be supported by knowledge bases storing domain specific ontologies.

2.3 CONSTRUCTING INTENSIONAL METADATA DESCRIPTIONS

Domain specific metadata can be used to construct intensional descriptions which capture information content of the underlying data. As discussed earlier, these descriptions are used for abstraction of representational details, or for representing domain knowledge on which inferences can be performed. Based on the desired goal, the intensional descriptions may be categorized as *m-contexts* and *c-contexts*.

2.3.1 METADATA CONTEXTS (M-CONTEXTS)

Metadata contexts primarily serve to abstract representational details such as format and organization of data. Typically they are boolean combinations of metadata items, where each metadata item captures some piece of information content in the underlying data. The terms used to construct these metadata are typically obtained from ontologies or vocabularies which do not support complex relationships between the various terms, e.g., definition of a term using other terms. Hence, each metadata item is independently mapped to the underlying data. At run time, when metadata corresponding to a query are evaluated, the mappings are computed independently and the results combined to satisfy the boolean combinations. An example of this type of metadata and how they may be used to interoperate across multimedia data (Sheth and Kashyap, 1996) is briefly described below:

Example: Consider a decision support query across multiple data repositories possibly representing data in multiple media.

Get all regions having a population greater then 500, area greater than 50 acres having an urban land-cover and moderate relief.

The m-context can be represented as:

(**AND** region (population > 500) (area > 50)
(= land-cover "urban")(= relief "moderate"))

- Each of the attributes population, area, land-cover and relief capture information about regions stored in the underlying data. The attributes population and area capture information stored in structured data, whereas land-cover and relief capture information stored in image data.

- The attributes population and area are computed independently, and consist of SQL queries which select the appropriate regions satisfying population and area constraints from the census data.

- The attributes land-cover and relief are also computed independently, and consist of image processing routines which analyze geological maps to select appropriate regions satisfying land-cover and relief constraints.

- The final answer is the intersection of regions returned after computing the different metadata, and reflects the semantics of the boolean operator **AND** used to construct the m-context.

2.3.2 CONCEPTUAL CONTEXTS (C-CONTEXTS)

The representation of m-contexts is the first step in abstracting representational details, and capturing information content. The information captured in m-contexts however is *data sensitive.* An alternative perspective to capturing information content is to capture information that is *application sensitive.* Conceptual contexts primarily serve to capture *domain knowledge*, and help impose a conceptual semantic view on the underlying data. C-contexts are constructed from terms (concepts, roles) in domain specific ontologies. They are richer in information as compared to m-contexts, and are constructed when terms are chosen from ontologies that support complex relationships between terms. These relationships are typically used in ontological inferences, that are performed before evaluating c-contexts. The relationships typically are definitions of a term based on other terms in the ontology, and domain/range constraints on metadata attributes. Ontological inferences may be used to determine relevance of the underlying data.

Example: Consider the m-context discussed in the earlier section. Suppose the ontology from which the metadata description is constructed supports complex relationships. Furthermore, let:

CrowdedRegion ≡ (**AND** region (population > 200))

Inferences supported by the ontology enable determination that the regions required by the query metadata discussed earlier are instances of CrowdedRegion. Thus, the metadata description can be rewritten as:

(**AND** CrowdedRegion (population > 500) (area > 50)
(= land-cover "urban") (= relief "moderate"))

Thus, when mappings corresponding to the metadata are computed only those repositories are consulted which are known to contain information about CrowdedRegion. C-contexts may be considered as more sophisticated versions of m-contexts, where ontological inferences are performed before computing mappings and determining the relevance of underlying data.

2.4 DESIGN AND USE OF ONTOLOGIES

We now discuss various approaches for choosing ontological terms for construction of metadata expressions. The terms are either chosen from a single global ontology, or from multiple ontologies. In the case of multiple ontologies, issues of transforming the various metadata expressions arise. If an ontology is not available for an information domain, either it is constructed by re-using existing classifications/taxonomies, or by combining pre-existing ontologies.

2.4.1 THE COMMON ONTOLOGY APPROACH

One approach has been to build an extensive global ontology. A notable example of a global ontology is Cyc (Lenat and Guha, 1990) consisting of around 30,000 objects. In Cyc, the mapping between each individual information resource and the global ontology is accomplished by a set of *articulation axioms*, which are used to map entities of an information resource to the concepts (such as frames and slots) in Cyc's existing ontology (Collet et al., 1991).

Another approach has been to exploit the semantics of a single problem domain (e.g., transportation planning) (Arens et al., 1993). The domain model is a declarative description of objects and activities possible in the application domain, as viewed by a typical user. The user formulates queries using terms from the application domain.

2.4.2 RE-USE OF EXISTING CLASSIFICATIONS

We expect that there will be numerous independent information resources providing information on the GII. In this context, it is unrealistic to expect any one existing ontology or classification to suffice. In such a case, the re-use of various existing classifications such as ISBN classification for publications, and botanical classification for plants, is a very attractive alternative. An example of such a classification is illustrated in Figure 2.1.

These classifications can be used to construct domain specific ontologies containing terms which can be used to construct semantic metadata expressions.

2.4.3 RE-USE OF EXISTING ONTOLOGIES

The wide variety of users and their differing world views on the GII require us to consider multiple pre-existing ontologies describing varying world views. These ontologies can be combined in different ways, and made available on the GII. However, these ontologies have been designed independently, and with different perspectives on the real world. Hence, re-use of existing ontologies gives rise to issues of combining them in a consistent manner. Consider two domain ontologies which we also use later in the book. The Bibliographic Data ontology (Figure 2.2), was designed as a part of DARPA's Knowledge Sharing Effort and the WordNet ontology (Figure 2.3) is based on the Wordnet 1.5 Thesaurus. Both these ontologies describe the same (bibliographic) information, but from different perspectives.

A critical issue in combining various ontologies is determining the overlap between them. One possibility is to define "intersection" and "mutual exclusion" points between the various ontologies. This can be done by identifying

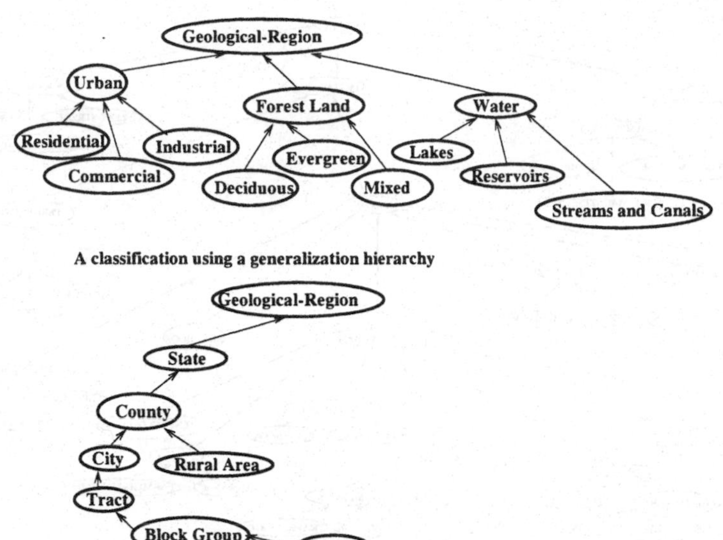

Figure 2.1. Examples of Generalization and Aggregation Hierarchies for Ontology Construction

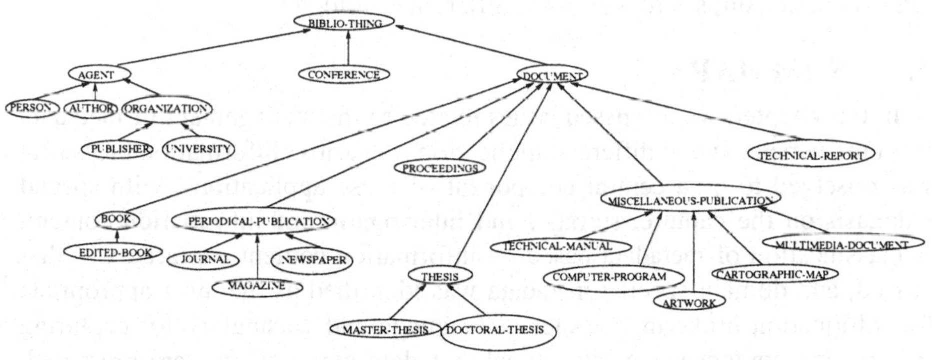

Figure 2.2. The Bibliographic Data Ontology (DARPA Knowledge Sharing Effort)

inter-ontological terminological relationships such as *synonyms*, *hyponyms*, and *hypernyms* between concepts in different ontologies.

Domain specific ontologies are an essential component of our approach to tackle heterogeneity and information overload on the GII. Future information systems will support semantic interoperability across different information domains, represented by various domain specific ontologies. Interoperation across different ontologies provides a way of supporting inter-domain semantic interoperability. Later in this book, we discuss techniques for inter-ontology

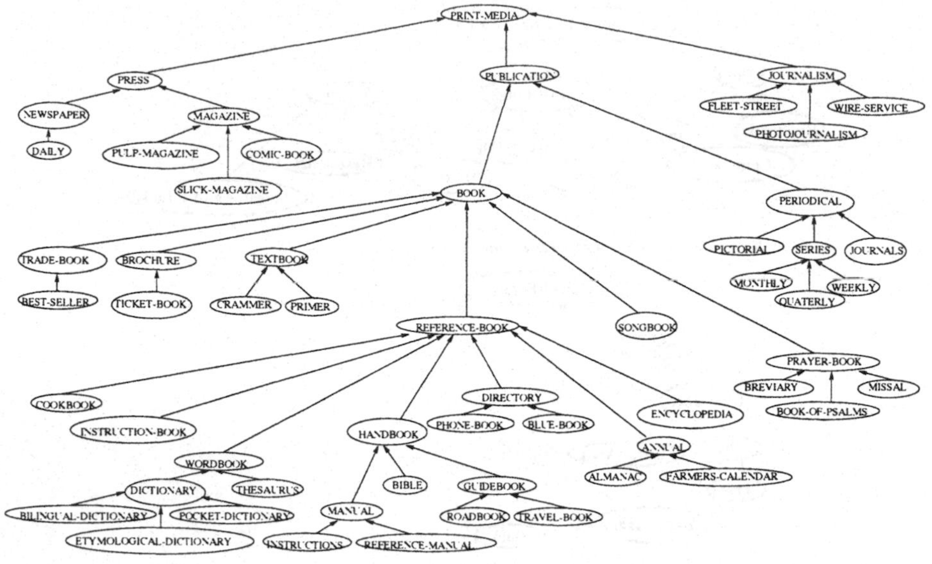

Figure 2.3. The WordNet 1.5 Thesaurus

interoperation based on identification, capture, and representation of terminological relationships across terms in different ontologies.

3. SUMMARY

In this chapter, we discussed issues related to the management of metadata from the perspective of different application scenarios. Information brokering was observed to be a central component of these applications, with special emphasis on the capture, storage, and interrogation of information content. A classification of metadata based on information content captured was discussed, and domain specific metadata was identified as the most appropriate for information brokering. Issues of language and vocabulary for capturing information content using intensional metadata expressions were presented. Also, an approach for re-use of terms in pre-existing domain specific ontologies, as the vocabulary for constructing intensional metadata expressions, was discussed. Metadata and ontologies form the twin pillars of our approach, and influence the design and architecture of brokering systems that are discussed in this book.

Chapter 3

METADATA-BASED ARCHITECTURES FOR INFORMATION BROKERING

In this chapter, an information brokering architecture with a focus on handling information overload is presented. The *metadata* and *vocabulary* components are the basic components of our approach (Chapter 1). In addition to discussing various components of the architecture, the "SEA" properties-*scalability*, *extensibility*, and *adaptability* for brokering systems are defined. The conditions under which the architecture would satisfy these properties are identified and discussed.

Finally, we trace the evolution of approaches for interoperability and discuss their relationship to the information brokering architecture. Interoperability-based approaches are mapped to the brokering architecture, and their drawbacks and limitations are discussed. Synergies between emerging agent-based information gathering and brokering systems are explored, and a *hybrid agent based brokering* architecture is presented.

1. AN (ABSTRACT) METADATA-BASED ARCHITECTURE

First, we describe an abstract metadata-based architecture organized around our two basic components (Figure 3.1):

Vocabulary Brokering Component The vocabulary component uses domain specific ontologies and terminological relationships between them, to reduce information overload and support a solution to the vocabulary problem. This component helps present to the user, a view of the GII as a collection of *vocabularies*, which may be used to construct metadata that characterize information content or specify an information request. The main sub-component is the *vocabulary broker*, which is responsible for translation of metadata descriptions (that capture information content) using terms in one

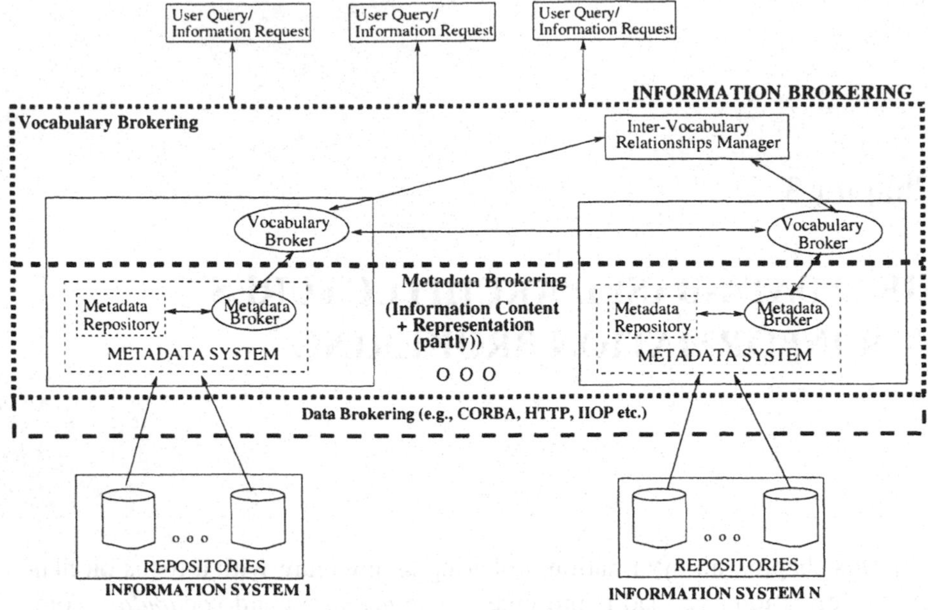

Figure 3.1. A High Level View of the Architecture

vocabulary into descriptions using terms from other vocabularies. For this purpose, it uses relationships between terms across different vocabularies provided by the *inter-vocabulary relationships manager*.

Metadata Brokering Component This component uses metadata descriptions to reduce information overload and capture information content. The main sub-component is the *metadata broker*, which is responsible for abstracting out representational details and capturing information content of the underlying data. It is also responsible for reasoning with metadata descriptions and combining information from the various underlying repositories, thus supporting information brokering at the level of *information content*. The metadata descriptions are stored in a *metadata repository*. Some metadata descriptions model representational details (e.g., structural organization) of the underlying data, and are used for brokering at the level of *representation*.

Each of the two basic components is a collection of various sub-components. We now describe the various sub-components in greater detail and discuss how they support a solution to the various problems enumerated in Chapter 1, Section 1.2

1.1 THE VOCABULARY BROKERING COMPONENT

The various sub-components of the vocabulary broker which enable information brokering at the *vocabulary* level (Figure 3.2) are:

- The *vocabulary broker*, the main sub-component
- The *inter-vocabulary relationships manager (IRM)*
- The *metadata system* which shall be discussed to the extent it supports vocabulary brokering functions.

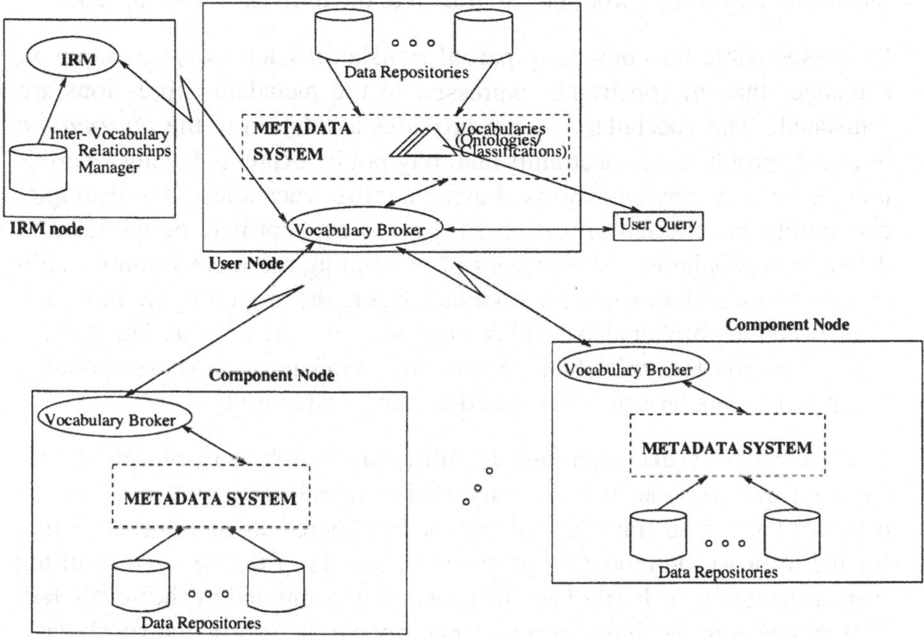

Figure 3.2. The Vocabulary Brokering Level of the Architecture

1.1.1 THE VOCABULARY BROKER

The Vocabulary Broker accepts as input a user query expressed in some metadata description language that may vary in sophistication (e.g., collection of keywords, attribute-value pairs, Description Logic expressions). The user vocabulary (represented as ontologies or classification taxonomies) used to construct the user query may be displayed using a Graphical User Interface (GUI). The functions performed by the Vocabulary Broker are as follows:

- It translates terms used in metadata descriptions, into vocabularies of other component systems. The vocabulary broker supports a limited solution to the *information resource discovery* problem based on the existence of a translation. For example, if a metadata description contains a request for a publication, identified as a book in another vocabulary, the vocabulary broker translates publication to book. *Information focusing* can be performed based on the resulting (possibly partial) translation of the query, which is used by the metadata system to determine the relevant subset of data in the underlying repositories. If a term translation does not exist, the vocabulary broker tries to translate the definition of the term based on other user vocabulary elements obtained from the metadata system. For example, if USGSPublication is defined as a publication produced by the organization USGS, the vocabulary broker would try to translate the term publication instead.

- It is responsible for combining partial translations across vocabularies in a manner that all constraints expressed in the metadata expressions are translated. The vocabulary broker provides a solution to the *information modeling* problem, as constraints that may not be expressed using a particular vocabulary may be expressed using another vocabulary. For example, constraints on different properties of a given concept may be modeled in different vocabularies. The process of combining these constraints would enable their translation into a vocabulary where the properties are modeled. The vocabulary broker also enables *information correlation*, as data satisfying various constraints is obtained from the metadata system corresponding to a given vocabulary, and then fused by the vocabulary broker.

- The vocabulary broker translates a conflicting term by substituting it with elements in a component vocabulary, which model similar information at a different level of abstraction, and may be considered an alternative solution for the information modeling problem. The *loss of information* resulting from a change in the level of abstraction is also computed by the vocabulary broker. For example, if the term student is not part of a particular vocabulary, the vocabulary broker might replace it with a term graduate student that might be present in that vocabulary. This leads to loss of information as only those instances of student that are graduate student are returned.

1.1.2 THE INTER-VOCABULARY RELATIONSHIPS MANAGER (IRM)

This component keeps track of terminological relationships between terms in different component vocabularies. It also stores transformer functions, that can convert/reformat data values using a vocabulary in one domain to another vocabulary in a semantically related domain.

1.1.3 THE METADATA SYSTEM

The Metadata System acts as the link between underlying data and terms of the vocabulary and is discussed in greater detail in the next section. Two functions performed by the metadata system that are useful for brokering at the vocabulary level are as follows.

- It provides the definition of a term based on other elements of a user vocabulary. It also provides information about vocabulary elements related to a particular term but at different levels of abstraction.
- It maintains mappings between terms in the vocabulary and underlying data structures in the repositories. It also combines these mappings in order to access and retrieve data corresponding to a metadata description from the repositories.

1.1.4 ENABLING SOLUTIONS TO THE VOCABULARY PROBLEM

The key problem handled at this level is the **vocabulary problem**. The two flavors of the vocabulary problem, namely, the *intensional* and the *extensional* are discussed next.

- At the intensional level, different terms might be used to describe similar but related information. If the terms are in different vocabularies, the relationship can be requested from the IRM. Descriptions and definitions of terms based on other elements in the same vocabulary can be retrieved from the metadata system. These are then used by the vocabulary broker to translate the original terms into terms in different vocabularies.
- At the extensional level, different terms may be used to describe instances or data values. An example is the use of semantically heterogeneous keys such as SS# and Employee No. to identify instances of employees in different databases. Transformer functions between various domains can be retrieved from the IRM. These transformer functions may be used to convert a SS# to the corresponding Employee No. (in the worst case it may be implemented as a table lookup). They are then used by the vocabulary broker to reformat and transform instances/values in one vocabulary to instances/values in another.

1.2 THE METADATA BROKERING COMPONENT

This component supports brokering both at the level of *information content*, and at the level of *representation*, depending on the metadata type used. It is a collection of metadata systems at each component node on the GII. Each component node is essentially a collection of information systems, the information content of data in which is captured by the metadata system. Each component node may or may not be described by a domain specific ontology. The main components of the metadata system at a component node (Figure 3.3) are described as follows.

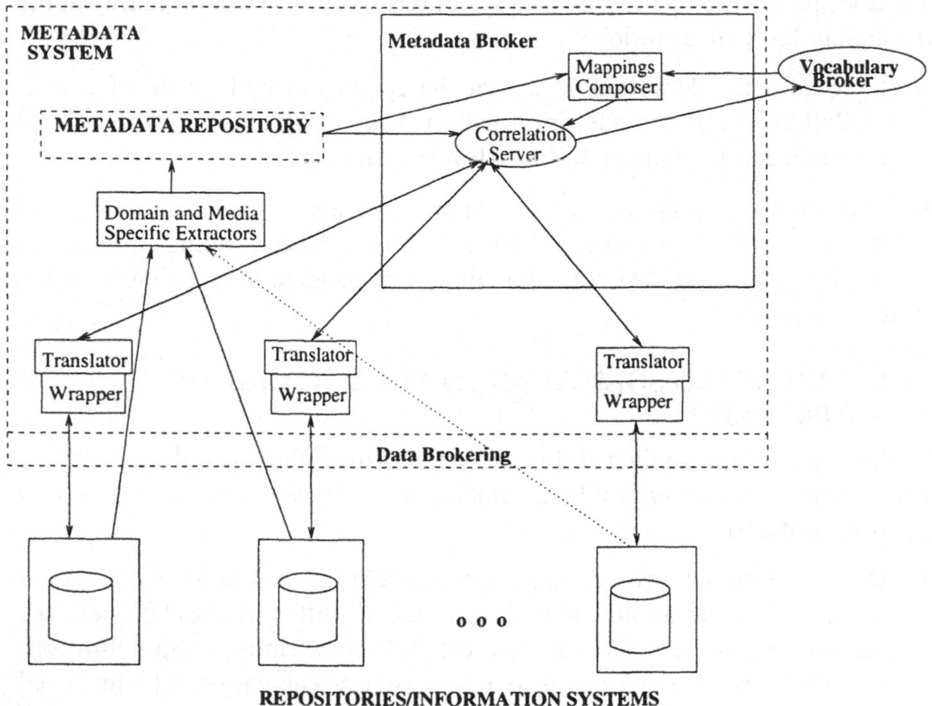

Figure 3.3. The Metadata System

1.2.1 THE METADATA BROKER

As discussed in the previous section, the metadata broker handles two kinds of requests: (a) requests for definitions of terms from the vocabulary broker; and (b) request for data corresponding to metadata descriptions from the vocabulary broker. The definitions of terms are obtained from the metadata repository. There are two major approaches for retrieving data corresponding to the metadata:

Bottom-Up approach In this approach, domain and media-specific metadata extractors are invoked off-line on the underlying data, and the computed metadata is stored in the metadata repository. The extraction process is responsible for identifying the relevant subset of data in the repositories. It also establishes relationships between various objects based on the different metadata supported by the metadata system, and relationships across the different metadata. Thus *information focusing* and *correlation* are performed by the extraction processes.

Top-Down approach In this approach, the metadata is computed at run-time, when the metadata broker attempts to answer a user query expressed as a metadata description. The various components of the metadata broker that enable this approach are described as follows.

Mappings Mappings between terms in the vocabulary and underlying data structures are stored in the metadata repository. For example, terms like publication may be mapped to appropriate tables in an underlying relational database. When evaluated at run-time, they result in retrieval of the relevant subset of data in underlying repositories. This helps in identifying the relevant subset of information and performs *information focusing*. A special case of mappings are *parameterized routines* that are invoked at run-time on the underlying data for metadata computation. An example of this case is an image processing routine associated with a term land-cover, that computes a region's land cover from a map.

Mappings Composer The mappings composer combines a set of mappings between terms in the metadata description and underlying data structures to give a composite mapping, that is logically equivalent to the metadata expression. For example, two terms in a vocabulary such as area and population, may map into the same underlying table (say Region). Suppose the metadata expression specifies the need for retrieving regions satisfying certain area and population constraints. The alternatives for the corresponding mappings are:

```
select * from Region where area > 1000 INTERSECT
select * from Region where population > 5000
```

(Without composition)

```
select * from Region where area > 1000 and population > 5000
```

(With composition)

It may be noted that the latter is a better alternative, as it eliminates the need for the metadata broker to redo work that is better done by the database system. In some cases (c-contexts), it may also perform inferences on the metadata description before mapping evaluation and composition. This enables *information correlation* at run-time. An example of this presented in Chapter 2, Section 2.3 demonstrates the utility of ontological inferences in identifying appropriate information sources.

Correlation Server The relevant data corresponding to the composite mapping constructed above may be spread across various repositories. The correlation server is responsible for:

(a) *Decomposition into mono-repository expressions.* After the composite mapping corresponding to a metadata description has been constructed, the pieces which can be computed at one repository have to be identified and dispatched to the appropriate repositories. The correlation server enables a partial solution to the *information resource discovery* problem within a component node, when it determines the relevant repositories as a part of the decomposition process.
(b) *Correlation of the data retrieved.* The data across various repositories is correlated according to the constraints specified in the metadata descriptions, thus performing *information correlation* within a component node.

Translator and Wrapper The mono-repository mapping expressions need to be translated to the local query languages used by underlying repositories. In case the repositories directly support a query language (e.g., SQL) then the mappings may be directly translated to SQL. If not, the mappings may be translated to a language supported by the wrapper around the repository.

1.2.2 THE METADATA REPOSITORY

The metadata repository is a (possibly) distributed system for storage and management of various types of metadata. It supports the metadata broker to compute metadata in response to a user query. Metadata requests to a metadata broker ultimately map into metadata queries against metadata repositories. In response, the metadata repository retrieves the appropriate stored metadata or invokes routines to compute metadata from the underlying repositories. It also provides definition of terms required by the vocabulary broker. The ability to deal with a wide variety of metadata suggests different possibilities for a metadata repository: a file system, a database management system and a knowledge base management system (Figure 3.4). For each possibility, we identify types of metadata requests that are best supported.

File Systems The metadata typically stored in file systems are direct content based metadata, examples of which are the inverted tree in WAIS (Kahle and Medlar, 1991) and document vectors in LSI (Deerwester et al., 1990). Typically *keyword-based queries* are used to query these types of metadata. Mappings between terms in a vocabulary and data structures in the underlying repositories may also be stored in a file system.

Databases A wide variety of metadata can (and should) be stored in structured databases. Examples of metadata, that may be stored in a structured database, are *type, location*, and *parent-child* relationships. The structured databases might have either a relational, object-relational or object oriented data model. Typically, *attribute-based queries* are used to query metadata

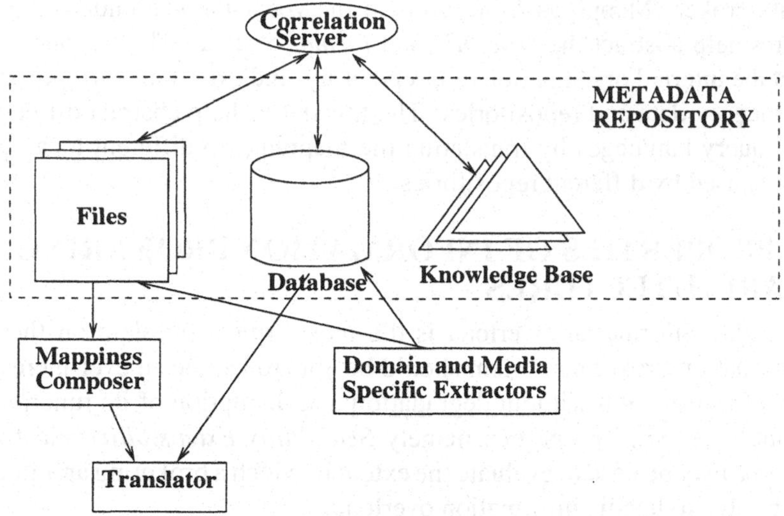

Figure 3.4. Different Possibilities for a Metadata Repository

stored in databases. As the amount of metadata increases, database indexing techniques may be used to improve performance. An object-relational or object oriented data model is essential to support storage and invocation of parameterized routines for run-time computation of metadata.

Knowledge Bases Domain specific metadata, such as ontologies and classification taxonomies may be stored in a knowledge base. The inference mechanisms supported by a knowledge base management system might be used to achieve reasoning with metadata descriptions. Typically, queries expressed as *c-contexts* are used to query metadata stored in a knowledge base. The request by the vocabulary broker for the definition of a term in the vocabulary (represented as an ontology in a knowledge base) is one request that can be supported by a knowledge base. Reasoning with metadata descriptions may also be implemented by subsumption inference supported by knowledge bases, one example of which is the classification of a metadata description into an ontology/classification taxonomy.

1.2.3 CONTRIBUTIONS AT THIS LEVEL OF ARCHITECTURE

A key contribution at this level of architecture is that of abstracting representational details to capture information content. *Domain* and *media specific* extractors help abstract media-specific characteristics to populate metadata. They also support modeling of information in a *domain specific* manner that enables domain specific requests for information. A similar contribution is made by the mappings composer and correlation server, which are components of the metadata broker. Mappings from terms in the vocabulary to underlying data structures help abstract the *structure* and *format* of data. The wrappers help abstract the internal organization of a repository, and export an *entity-attribute* view of legacy data and repositories. The translators help abstract differences in local query languages by translating the mappings to different local query languages used by different repositories.

2. PROPERTIES OF INFORMATION BROKERING ARCHITECTURES

Given that information overload is the most critical problem on the GII, any information brokering system should be able to handle an ever increasing amount of information without degradation and disruption of its functioning. We define three "SEA" properties, namely, *Scalability, Extensibility*, and *Adaptability*, that may be used to evaluate the extent to which a brokering architecture would be able to handle information overload.

Scalability The scale at which a system performs brokering is determined by the amount of data, and the number of data types/formats, information resources, and vocabularies handled by the system. An increase in the scale of brokering would necessarily lead to an increase in time for location of relevant information sources, translation of information requests into queries over multiple information sources, and correlation of related information. Scalability is the ability of the system to minimize increase in time for the above tasks as the scale of the brokering activities increases.

Extensibility Extending a brokering system to handle diverse information involves:

- registration of types/formats of data, information sources and vocabularies with the system
- complex mapping of terms in a (new) vocabulary to data types, data structures and query languages of information sources
- mapping of terms in a (new) vocabulary to other vocabularies registered with the brokering system.

A unit increase in the extent of the system may then be defined as enhancement of the system to support a new data type, information source, or vocabulary, and may lead to system non-availability for some period of time. Extensibility is the ability of the system to minimize the time of non-availability for a unit increase in the extent of the system.

Adaptability A brokering system should be able to handle situations where the user expresses his information request using terms of a vocabulary which is different from the one used by an information source to describe its information. Adapting an information request involves handling polysemy effects and differences in modeling and abstraction between two vocabularies. This leads to a loss of information, precision, and recall in the answer returned by the system. Adaptability is the ability of the system to minimize the loss of information incurred when transforming an information request using terms in one vocabulary into one using terms from a different vocabulary.

We now discuss the conditions under which, and to what extent, the architecture discussed in the previous section would satisfy the "SEA" properties.

2.1 ISSUES OF SCALABILITY

Issues related to scalability in the two components of the metadata-based architecture are discussed in this section.

2.1.1 ISSUES OF SCALABILITY IN THE VOCABULARY BROKERING COMPONENT

One of the key issues that affect the scalability of the architecture in this component, is what has been known as the *global ontology assumption.* A global ontology [of which Cyc (Lenat and Guha, 1990) is the most popular example] has been used for resource integration as in the Carnot project (Collet et al., 1991). In our approach, we visualize the vocabulary brokering component as a collection of *domain specific ontologies.* Interoperation across different ontologies is achieved by means of terminological relationships between terms across ontologies. This enhances the scalability of the system due to the following reasons.

- When similar terms in a global ontology are mapped into data structures of a large number of repositories, the complexity and heterogeneity of the mappings can increase significantly as the number of repositories increases. In our approach, data corresponding to similar terms in component ontologies can be combined, based on the nature of relationship between the terms. As an example, database object instances corresponding to two synonym terms in different ontologies may be combined using the *set union* operation. This enhances scalability as less computation is required to combine data, as opposed to the computation of complex mappings to an increasing number of repositories.

- Vocabulary brokering is achieved by translating from the user vocabulary into component vocabularies with the help of terminological relationships. This process can be terminated on input from the user. This enhances scalability as computation of complex relationships between terms in a global ontology would take more time and may often give inconsistent answers.

It may be noted that the key assumption in our approach is that, the number of relationships across similar terms in component ontologies is an order of magnitude less than the total number of terms and relationships in a global ontology. Thus, it would be more scalable to manage these smaller number of terminological relationships as opposed to the large number of terms in a global ontology.

2.1.2 ISSUES OF SCALABILITY IN THE METADATA BROKERING COMPONENT

As discussed earlier, one of the key functions of metadata layer, is to retrieve data in underlying repositories satisfying constraints in the metadata descriptions. Issues of scalability in this layer are dependent on issues of scalable processing by individual components (see Figure 3.3) of the architecture in this layer.

Metadata Repository As noted earlier, requests for attribute-based metadata typically stored in structured databases, can be speeded up by building indices on frequently queried and selective attributes. Schemas to store metadata should also be designed with care, as choice of a certain schema definition may make it more expensive to query the metadata, even though it may be possible to add more metadata types easily. This trade-off is an instance of the typical *scalability* versus *extensibility* trade-offs seen in information brokering. Constructs in a knowledge representation language used to represent domain specific ontologies should be carefully chosen so as to permit tractable computation of inferences (e.g., definitions of terms, least common subsumers) on terms stored in the knowledge base.

Correlation Server As discussed earlier, the function of the correlation server is to correlate data across various repositories satisfying constraints specified in the metadata descriptions. The correlation server may be made more scalable by using the following approaches.

- A control strategy can be used to order the evaluation of metadata constraints. Metadata that require expensive computation to be performed on the underlying media (e.g., image), may be computed after the number of objects under consideration are reduced, as a result of computing constraints on metadata requiring less computation (e.g., structured data). This may be viewed as a generalization of the famous semi-join technique in distributed databases. Planning-based approaches for evaluations of constraints across multiple information sources (Arens et al., 1993) have a similar purpose.

- Trade-offs can be made between pre-computation (or static extraction) of metadata, storage of frequently used metadata in the metadata repository, and computing them at run-time. In the case where metadata changes rapidly (e.g., cloud cover in weather maps), and where a huge amount of space is required for storage, pre-computation may not be a feasible option. This trade-off is another instance of the typical *scalability* versus *extensibility* trade-offs seen in information brokering.

- One way to ensure scalability of an information brokering system is to anticipate the types of metadata descriptions in advance, and ensure support for efficient computation for those metadata. One approach to ensure this, is to support *querying at multiple levels of abstraction* within a particular domain. Here, it would be advantageous to model metadata computations at a particular level of abstraction, as a function (e.g., aggregation) over pre-computed metadata at the preceding or succeeding level(s) of abstraction. An important issue here is the level of abstraction at which metadata may be computed. Using this approach to ensure scalability leads into issues of *adaptability*, which shall be discussed in a later section.

2.2 ISSUES OF EXTENSIBILITY

We now discuss issues related to extensibility of the brokering architecture at both, the vocabulary and metadata levels. In particular we shall discuss how disruption in the functioning of the system may be minimized when new repositories and component ontologies are added.

2.2.1 ADDITION OF NEW REPOSITORIES

The addition of new repositories requires design of new mappings from terms in the component vocabulary to its data structures, a wrapper for supporting an *entity-attribute* view of the repository, and a translator to translate mapping expressions into the local repository query language. It may be noted that all these changes may be implemented at the repository site without affecting the functioning of the system. System level information required by the correlation server such as *locations of the data/repositories, wrappers, authorization information needed by the wrappers, translators, data organization*, etc. may be stored and obtained from the metadata repository.

We may want to add repositories to the system which may be queried using a *keyword-based query* thus exporting a full-text view. One way of achieving this is to *re-use* and *plug in* third party indexing technologies. Indexing technologies come with their own search modules, which operate on metadata stored in particular formats. All we need to do in our architecture is to write appropriate domain and media specific extractors, which would extract and store textual metadata from the text repositories in the same way the indexing technology would.

2.2.2 ADDITION OF NEW ONTOLOGIES

The key problem in adding a new vocabulary to the system is that of interoperating the ontology of the new component with the other component ontologies. Conforming to the *global ontology* assumption would require integration/assimilation of the existing ontology with the new component ontology. This is a complex task and would require disruption of the functioning of the system. In our architecture, all we need to do is add relationships between terms in the new vocabulary and terms in existing vocabularies in the IRM repository. This can be done without disruption as the IRM is an independent unit.

2.2.3 EXTENSIBILITY OF METADATA REPOSITORY

There are two conditions under which the metadata repository can be considered extensible with respect to new data and media types and new metadata.

- When new domain specific metadata or terms are added to a component vocabulary, the knowledge base should support mechanisms to appropriately classify them in the ontology/classification.

- The *top-down approach* of metadata computation leads to an increased extensibility of the system. It enables easy addition of metadata, which require processing on new media or data types, and processing of dynamically changing data. Addition of new data corresponding to already supported data types does not require any changes to the metadata. The schema of the metadata repository should support *parameterized routines*. All that needs to be done is to add appropriate parameterized routines corresponding to new data and media types, to the metadata repository. Contrast this with the *bottom-up approach*, where domain and media specific extractors would have to be executed again to re-populate the metadata.

2.3 ISSUES OF ADAPTABILITY

We have discussed in the previous section, an approach for ensuring scalability, that anticipates all metadata descriptions that might be generated. This can be achieved by providing support for efficient computation of metadata, and depends on terms in the vocabulary of a particular information domain. Thus, adaptability of a system may be seen as a logical outgrowth of enhancing its scalability. We now discuss conditions under which the architecture discussed in the previous section may be considered adaptable.

Intra-Domain Adaptability This type of adaptability is displayed in the *metadata brokering component*, and arises from the need to support efficient metadata computation for all terms in a specific domain of information. Support is provided for querying at different levels of abstractions within a domain, and is enabled by a *top-down* approach for metadata computation. Adopting the *bottom-up* approach for metadata computation would entail pre-computing metadata at all levels of abstraction which is not a feasible option. The top-down approach can be applied to any set of domain specific terms in a vocabulary as all that is required is definition of appropriate mappings, translators, wrappers, and parameterized routines. This enables adaptability of the metadata brokering component within the vocabulary of an information domain.

Inter-Domain Adaptability This type of adaptability is displayed at the *vocabulary brokering level*. In this case, there is a need to support computation of metadata expressing similar information, but characterized using a set of terms from a (slightly) different domain specific vocabulary. In this case too, considerations of scalability lead us to design a scheme of interoperation across different component vocabularies. A critical issue in supporting the above approach for interoperation, is that of using *inter-ontology relationships* to transform metadata descriptions using terms in one ontology, into one using terms in a different but related ontology. This is achieved by the management of inter-ontology relationships by the IRM, and translation of metadata descriptions by the vocabulary broker. This enables adaptability of the vocabulary brokering component across different but related domains of information.

3. ARCHITECTURAL EVOLUTION AND PROPERTIES

Interoperability across disparate information systems spread over a networked infrastructure has been the subject of research and development since the 1970s. We now trace the evolution of various approaches by discussing representative architectures based on these approaches in the context of our brokering architecture (Section 1.). The properties of these architectures based on "SEA" criteria (Section 2.) are also discussed. Finally, a new paradigm of interoperability based on agent systems, that attempts to exploit the synergy between brokering and agent systems, is explored in the context of a *hybrid agent-based brokering* architecture.

3.1 FEDERATED MULTIDATABASE SYSTEMS

The predominant architectural framework for interoperation of database management systems, was that of federated multidatabase system (Heimbigner

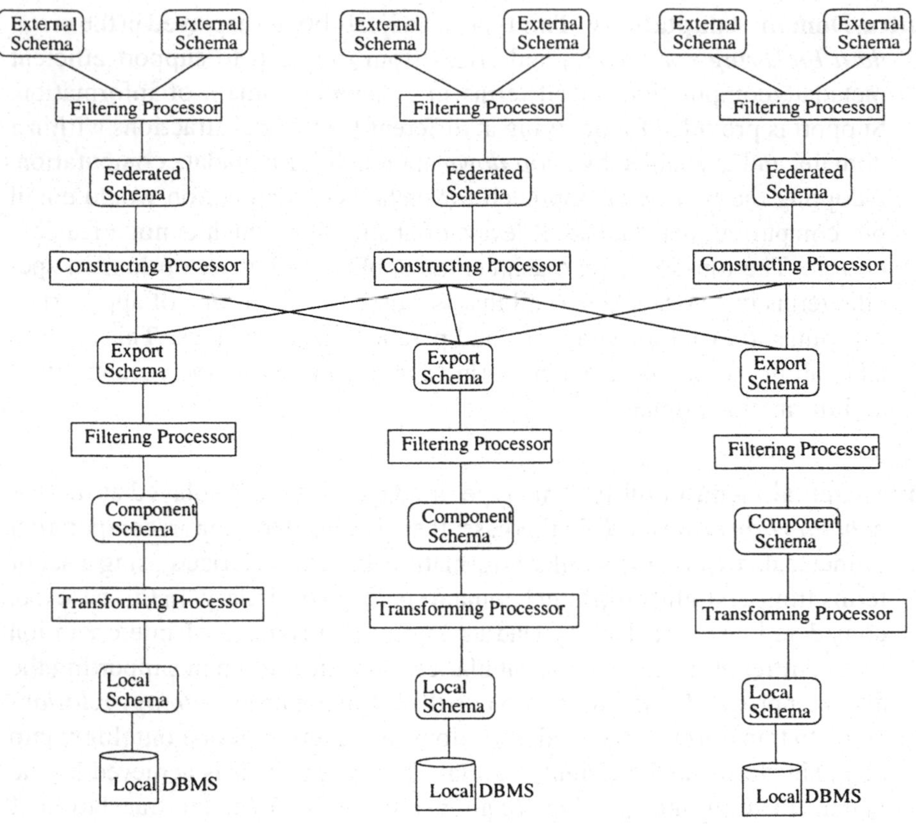

Figure 3.5. Federated Architecture for Multidatabase Interoperability

and McLeod, 1985; Litwin and Abdellatif, 1986; Sheth and Larson, 1990). The five level federated architecture illustrated in Figure 3.5 consists of the following components.

Local Schema A local schema is the conceptual schema of a local DBMS. Different local schemas may be expressed in different data models. In our information brokering architecture, we do not require information sources such as text and image databases to have a conceptual schema.

Component Schema A component schema is derived by translating local schemas into the *canonical* or *common data model* (CDM) of the federated system; and describes diverging local schemas using a single representation. This component schema is implicitly captured by terms in the domain specific ontology. The common data model corresponds to the data model or meta-model in which the ontology is represented.

Transforming Processor The process of schema translation from a local schema to a component schema generates mappings between component and local schema objects. Transforming processors use these mappings to transform commands on a component schema, to commands on the corresponding local schema. This functionality can be found in the *translator/wrapper* component of the *metadata broker*. The mappings between the component and local schema objects are special cases of mappings between terms in the vocabulary and data structures in the information sources, and are stored in the *metadata repository*.

Export Schema For reasons of security and privacy, not all data of a component schema may be available to the federation. An export schema represents a subset of a component schema that is available to the federation. The export schema is implicitly specified in the information brokering architecture by the set of term mappings supplied by the information sources.

Filtering Processor A filtering processor provides the access control as specified in the export (or external) schema by limiting the set of allowable operations on the corresponding component (or federated) schema. This is again done implicitly by specification of appropriate term mappings.

Federated Schema A federated schema is an integration of multiple export schemas. Is also includes information on data distribution that is generated when integrating export schemas. The federated schema is implicitly captured by terms in the domain specific ontology.

Constructing Processor A constructing processor transforms commands on the federated schema into commands on one or more export schemas. This functionality is found in the *mappings composer* and *correlation server* components of the *metadata broker*. However, the constructing processor is dependent on pre-defined mappings to the federated schema, and cannot respond to a dynamic environment where external schemas are being added and deleted from a federation.

External Schema An external schema defines a schema for a user, and/or application, or a class of users/applications. It provides a customization of the federated schema targeted towards a class of users/applications. The external schema may be created by defining views, and subsets of domain specific ontologies.

These systems deal with interoperability at the level of *information content*, especially the content captured in structured databases having a well defined schema. They lack the ability to support interoperability at the vocabulary level, and thus, lacking in *adaptability* within and across information domains.

The federated schema in the above architecture needs to be designed statically or prior to query formulation, and is based on the integration of the underlying export schemas. This makes easy addition and removal of information resources from the federation, a difficult task. Each time a new system is added or removed, the federated schema has to be re-constructed and the mappings redefined. This results in the lack of *extensibility*. Integration of external schemas is a complex task and the architecture supports some *scalability* by allowing for the definition of multiple federated schemas. However, the approach involving pre-integration of schemas is not known to scale beyond tens of schemas. This is a definite limitation with respect to the global scope of current information systems.

3.2 MEDIATOR-BASED SYSTEMS

As a wide variety of multimedia data began to proliferate, the federated multidatabase architecture was adapted to become a federated information systems architecture, where the database systems were replaced by a broader variety of information systems. These included simple data access protocols, a broad variety of databases (network, relational, and object oriented), specialized databases to handle specific digital media (predominantly images and video), web servers for semi-structured data management, and even expert systems. These systems are likely to face some of the shortcomings seen in the federated architectures discussed above.

Mediator architectures (Wiederhold, 1992) were clearly the dominant ones for these systems. They consisted of wrappers for encapsulating heterogeneous information sources to provide a uniform interface to the rest of the world, and mediators to provide a broad variety of value added services. Most implemented mediator systems, however, consider scenarios with one central mediator module collaborating with a collection of wrapper modules. We now discuss a representative mediator architecture (Figure 3.6) and compare it to the brokering architecture discussed in an earlier section of this chapter.

Translators A translator logically converts the underlying data objects in an information source to a common information model. Queries over information in the common model are converted into requests that the source can execute, and data returned by the source is converted into the common model. A translator in the mediator architecture, and *translators/wrappers* in the brokering architecture, may be considered generalizations of the *transformation processor* in the federated architecture. Whereas the transformation processor transforms queries and data from one structured data model to another, translators in the mediator architecture transform unstructured data into a structured information model.

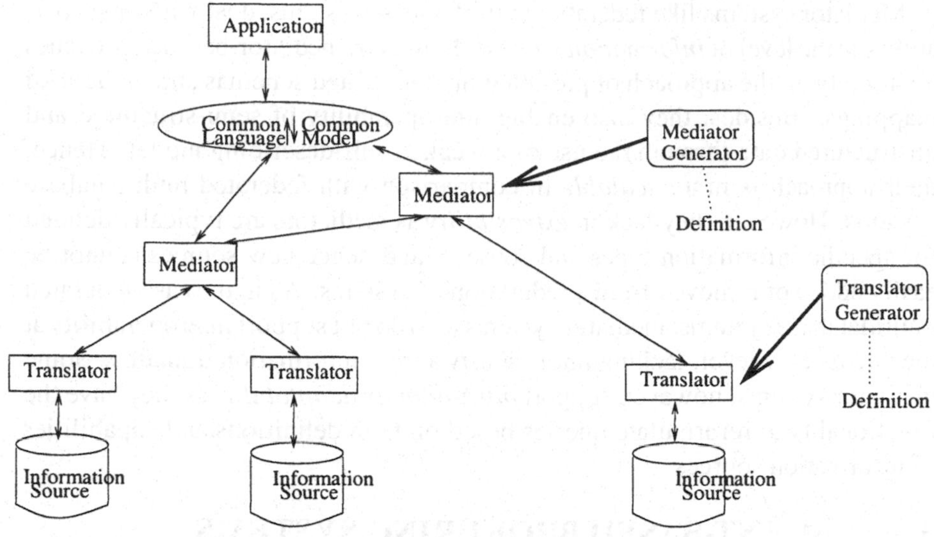

Figure 3.6. A Standard Mediator Architecture

Common Model A common object model serves to convey information among components, and typically they are simple, self describing models with nesting. This is a generalization (or a weaker version of) the *common data model* in the federated architecture as it does not have strong typing of objects. It corresponds to the *meta-model* for storing ontologies in the brokering architecture.

Common Query Language A common query language is used to link components and query substructures in the objects represented in the common information model. This is a more powerful version of the query language used in the federated architecture, and corresponds to the language used by the *metadata broker* for representing metadata expressions in the brokering architecture.

Mediators A mediator is a system that refines in some way, information from one or more sources (Wiederhold, 1992). A mediator embeds the knowledge that is necessary for processing a specific type of information. It may be considered a generalized form of the *construction processor* and *federated schema* of the federated architecture. However, it is dependent on the type and sources of information. This functionality may be found in the *correlation server* and *mappings composer* components of the *metadata broker*, but mediators lack the capability of dynamic composition of mappings in response to new information sources being added to the system. Mediators can perform simple functions such as *date transformation* or complex functions such as *capability based query reformulation.*

Mediator systems like federated multidatabase systems, deal with interoperability at the level of *information content*. However, mediator-based approaches do not rely on the approach of pre-integrated federated schemas and predefined mappings. Besides, they also enable interoperability of semi-structured and unstructured data through the use of a weaker, self-describing model. Hence, their approach is more *scalable* in comparison with federated multidatabase systems. However, they lack in *extensibility* as mediators are typically defined for specific information types and sources, and hence new sources cannot be easily added or removed from a federation of systems. As in the case federated multidatabase systems, mediator systems also do not support interoperability at the *vocabulary* level, lacking *adaptability* across information domains. Some mediator systems, however, support *intra-domain adaptability* as they have the functionality to reformulate queries based on term definitions and capabilities of information sources.

3.3 AGENT-BASED BROKERING SYSTEMS

There has been a lot of research in identifying and describing essential features of multi-agent systems from different perspectives (Huhns and Singh, 1998; Klusch, 1999). Various features of multi-agent systems make them an appropriate choice for implementing information brokering techniques on the GII. Some extensions to agent functionalities that enable support for information brokering (Sheth et al., 1999) are:

- ability to capture, view and interrogate semantics of the underlying (multimedia) data. An information agent should be able to extract and associate semantic metadata descriptions, and design mappings from the underlying data

- ability to support information requests independent of the type, structure, format or media in which the information may be stored. An information agent should be able to locate and correlate pieces of relevant information that may be distributed on the GII.

- ability to support interoperation across multiple terminologies or domain specific ontologies. An information agent should be able to merge ontologies and reformulate information requests across different ontologies.

We now discuss an agent system designed to handle typical information brokering functions (Figure 3.7). An example of agent system that instantiates part of this architecture will be discussed later in this book.

Consumer Agent This agent interacts with the user by helping it to specify an information request. It also communicates with vocabulary brokers known to it, and receives information about the various vocabularies/classifications

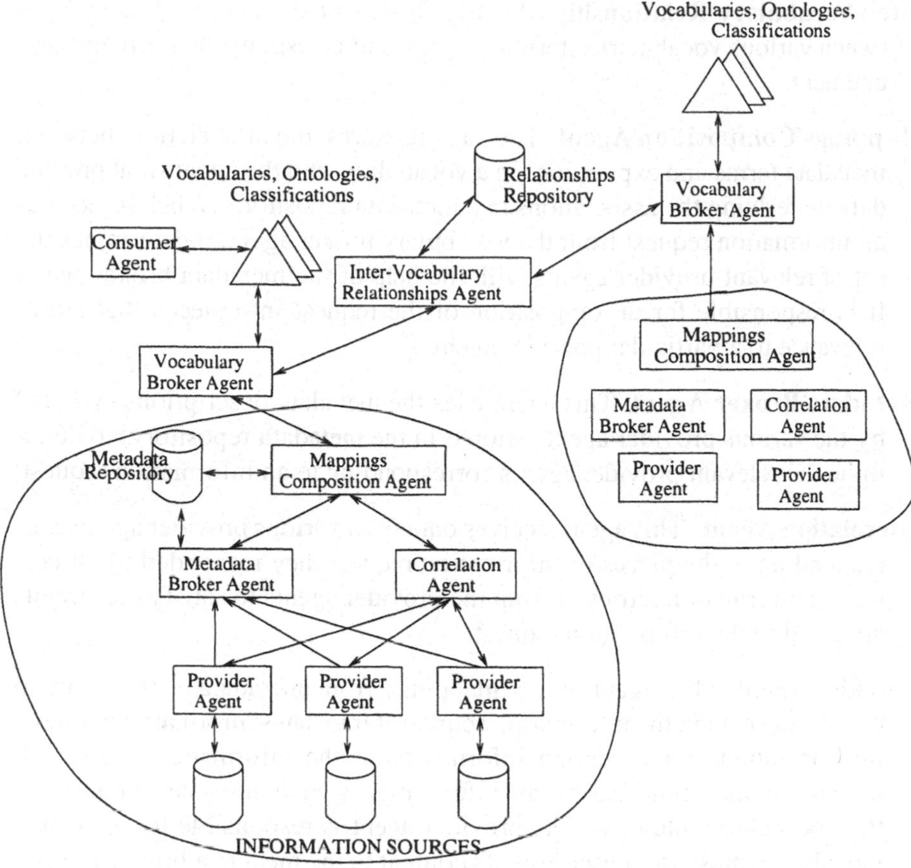

Figure 3.7. Agent-based Information Brokering

and ontologies. Information requests are constructed using concepts from vocabularies/ontologies and forwarded to the vocabulary broker agent.

Vocabulary Brokering Agent This agent tries to satisfy the information request in one of the following two ways.

- It forwards the information request to a metadata broker agent which retrieves the relevant information.
- It retrieves linkages with other vocabularies/ontologies from the inter-vocabulary relationships agent, and reformulates the information request using terms and concepts from other vocabularies/ontologies. It forwards the reformulated information request to relevant vocabulary broker agents, and is responsible for correlating information received from them.

Inter-Vocabulary Relationships Agent This agent stores cross-linkages between various vocabularies/terminologies, and is responsible for their management.

Mappings Composition Agent This agent stores the association between metadata terms and expressions in a vocabulary, and the agents that provide data underlying the associations in a metadata repository. When it receives an information request from the vocabulary broker agent, it determines the set of relevant provider agents with the help of the metadata broker agent. It is responsible for decomposition of the request into pieces that are of relevance to a particular provider agent.

Metadata Broker Agent This agent uses the metadata descriptions exported by the various provider agents (stored in the metadata repository) to determine the relevant provider agents corresponding to an information request.

Correlation Agent This agent receives data from various provider agents corresponding to the pieces of information request they responded to. It correlates information retrieved from the provider agents to satisfy constraints specified in the information request.

Provider Agent This agent stores mappings from metadata expressions to underlying data in the information source. It translates information requests into operations for accessing information at the information source. It transforms data returned by an information source into the language of the vocabulary/ontology. The provider agent is responsible for exporting metadata expressions describing its content to the metadata broker agent.

4. SUMMARY

A metadata-based architecture for information brokering was described in this chapter. We identified and discussed two basic components of this architecture, *metadata* and *vocabulary*. These components were described in greater detail by describing their sub-components and their respective functionalities. The contributions made by each of the components towards tackling information overload were also discussed. A set of "SEA" properties, *scalability*, *extensibility*, and *adaptability* that brokering systems should have, were identified and defined. Issues relating to the above properties as relating to the different components of the architecture were also discussed.

We also discussed the evolution of architectures to support interoperability. Reference architectures for federated multidatabase systems and mediator-based systems were compared to the brokering architecture. The "SEA" properties of these architectures were also discussed. We concluded by presenting a *hybrid agent based brokering* architecture for information brokering.

Chapter 4

METADATA-BASED BROKERING FOR DIGITAL DATA

We now discuss, with the help of an illustrative example, how different types of metadata may be utilized for responding to information requests. The information required is stored in different types of digital media, viz., text, image and structured databases. *Domain specific metadata* is the most important component of metadata for brokering at the level of information content. Domain specific metadata support retrieval and correlation of information independent of the underlying media of representation. This approach may be characterized as follows.

- Use of domain specific metadata descriptions for capturing information content of data stored in heterogeneous data/media types.
- Establishing relationships between metadata descriptions. These relationships might be specified in the information request, or may be inferred from the domain specific ontology.
- Fusion and presentation of the retrieved data represented in multiple media.

This chapter deals with the *metadata brokering component.* We use an example information request to illustrate various roles played by different types of metadata in responding to a request involving multimedia data. A succession of information brokering prototypes are discussed in this context.

1. A MULTIMEDIA INFORMATION REQUEST

Consider the following query, that is representative of information needed by decision makers trying to evaluate areas for evacuation in the case of large fires. In particular, this query identifies those areas where the fire is "contained" so that emergency response teams can focus on other areas.

Get me all **regions (states, counties, blocks)** having a **population** greater than 500 and **area** greater than 50 acres having an **urban land cover** and such that all the nearby fires have **excellent containment**

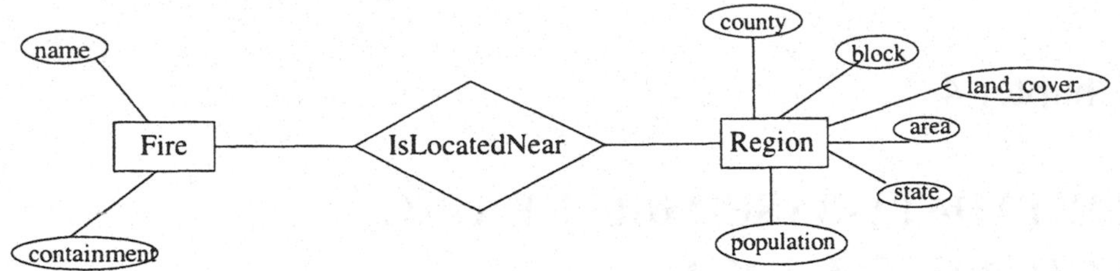

Figure 4.1. The Domain Ontology for the Multimedia Query

The words in bold represent terms from a user's vocabulary (Figure 4.1) used to construct a query expression consisting of *domain specific* metadata. It may be noted that the relationships and constraints are *media independent* in nature. The information brokering problems that arise in trying to respond to the above information request are discussed next.

Representational Heterogeneity In the above information request, *population* and *area* are computed from a structured database, *land cover* is computed from a GIS image database, and *excellent containment* of fires is computed from a text database. In order to perform correlation, the brokering system also needs to compute the *boundary* and *spatial location* of a region which is transparent to the user. Also, since the constraints in the information request are *media independent*, it is not necessary for decision makers to be aware of this heterogeneity. The following repositories are used to respond to this information request:

- A Census database containing area and population characteristics obtained from the US census bureau.
- A repository containing land use maps (image data) from the USGS.
- The TIGER/LINE database containing the boundaries of various regions in the US.
- A repository containing daily reports on major fires in the US. This is provided by the USGS, and is in the form of textual documents containing structured phrases and free form text.

Information Overload It is unrealistic to expect decision makers to keep track of repositories that can satisfy a particular information need. In the above situation, the user would need to manually look up fire reports and land cover maps, and correlate them with area and population characteristics of regions that are close to the fire. We use metadata as the basis to enable correlation across structured, text, and image data.

The overall brokering approach involved in responding to the information request discussed above is illustrated in Figure 4.2. The functionality required to respond to the information request involves dealing with different types of metadata. This is done by different brokering systems identified in the figure.

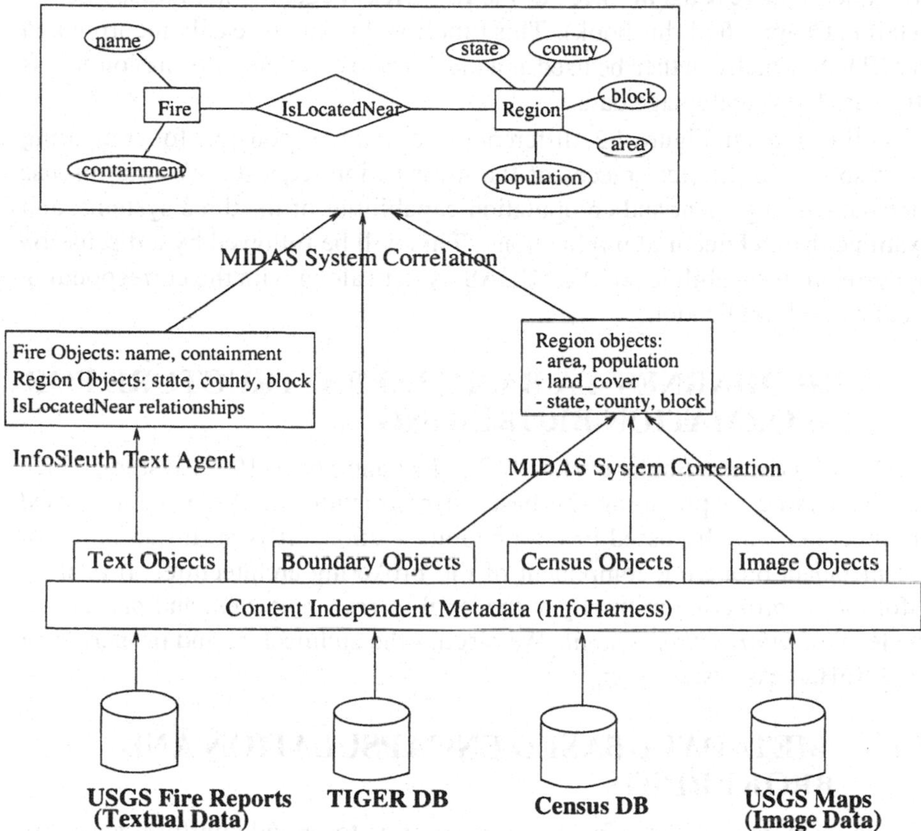

Figure 4.2. Metadata Brokering for Multimedia Information Requests

The **InfoHarness** system provides uniform access to information independent of formats, location, and organization of information in the individual information sources. Content independent metadata are used to encapsulate the underlying data and media heterogeneity, and represent information in an object model. This provides a basic metadata-based brokering infrastructure, which is used to implement techniques for handling domain specific metadata. The **MIDAS** system is essentially an extension of the InfoHarness system, designed to handle a richer variety of domain specific metadata, especially those describing data stored in different media types. It also provides a metadata-based platform to correlate information stored in different media types.

The MIDAS system manages metadata and its associations with structured and image data. We use its metadata-based platform to correlate information stored in structured and image data with information stored in text data. The ability of managing metadata associated with textual documents requires functionality to store and combine mappings of domain specific metadata, and can be found in the **text agent** piece of the **InfoSleuth** agent system (discussed in detail in Chapter 6 of this book). This functionality can be easily incorporated in MIDAS, which can then be used as a platform to correlate information across structured, text and image data.

As illustrated in Figure 4.2, different systems are responsible for computing the response to different pieces of the information request. We first discuss metadata management and computation capabilities of the three systems, and examine the architectural implications. This will be followed by a discussion of correlation capabilities of the MIDAS system along with the corresponding architectural implications.

2. INFOHARNESS: A BASIC INFRASTRUCTURE FOR INFORMATION BROKERING

The InfoHarness (Shklar et al., 1995c; Shah and Sheth, 1999) system, which can be viewed as providing the basic infrastructure for the metadata-based architecture, was discussed in the previous section. It is an instantiation of the metadata brokering component of the brokering architecture. It enables information brokering primarily at the level of *representation*, and partially at the level of *information content*. We discuss the architecture and properties of the InfoHarness system next.

2.1 METADATA-BASED ENCAPSULATION AND BROKERING

The main goal of the InfoHarness system, is to provide uniform access to information independent of the formats, location, and organization of information in the data repositories. We discuss how content-independent metadata (e.g., type, location, access rights, owner, creation date, etc.) may be used to encapsulate the underlying data/media heterogeneity and represent information in an object model. Brokering functions supported by the InfoHarness system are also discussed.

2.1.1 METADATA-BASED ENCAPSULATION

A metadata entity that is associated with the lowest level of granularity of information available to the InfoHarness system is called an *information unit*

(IU). An IU may be associated with a file (e.g., a man page, a usenet news item), a portion of a file (e.g., a C function or a database table), a set of files (e.g., a collection of related bitmaps), or any request for the retrieval of data from an external source (e.g., a database query). An InfoHarness Object (IHO) may be one of the following:

- a single information unit
- a collection of InfoHarness objects (indexed or non-indexed)
- a single information unit and a collection of InfoHarness objects

Each IHO has a unique object identifier that is recognized and maintained by the system. An IHO that encapsulates an IU contains information about the location of data, retrieval method, and any parameters needed by the method to extract the relevant portion of information. In addition each IHO may contain an arbitrary number of attribute-value pairs for attribute-based access to the information. An InfoHarness Repository (IHR) is a collection of IHOs. Each IHO that encapsulates a collection of IHOs stores unique object identifiers of the members of the collection. These members are called *children* of the IHO, and the IHOs that are associated with these collections are called *parents*. Each IHO that has one or more parents always contains unique object identifiers of its parent objects.

2.1.2 METADATA-BASED BROKERING

The types of brokering functions supported by the InfoHarness system are discussed next.

Logical structuring of the Information Space

We illustrate with an example how extraction of content and domain independent metadata can enable logical structuring of the information space. Information can be browsed according to units of interest, as opposed to the physical organization of the underlying data repositories.

Consider the scenario illustrated in Figure 4.3. Case I depicts actual physical distribution of various types of documents required in a large software design project. The different documents are spread all over the file system as a result of different members of the project putting files where they were deemed appropriate. Appropriate metadata extractors pre-process these documents, and store important information like *type* and *location*, and establish appropriate parent-child relationships. Case II illustrates the desired logical view seen by the user.

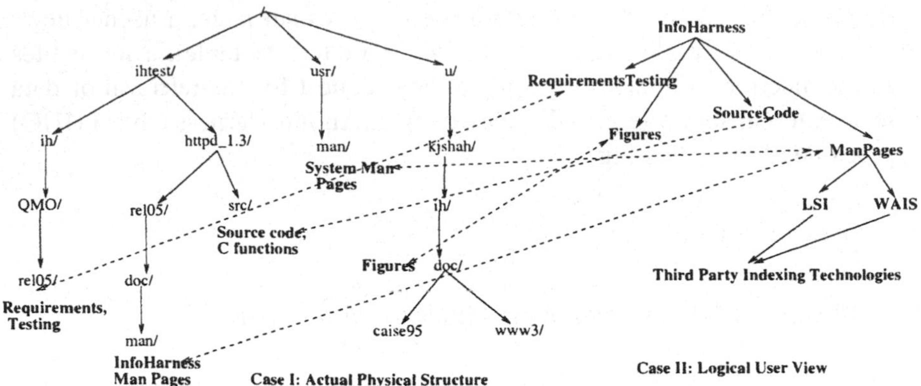

Figure 4.3. Logical structuring of the Information Space

Use of third party indexing technologies for keyword-based access

One of the key capabilities of the InfoHarness system, is that it provides an infrastructure for the use of third-party indexing technologies to index document collections. This is illustrated in Figure 4.3, Case II where the same set of documents are indexed using different third party indexing technologies. Each of these document collections so indexed can be now queried using a *keyword-based query* without the user having to worry about details of the underlying indexing technology.

Attribute-based access

Attribute-based access provides a powerful complementary or alternative search mechanism to traditional content-based search and access (Sheth et al., 1995). While attribute-based access can provide better *precision* (Salton, 1989), it can be more complex as it requires that appropriate attributes be identified, and the corresponding metadata instantiated before accessing data.

In Figure 4.4, we illustrate an example of attribute-based access in the InfoHarness system. Attribute-based queries by the user result in SQL queries to the metadata repository (stored in an Oracle database in this case), and result in the retrieval of news items which satisfy the conditions specified. The InfoHarness system supports bottom-up extraction of attribute-based metadata from text documents. However, it does not have the capability of associating domain specific concepts and attributes with underlying data. This capability is present in the text agent of the InfoSleuth system.

2.1.3 TYPES OF METADATA

The brokering performed by the InfoHarness system is primarily at the level of *representation*, and is reflected in the organizational structures of the IHOs

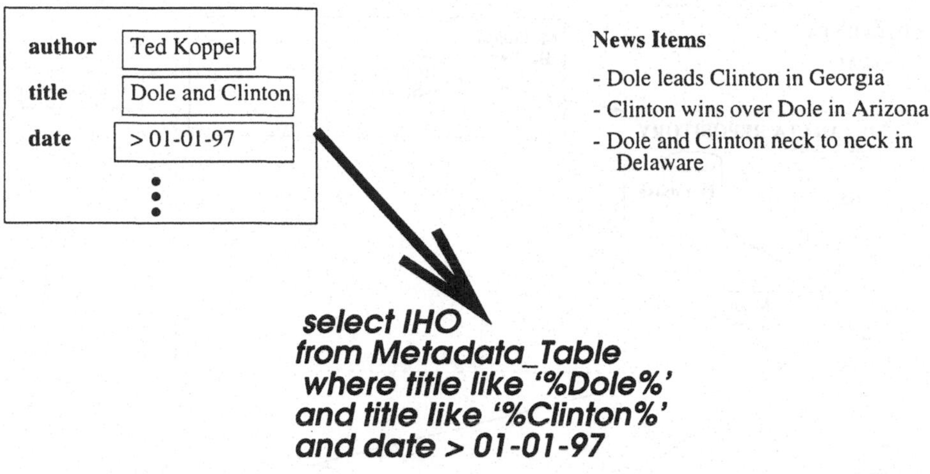

Figure 4.4. Attribute Based Access in InfoHarness

encapsulating them. A small but significant part of the brokering is performed at the level of *information content*. This is reflected in the metadata types extracted and managed by the InfoHarness system. We enumerate various types of metadata and identify the purpose for which they are extracted in Table 4.1.

Metadata	Metadata Type	Purpose
location, type, owner, permissions	content independent	encapsulation
size	content dependent	brokering at the level of representation
document vectors, inverted trees	direct content based	brokering at the levels of representation and content
parent-child relationships function-file relationships in C class-subclass relationships in C++	domain independent	brokering at the level of structural organization/ representation
attributes of netnews posts like date, author, title	domain specific	brokering at the level of information content

Table 4.1. Metadata Types in the InfoHarness System

2.2 THE INFOHARNESS SYSTEM ARCHITECTURE

The architecture of the InfoHarness system (Figure 4.5) is described next.

InfoHarness Server This represents the metadata broker identified in the brokering architecture. It is responsible for handling metadata requests generated as the result of a user query. It passes metadata requests to the metadata

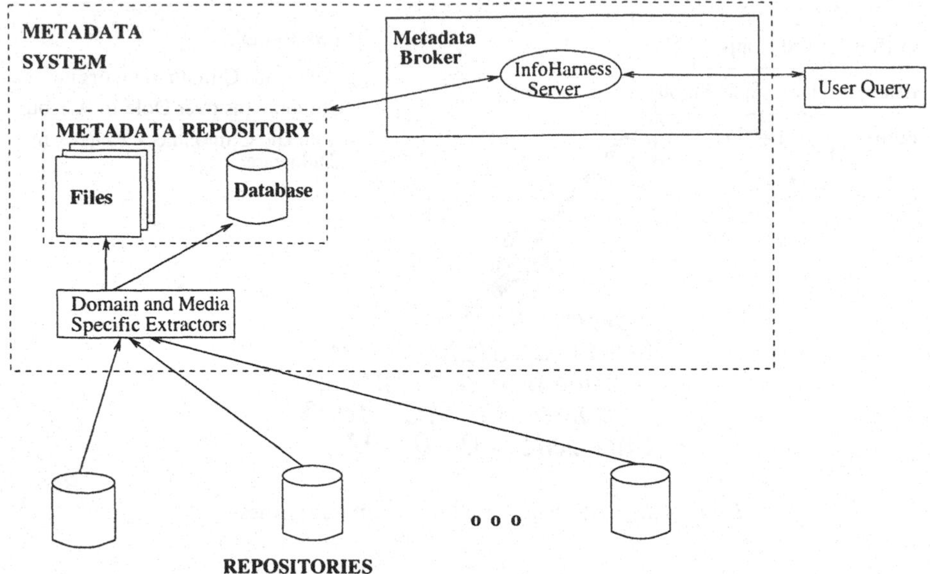

Figure 4.5. The InfoHarness System Architecture

repository, and reformats results for presentation on the user interface. Typically, relevant metadata is displayed on the user interface, and if actual data is required by the user, the server consults *type* and *location* information stored in the metadata repository for data retrieval.

Metadata Repository The metadata repository is responsible for the storage of metadata, and efficient processing of queries on the metadata. The repositories may either be *File systems* or *Database Management Systems (DBMSs)* and are discussed in detail, later in this section.

Domain and Media Specific Extractors This represents the **bottom up** approach for metadata computation. A library of media and domain specific metadata extractors is used to pre-process underlying data. The metadata is pre-computed and stored in the metadata repository ahead of time.

The above architecture does not have a vocabulary brokering component, and hence lacks adaptability. Since it only supports the bottom-up approach of metadata computation, it is not an extensible architecture, as introduction of new data requires renewed pre-processing to compute the corresponding metadata. We now discuss *domain and media specific extractors*, and the *metadata repository* in greater detail.

2.2.1 METADATA COMPUTATION: A BOTTOM-UP APPROACH

In the InfoHarness system, we follow a bottom-up method of metadata computation, where extractors pre-process the raw data and store relevant metadata as attribute-value pairs in an IHO. The extractors accept as inputs, both the location and desired representation of data, and outputs the set of IHOs and their relationships. The extractors may either be written by InfoHarness administrators, or created automatically by interpreting InfoHarness Repository Definition Language (IRDL) statements. A detailed discussion of IRDL can be found in (Shklar et al., 1995a), and its use in modeling heterogeneous information is discussed in (Shklar et al., 1995b).

Consider the metadata extraction process for C programs (Figure 4.6). To encapsulate individual functions and perform indexing based on comments and function names, the extractor has to perform some basic parsing to recognize comments, function blocks, etc. Function signatures, which uniquely identify individual functions, are stored as values of the *name* attribute of encapsulating objects. Function names are used to qualify file names in the *location* attribute.

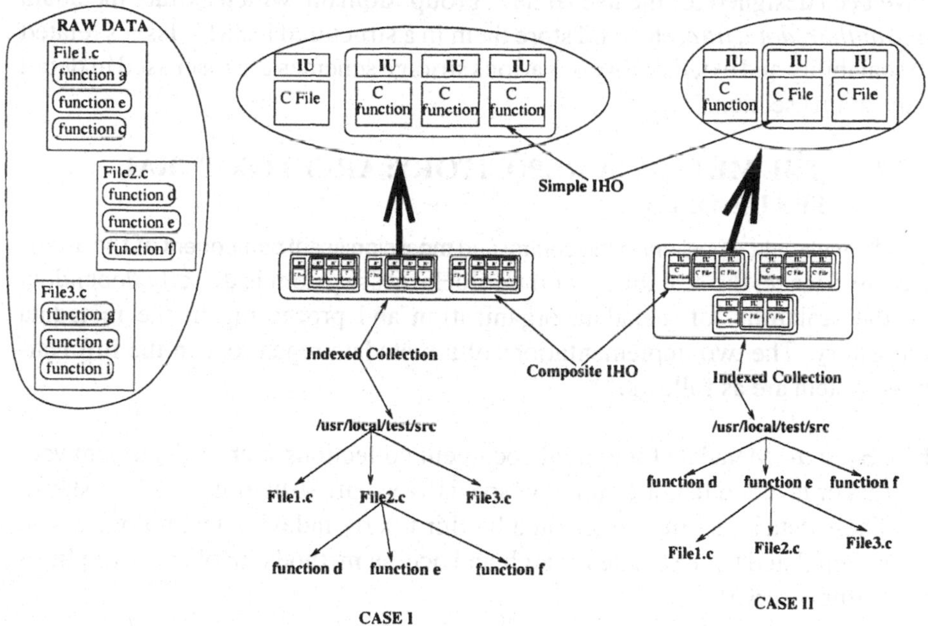

Figure 4.6. Metadata Extraction for a C Program

The next step is to encapsulate and index C files, and create parent-child relationships between collection and child IHOs (Figure 4.6, Case I). Alternatively (Figure 4.6, Case II), it may be desirable to index the individual functions and establish parent-child relationships between the indexed collection and function IHOs, as well as between function IHOs and file IHOs.

Extraction of Keyword-based Metadata

IHOs that encapsulate indexed collections store information about locations of the index and query method. Any indexed collection may use its own data retrieval method that is not a part of the InfoHarness system. Also, metadata created by various indexing technologies are stored separately in file systems, exactly the way it is required by the indexing technology. This information can be easily encoded in the metadata extractor used to create a collection from a set of documents. As a result, third party indexing technologies can be easily plugged into the infrastructure supported by the InfoHarness system, thus, enhancing the **extensibility** of its architecture.

Extraction of Attribute-based Metadata

Domain and media specific information can also be encoded in the metadata extractor which can be used to extract and represent *domain specific* information as attributes associated with the IHO. These attributes can then be queried appropriately to determine the IHO of interest to the user. Metadata extractors have been designed for the usenet newsgroups domain, which extract metadata like *author*, *date*, *title*, etc., and store them in a structured DBMS. Issues related to scalability and extensibility of various storage schemes are discussed in detail later in this section.

2.2.2 THE METADATA REPOSITORY: ARCHITECTURAL TRADE-OFFS

The metadata repository is the central and most significant component of the architecture. Hence, the scalability of the InfoHarness system is directly dependent on the scalability of metadata organization and processing in the metadata repository. The two implementations of a metadata repository in the InfoHarness system are as follows.

File System Metadata for textual document collections such as document vectors or inverted lists are stored in specialized data structures on file systems. These data structures are created by third-party indexing technologies, and manipulated by associated search and access methods invoked by the InfoHarness server.

Database Management System (DBMS) Metadata for attribute-value pairs and parent-child relationships are stored in a database table with B-tree indices created over appropriate attributes.

Since metadata stored in file systems is created and processed independently by third-party indexing technologies, only storage and processing of metadata in the database can be controlled. We now discuss how schema for metadata storage in the database impacts scalability and extensibility of the metadata repository, and hence, the system.

Storage Schema: The Attribute-Value approach

Metadata is viewed as a set of attribute-value pairs independent of the data or media-type of the objects. This perspective is reflected in the schema Metadata_Table(Oid, Attribute, Value). An extension of this schema is illustrated in Table 4.2. The properties of the metadata repository having such a schema are:

Oid	Attribute	Value
59716	location	http://www.xx.yyy/database?query
59716	county	59
59716	block	716
59716	population	73
59716	area	34
59716	boundary	$\{Poly_1, Poly_2\}$
59716	land_cover	{(mixed_forest, 0.6), (wetland, 0.4)}
59716	relief	moderate
⋮	⋮	⋮
12345	location	http://www.xx.yyy/file_path
12345	newsgroup	clari.news
12345	author	kilpatrick
12345	title	Clinton's Ratings
⋮	⋮	⋮

Table 4.2. Metadata Storage Using the Attribute-Value Approach

Extensibility The repository is highly extensible as it is very easy to add or drop attributes characterizing various datatypes. In the schema illustrated in Table 4.2, the attributes may be added or dropped as follows:

- Addition of the attribute location can be easily accomplished by the following SQL statement:

```
insert into Metadata_Table values(59716, 'location',
                        'http://www.xx.yyy/database?query')
```

- Deletion of the attribute location from the schema can be easily accomplished by the following SQL statement:

```
delete from Metadata_Table where Attribute = 'location'
```

Scalability The repository is not scalable for a large collection of metadata as it is very expensive to query this schema. Consider the following example query:

Get all blocks having a population greater than 500 and area greater than 50 acres having an urban land cover and moderate relief

The above can be expressed as follows.

select Oid from Metadata_Table where Attribute = 'population' and Value > 500
INTERSECT
select Oid from Metadata_Table where Attribute = 'area' and Value > 50
INTERSECT
select Oid from Metadata_Table where Attribute = 'land_cover'
and Value.type = 'urban' and Value.percentage > 50
INTERSECT
select Oid from Metadata_Table where Attribute = 'relief' and Value = 'moderate'

In general, if there are K constraints in the query, it will be translated into K-1 intersections. The performance of the system can be adversely impacted if the metadata size is large.

Redundancy Another major defect of this schema is that the attribute name is repeated for each object instance in the system. If K_{min} and K_{max} are the minimum and maximum number of attributes of any object type, and S is the total number of instances, the storage redundancy can be given as follows.

$$S \times K_{min} \leq \text{Redundancy} \leq S \times K_{max}$$

Storage Schema: The Entity-Attribute approach

All objects in the system are viewed as *entities*, and metadata extracted as *attributes* are associated with these entities. This leads us to identify a table/type with each new data and media type. Each entity is represented as a tuple in the table, with attributes specific to it represented as fields of the tuple. An example schema for two data types is as follows.

GeoSpatial_Table(Oid, Location, County, Block, Boundary, Land_cover, Relief, ...)
Newsgroup_Table(Oid, Newsgroup, Author, Title, ...)

An extension of this schema is illustrated in Tables 4.3 and 4.4. The properties of the metadata repository having such schemas are:

Scalability Both schemas discussed above are scalable, as appropriate indices can be built on the attributes reducing the search time to a constant. Part of the example information request discussed can be expressed as follows.

select Oid from GeoSpatial_Metadata
where Population > 500 and Area > 50
and Land_cover.type = 'urban' and Land_cover.percentage > 50

Extensibility Both schemas are partially extensible, as it is easy to add an attribute. Deletion of an attribute would require re-creating the table again. Addition of an attribute can be done using the following SQL statement:

```
alter table GeoSpatial_Metadata add column new-attribute attr-type
```

Redundancy The values for the common attributes for object instances belonging to more than one type (e.g. oid = 59777) are repeated.

Oid	Location	County	Relief	...
59716	http://...	59	moderate	...
59777	http://...	59	steep	...
⋮	⋮	⋮	⋮	⋮

Table 4.3. Geo-Spatial Metadata Stored Using the Entity-Attribute Approach

Oid	Location	Newsgroup	Title	...
12345	http://...	clari.news	Clinton's ratings	...
59777	http://...	sci.geology	A Steep Region	...
⋮	⋮	⋮	⋮	⋮

Table 4.4. Newsgroup Metadata Stored Using the Entity-Attribute Approach

The Scalability versus Extensibility trade-off

The two choices of storage schemas give rise to trade-off between the scalability and extensibility of the metadata repository. The schema mirroring the *attribute-value* approach is more extensible than the schema mirroring the *entity-attribute* approach. However, the latter schema design is more scalable as it offers the possibility of constructing indices on the most frequently queried attributes. The better alternative ultimately depends on the size of the metadata collection, and type of metadata queries handled by the metadata repository.

3. ISSUES OF METADATA AND ARCHITECTURE IN THE MIDAS SYSTEM

The MIDAS system is an enhanced version of the InfoHarness system, and supports association of domain specific metadata with structured and image data. The MIDAS system provides support for a wider and richer variety of domain specific metadata compared to the InfoHarness system. It also provides support for image data that is missing in the InfoHarness system.

We now discuss the MIDAS system *wrt* to the role of metadata, techniques to compute them, the architecture, and properties of the architecture. A more detailed discussion related to correlation of metadata across different media and the impact they have on the "SEA" properties of the system is presented later in this chapter.

3.1 ROLE OF METADATA IN MIDAS

We review various types of metadata used in MIDAS and identify the purpose of each metadata. The advantages of associating intensional domain specific metadata descriptions to capture information content of the underlying data repositories are also discussed.

3.1.1 METADATA TYPES IN MIDAS

The information brokering performed by the MIDAS system is primarily at the level of *information content*. This is reflected in the metadata types used to perform brokering. We enumerate and discuss only those metadata not handled by the InfoHarness System (Table 4.5).

Metadata	Metadata Type	Purpose
colors in image, number of rows number of columns	content dependent	brokering at the level of representation
image format (GIF, PPM)	domain independent	extraction of metadata
coordinate system, boundary, map-type (LULC, DEM), land-cover, relief	geo-spatial information domain specific	brokering at levels of information content and structural organization (partially)
area, population statistics	census information domain specific	brokering at the level of information content

Table 4.5. Additional Metadata Types in the MIDAS System

The MIDAS system concentrates on metadata specific to the domains of Geo-spatial and Census information. The intensional metadata descriptions primarily serve to abstract representational details in the underlying data, and are typically boolean combinations of individual metadata items. These are referred to as *m-contexts*, and are instrumental in

- enabling correlation without requiring the user to establish physical links between image and structured data, and
- improving the performance of the system by minimizing (costly) image processing.

3.1.2 UTILIZING METADATA TO ENABLE CORRELATION

Level of abstraction and modeling are two basic issues associated with correlating information stored in structured and image data.

Level of Abstraction The first step is to be able to perform correlation at a higher level of abstraction, independent of the representation of data, as either a tuple in an object-relational database, or as a set of pixels in an image. *Metadata descriptions* enable us to provide a uniform view of the image or structured data. Correlation would not be possible without this uniform view provided by the metadata descriptions. Consider the illustrative information request discussed in Section 1 of this chapter.

- The metadata area and population help view tuples in the structured database as a set of regions having an area and a population.
- The metadata land cover helps view pixels in an image database as a set of regions with a particular land cover.

Level of Modeling The metadata descriptions model information at the *intensional level*, i.e., at the level of the database schema. The metadata descriptions serve as a rudimentary schema for image data. The correlation between metadata descriptions (defined as the conjunction of constraints expressed in the descriptions) may be expressed as a join between the two schemas, and results in automatic association of individual regions in the structured data with regions in the image data. This avoids the need for manually adding links between the structured data and corresponding image objects [see (Sheth and Kashyap, 1996) for further details on this issue]. Consider the example information request discussed in the beginning of this chapter.

Structured Metadata The metadata area and population define a schema for structured data:

Structured_Metadata(county, block, area, population)

Image Metadata The metadata land_cover defines a schema for image data:

Image_Metadata(county, block, land_cover)

Correlation Correlation between image and structured data may then be viewed as a join between these two schemas:

Regions = Join[county, block](Structured_Metadata, Image_Metadata)

followed by a select based on the conditions input by the user.

Answer = Select(Conditions, Region) where

$$\text{Conditions} \equiv (\text{minArea} \leq \text{area} \leq \text{maxArea}) \wedge (\text{land\_cover} = \text{land\_cover\_type})$$

...

The advantages of this approach are as follows.

- The user does not have to manually add links between each region represented in the structured data and its image represented in the image data. This is done at the intensional level by the join condition.
- The user does not have to traverse each link and verify the input conditions. Again, this is done at the intensional level by the select condition.

3.1.3 UTILIZING METADATA TO IMPROVE PERFORMANCE

Image processing techniques used to compute image metadata are significantly more costly compared to processing in structured databases. We now discuss how information from structured metadata may be used to reduce image processing.

- Reducing the number of objects to be processed. Consider the metadata land cover, which is computed from image data. Instead of computing them for all regions, we compute them only for those regions that satisfy constraints in the information request corresponding to the structured metadata area and population.

- Reducing the number of images to be processed. Consider the metadata boundary, which is evaluated for a particular region before its image metadata are computed. This information is used to determine which regions are found in which maps. Thus, all the images need not be processed unnecessarily. This is an example of *spatial indexing*.

- Reducing the area of an image to be processed. Instead of computing the land cover of a region corresponding to the whole image, only the portion determined by computation of the metadata boundary is subjected to image processing.

3.2 THE MIDAS SYSTEM ARCHITECTURE

We now describe the architecture of the MIDAS system, and discuss it from two perspectives. The first perspective is that of the MIDAS architecture as an instantiation of the metadata brokering component of the brokering architecture (Figure 3.1). As discussed earlier, the MIDAS system performs brokering, primarily at the level of information content. However, the MIDAS system also performs a limited form of vocabulary brokering. Though the MIDAS system has been implemented independently of the InfoHarness system, the functional architectures of the two systems can be compared. Thus, we identify enhancements that need to be made to the InfoHarness system architecture to support this level of information brokering. The components of the MIDAS system architecture are are shown in (Figure 4.7).

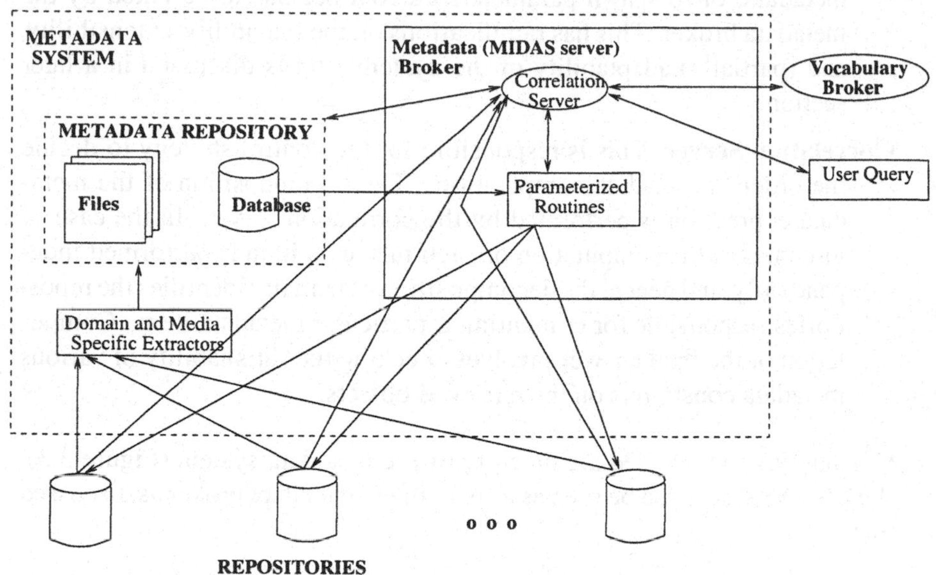

Figure 4.7. Architecture of the MIDAS System

MIDAS Server The MIDAS server represents the metadata broker identified in the brokering architecture. It shares with the InfoHarness server, the basic functionality of a metadata broker, which is the capability of handling metadata requests from either a vocabulary broker or as a result of processing the user query. It passes metadata requests to the metadata repository, and reformats results for presentation on the user interface. However, in order to support brokering at the level of information content and partially at the level of vocabulary, the MIDAS server needs to have additional capabilities. These capabilities are supported by the following components not present in the InfoHarness server.

Parameterized Routines The storage of data in digital (e.g., image) formats makes the bottom-up approach of metadata pre-computation infeasible, as it takes a lot of time. The metadata so computed might change in shorter intervals of time. The metadata broker should have the capability of computing metadata at run time either directly from the underlying data, or from already existing metadata stored in the metadata repository. The capability to execute parameterized routines is the first step in this direction, and has been incorporated in the MIDAS server. In some cases, the parameterized routines may be executed by the server, while in others, it may be delegated to the DBMS managing the metadata repository. The decision of whether to pre-compute metadata, or to spawn parameterized routines has to be taken by the metadata broker. This has ramifications on the scalability, extensibility, and (partially) adaptability of the system, and is discussed in a later section.

Correlation Server This is responsible for the control strategy to decide the order of metadata computation. The decomposition of the metadata expression is performed by the correlation server. In the case of m-contexts, the computation of each metadata item is performed independently, and hence, the decomposition essentially identifies the repositories responsible for computing a particular metadata item. Computation of the final answer involves checking the satisfiability of various metadata constraints on the retrieved objects.

Considering the detailed architecture of the metadata system (Figure 3.3), the MIDAS server can be seen as a specialized metadata broker as discussed next.

- All the repositories for which the MIDAS system is responsible (Figure 4.2) are stored in object relational DBMSs, and hence, do not need wrappers. The exception is the InfoSleuth text agent, which may be viewed as a wrapper around a text database.
- The information related to the location of repositories and their local query languages (SQL in this case) are hard coded in the parameterized routines. The mappings between the metadata and underlying data are also encoded in the form of SQL expressions.
- In the MIDAS system, we use m-contexts, where metadata descriptions can be viewed as simple boolean combinations of component metadata. Mapping composition is a simple process and is implemented by the correlation server using an appropriate control strategy, and corresponding operations over objects to check satisfiability of metadata constraints.

Metadata Repository The metadata repository is responsible for storage and efficient processing of queries on the metadata. The repositories are implemented using File Systems and DBMSs. In the MIDAS system, procedural fields (Stonebraker and Rowe, 1986) are used to support parameterized routines executed by the server. This is especially useful when the server delegates execution of parameterized routines to the metadata repository.

Domain and Media Specific Extractors A library of domain and media specific extractors is used to compute metadata from the underlying data. In the MIDAS system, these extractors encode domain specific knowledge and invoke image processing routines on image data. They process data across different repositories, and establish partial correlation when computing the metadata.

3.2.1 DOMAIN AND MEDIA SPECIFIC EXTRACTORS

In this section, we discuss how metadata may be pre-computed by domain and media specific extractors. For structured data stored in relational databases, we do not need to write metadata extractors as it is much easier to provide a mapping from metadata exported by the MIDAS system to the schema corresponding to the structured data. Therefore, we only discuss extractors for Image Data. We now discuss storage of pre-computed metadata, and illustrate the metadata extraction process.

Storage of Pre-computed Metadata

Consider the table Extracted_Metadata illustrated below (Table 4.6). We use object-relational capabilities of the underlying DBMS to define the types of some of the attributes.

- county, block and population have the type integer,
- area has the type real,
- boundary has the type setOf(polygon), where the type polygon represents the boundary polygon, and
- land_cover has the composite type setOf(<string, real>)

county	block	population	area	boundary	land_cover
59	716	73	34	{$Poly_1$, $Poly_2$}	{(mixed_forest, 0.6), (wetland, 0.4)}
⋮	⋮	⋮	⋮	⋮	⋮

Table 4.6. Storage of Pre-computed Metadata in the MIDAS System

A Metadata Extractor for Image Data

Consider the example information request discussed in the beginning of this chapter. The domain specific metadata used in the query for image data is land cover. In this section, we discuss an extractor which reads in all regions from **Census DB**, analyzes images in **Image DB**, and for each region in **Census DB** populates the metadata for land cover in the metadata repository. The extraction process is illustrated in Figure 4.8.

The implementation details of the extractor are presented in Appendix 4.A. Information related to the geo-spatial nature of metadata and transformations

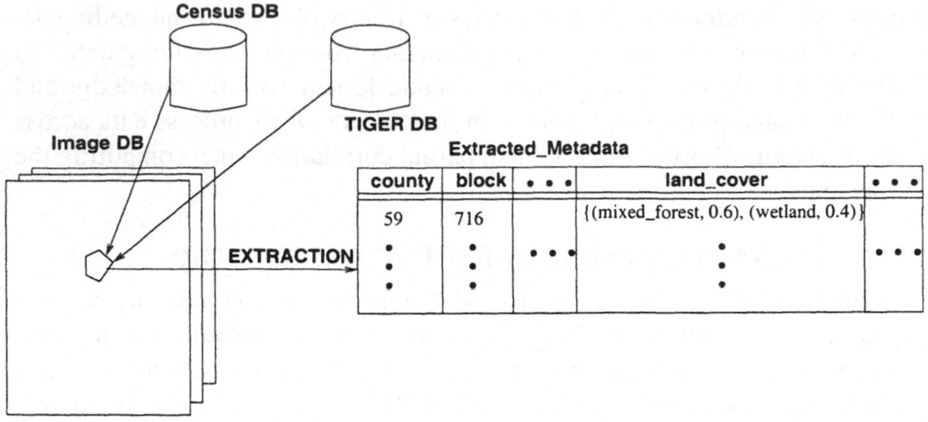

Figure 4.8. Extraction of Land Cover Information in MIDAS

across coordinate systems is encoded in the routines compute_region_boundary and convertSphericalPlanar. Domain specific knowledge, that land cover can be computed only in a Planar coordinate system, is embedded in the extractor. The conversion routine convertPlanarImage encodes image-specific knowledge about sampling scale and geo-spatial location of the image. The routine compute_cover encodes knowledge of media specific operations (such as how to determine colors of pixels) and domain specific categories corresponding to various colors in the map. This is an example of how domain and media specific extractors can help relieve information load, and encapsulate media heterogeneity for enabling specification of information requests at a higher level of abstraction.

3.2.2 PARAMETERIZED ROUTINES

We now discuss how metadata may be computed at run-time either by the MIDAS server, or by the metadata repository manager. Two ways of storing parameterized routines in the metadata repository are also discussed.

Storage of Parameterized Routines

The storage of parameterized routines depends on the component that invokes them.

- Parameterized routines may be used to compute metadata, and identify a set of objects that satisfy constraints on the metadata specified by decision making agents, e.g., get all regions having area between a <minArea> and a <maxArea>. We store these routines, their parameters, and associated metadata in the Parameterized_Routine table illustrated below (Table 4.7). At run time when the metadata constraints are evaluated, the MIDAS server spawns the parameterized routines.

metadata	function	param_list	...
area	compute_area	<minArea, maxArea>	...
population	compute_population	<minPopulation, maxPopulation>	...
⋮	⋮	⋮	⋮

Table 4.7. Parameterized Routines Stored in the Metadata Repository

- Parameterized routines may be used to compute metadata of a given object, e.g., land cover of a particular region, to determine if it satisfies metadata constraints specified by the decision making agent. The storage of parameterized routines as procedural fields in a table is illustrated in Figure 4.9. When metadata constraints are evaluated at run time, the MIDAS server delegates the execution of these routines to the DBMS, which activates stored procedures to compute the metadata.

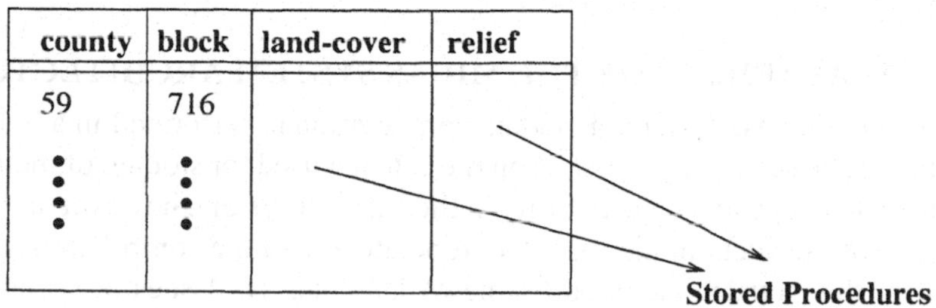

county
block
land-cover
relief
59
716
Stored Procedures

Figure 4.9. Parameterized Routines as Procedural Fields in the Metadata Repository

Parameterized Routines for Run Time Metadata Computation

Consider the example information request discussed in the beginning of this chapter. The domain specific metadata *population* corresponding to structured data, and *land cover* corresponding to image data, are invoked at run-time to evaluate the respective metadata.

Metadata for Structured Data Whenever values of the metadata *population* need to be evaluated for a region, the associated routine opens a connection to the **Census DB** and executes an SQL query to retrieve the population for that region. This routine implements the mapping between the metadata *population* and the corresponding data stored in **Census DB**. It also has the local query language (SQL) of the repository hard-coded. The detailed implementation is presented in Appendix 4.B.

Metadata for Image Data Whenever values of the metadata *land cover* need to be evaluated for a region, the associated routine gets boundary information from the **TIGER DB**. Based on the boundary information, it identifies the appropriate map and region from the **Image DB**, and executes image processing routines to compute the land cover for that region. This routine has the location and local languages of various repositories hard-coded in it. It also encodes domain specific knowledge related to geo-spatial nature of the data, and transformations across coordinate systems. The detailed implementation is presented in Appendix 4.C.

3.3 PROPERTIES OF THE MIDAS SYSTEM ARCHITECTURE

The MIDAS system architecture does not have a vocabulary brokering component as brokering is performed primarily at the level of information content (Figure 3.1). However, issues related to adaptability, arise in the metadata brokering component itself. We now discuss the extent to which the MIDAS system architecture possesses "SEA" properties, and discuss trade-offs that arise.

3.3.1 SCALABILITY OF THE MIDAS SYSTEM ARCHITECTURE

In the InfoHarness system, metadata computation is performed in a bottom-up manner. The scalability depends on the schema used for storage of metadata in the metadata repository. Scalability in the MIDAS system, however, depends on storage of metadata in the metadata repository, and the control strategy for computing the metadata adopted by the MIDAS server. Issues of scalability, dependent on the control strategy for metadata computation are discussed in detail later in this chapter. This dimension arises due to the use of parameterized routines to compute metadata. The scalability of the system can be enhanced by the following techniques.

- Using domain and media specific extractors to completely pre-compute metadata corresponding to the underlying heterogeneous data. Thus, any metadata query can be processed locally at the metadata repository without the need to access different repositories over the network.

- In the case where parameterized routines are used, a judicious control strategy may be used. In the MIDAS system, the results of metadata computation corresponding to structured data are used to limit metadata computation corresponding to image data, as this involves costly image processing.

On the face of it, the alternative of pre-computing all metadata ahead of time appears to be the most attractive in terms of enhancing scalability of the system. However, there are other considerations which make this option less desirable.

- Since the MIDAS system supports brokering at the level of information content, it should support querying at different levels of abstraction. In the context of the example information request, it should be able to help locate appropriate counties as well as blocks (to name two of the abstraction levels) satisfying the required land-cover constraints. This would amount to pre-computing metadata at all levels of abstraction, which will usually be undesirable in terms of storage needs.

- Another disadvantage of the above approach is that if new data is added to the underlying repositories (addition of new maps), or if the data changes dynamically (cloud cover in weather maps), the extractors have to be executed again and the metadata re-computed. The amount of metadata that might actually be used may be small, and hence, it may be too expensive to compute all that unused metadata.

3.3.2 EXTENSIBILITY OF THE MIDAS SYSTEM ARCHITECTURE

In the InfoHarness system, metadata computation is performed in a bottom-up manner, and this entails pre-computation of all the relevant and required metadata. As discussed earlier, addition of new data, and changes in the data in underlying repositories requires re-computation of metadata. During this time, the metadata repository is not available to the MIDAS server for satisfying metadata requests, hence affecting extensibility of the system. Another disadvantage discussed previously, is the large amount of storage space required.

The use of parameterized routines in MIDAS makes the system more extensible than the InfoHarness system. Parameterized routines are used to compute metadata for both structured and image data. In the case of structured data, they encode mappings from system metadata to schema metadata. In the case of image data, they encode image analysis and processing routines. Thus, in the case of a change in data, the latest snapshot of the repository is reflected, when the parameterized routines are processed. Addition of new data types can also be easily handled by addition of appropriate parameterized routines. The overhead involved in this is typically much less compared to re-computation of metadata required in the InfoHarness system.

Another advantage is that the space required to store parameterized routines is negligible, compared to storage required for all relevant metadata. However, the major disadvantage in using parameterized routines is that of the time required to execute parameterized routines for each metadata. This is an optimization issue, which is partially taken care of by deciding which metadata should be computed first, and is another manifestation of the inherent scalability-extensibility trade-off in information brokering.

3.3.3 THE SCALABILITY VERSUS EXTENSIBILITY TRADE-OFF

The trade-off between scalability and extensibility in the MIDAS system manifests itself as follows:

Enhancing Scalability As discussed in Section 3.3.1, scalability of the system can be enhanced by pre-computing all relevant metadata. Even if we assume that data in the underlying repositories does not change much, the space required to store all relevant metadata, and the astronomical time required to pre-compute, usually makes it an infeasible proposition. Besides, as new data is added and the old data changes, a re-computation of the metadata is required.

Enhancing Extensibility Parameterized routines are appropriate for enhancing extensibility of the system. They also occupy negligible space, but executing them for each metadata computation may take a long time.

The Trade-Off The scalability-extensibility trade-off thus translates into a space-time trade-off where the issue boils down to: How much and which metadata should be pre-computed given a limited amount of space? Later in the chapter, we discuss various caching strategies to handle the above problem.

These trade-offs are typically observed when the MIDAS system attempts to correlate information, and will be discussed in detail later in this chapter.

3.3.4 SCALABILITY: THE STEPPING STONE FOR ADAPTABILITY

The need to support enhanced scalability is primarily responsible for issues of adaptability. We have discussed (disk) caching of metadata as a means of enhancing scalability and extensibility of the system. A complementary method of enhancing scalability is to anticipate in advance, the metadata requests and to support efficient query processing for them. One way to achieve this is to support efficient metadata computation for all **vocabulary elements** of an information domain. This is referred to as **intra-domain adaptability**, and arises as a consequence of enhancing scalability of the system. We assume that an information domain is characterized by concepts at different levels of abstraction. This gives rise to the following possibilities:

- Express metadata computations at one level of abstraction, as functions of pre-computed metadata at a higher/lower level of abstraction.
- Compute metadata directly from the underlying data.
- Pre-compute metadata at all levels of abstraction.

In any information brokering system, enhancing intra-domain adaptability would mean determining: At what level of abstraction should metadata be pre-computed? This is discussed in detail later in this chapter.

4. THE INFOSLEUTH TEXT AGENT

In this section, we discuss how domain specific metadata can be mapped to underlying textual data based on a well standardized set of *media-specific* metadata, supported by a large variety of textual indexing schemes. We shall consider a subset of the user vocabulary discussed in the beginning of this chapter (Figure 4.1), and illustrate how a part of the example information request can be processed. We shall only discuss the functionality of the text agent *wrt* its ability to capture information content in text documents using domain specific metadata. Issues related to the architecture and related "SEA" properties are more appropriately discussed in the context of the InfoSleuth system (Chapter 6).

4.1 METADATA-BASED VIEW OF THE INFORMATION SPACE

Data models and query languages have been proposed for semi-structured documents (Abiteboul, 1997). The domain ontology is viewed as a *data guide* that provides a loose description of the structure of data. An information source is viewed at the level of the domain specific metadata supported by it, and information requests are specified in terms of the metadata in a *media independent manner*. Thus, users can specify a query containing terms from a domain ontology in SQL, and get back tuples from a structured database, text documents, or images from various information resources. The above approach facilitates the integration and querying of multimedia data in a seamless manner, at the level of domain specific metadata constructed from terms in a domain ontology. A critical challenge in this approach is to map domain specific metadata to the underlying textual and image data.

In our approach, we map domain specific metadata into a set of *potential structures* that may appear in the text body, and implement a *relevance measure* based on their existence. This is accomplished in a *domain specific* manner and provides a collection of domain specific metadata based on which a textual database can be queried. This is in contrast to concept based searches supported by indexing engines such as Excite (Excite,), where concepts are constructed by statistical methods, and are generic in nature. Consider the user vocabulary illustrated in Figure 4.1. The vocabulary subset supported by the text agent is illustrated below in Figure 4.10.

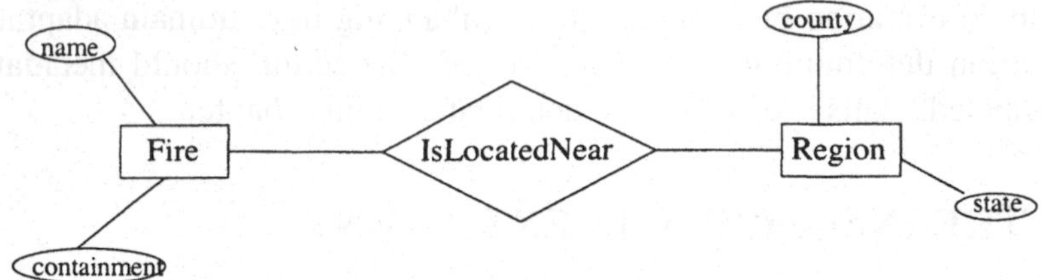

Figure 4.10. Vocabulary Subset Supported by the Text Agent

4.2 MAPPING DOMAIN SPECIFIC METADATA TO TEXTUAL DATA

In the case of structured data, entities, attributes, and relationships captured in domain specific metadata are mapped to the underlying tables (relational model) or objects (object-oriented model). We first discuss a relevant subset of media specific metadata based on information retrieval operations. These media specific metadata expressions are collectively referred to as topic expressions, and are supported by the Verity Indexing engine (Inc., 1994). With the help of the example information request, we demonstrate how domain specific metadata can be mapped to these topic expressions.

4.2.1 TOPIC EXPRESSIONS: MEDIA SPECIFIC METADATA

We now enumerate some of the information retrieval operators, which can be used to construct the topic expressions (Inc., 1994). Each of these operations by themselves define a **topic** and can be combined in different ways to define richer topics. These topic expressions are used to query document collections based on content, and can be considered as *views* on the underlying textual data.

<WORD>(W_1) Checks whether W_1 is a word in the text body.

<PHRASE>($W_1, W_2, ..., W_k$) Checks whether W_1, W_2, ..., W_k form a phrase (in the same order) in the text body.

<SENTENCE>($W_1, W_2, ..., W_k$) Checks whether W_1, W_2, ..., W_k appear in the same sentence (in any order) in the text body.

<THESAURUS>(W_1) Checks whether a thesaurus expansion of W_1 appears in the text body.

<STEM>(W_1) Checks whether the root/stem of a word appears in the text body.

<TOPIC>(T_1) This may be a pre-defined topic defined using the above and following operators.

<ACCRUE>($T_1, T_2, ..., T_k$) Checks whether the topics $T_1, T_2, ..., T_k$ appear in the text body. Each of the topics can have a weight associated with it and depending on the presence of the topics, the weights can be "accrued".

4.2.2 MAPPING DOMAIN METADATA TO TOPIC EXPRESSIONS

With the help of the example in Figure 4.11, we now illustrate the mapping from domain specific metadata expressed as entities, attributes, and relationships to media-specific metadata expressed as topics in the underlying textual database. The following cases arise:

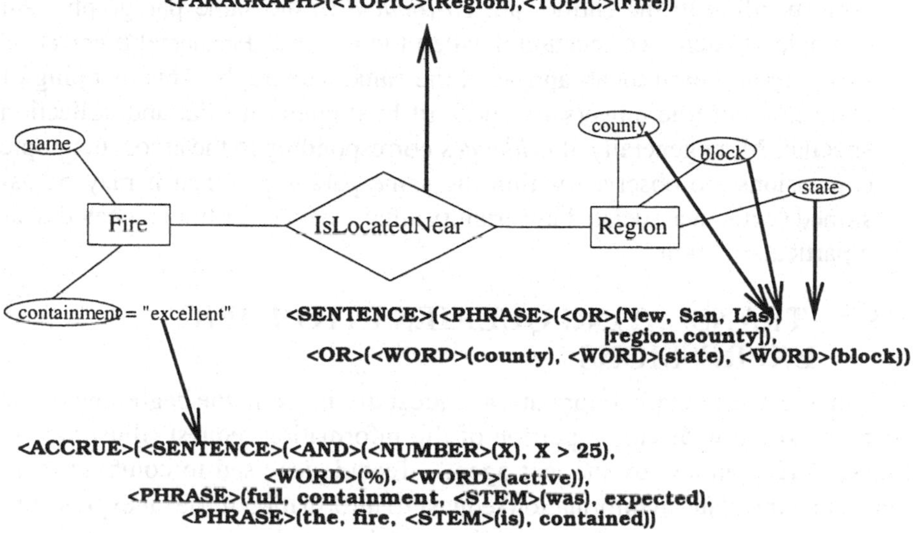

Figure 4.11. Mapping Domain Specific Metadata to Media Specific Metadata

Entity Mapping In the case of structured data, the entities Region and Fire may be mapped to a *table*, whereas for textual data, they are mapped to *topic expressions*. In the case of structured data, the instances of an entity are a *set of tuples*, whereas for textual data, the instances are a *set of words/patterns* appearing in documents.

Attribute Mapping In the case of structured data, the attribute containment may be mapped to a *table column*. However, in the case of textual data it is mapped to a *parameterized topic*. In the above example, whenever we want to evaluate a condition like containment = "excellent", we search for patterns like [Fire.name] is 10% active, [Fire.name] is contained, etc. As discussed in (Abiteboul, 1997), one could possibly parse semi-structured documents to infer the containment of a fire. But in the case of unstructured data, we make the indexing engine *search* for the above-mentioned patterns, and this gives rise to *uncertainty* in the answers. The two main reasons for this are: lack of structure in underlying data leading to the absence of the notion of a key attribute; and search for patterns at run-time as opposed to parsing/extraction of documents resorted to for semi-structured documents.

Relationship Mapping The relationship isLocatedNear models association between the entities Fire and Region. In the case of structured data, the relationship may be mapped to a table which contains object identifiers of the entities as *foreign keys*. In the case of textual data, since there is no notion of object identity, we search for situations where topic expressions corresponding to the entities are *co-located* in the same paragraph. An example of such a co-location is when the patterns [Fire.name] is contained and [Region.county] county appear in the same paragraph. This mapping of course, is not true universally and will be domain, media, and collection specific. More generally, if *evidences* corresponding to the associated topic expressions are observed within the same paragraph, then it may be assumed (with an associated uncertainty) that a particular fire is located near a particular region.

4.3 TRANSLATING QUERIES INTO TOPIC EXPRESSIONS

Consider the example information request discussed in the beginning of the chapter. We now discuss a portion of the information request (illustrated in Figure 4.12) handled by the text agent. Techniques used to combine mappings, and translate an information request to information retrieval expressions supported by the Verity indexing engine are illustrated.

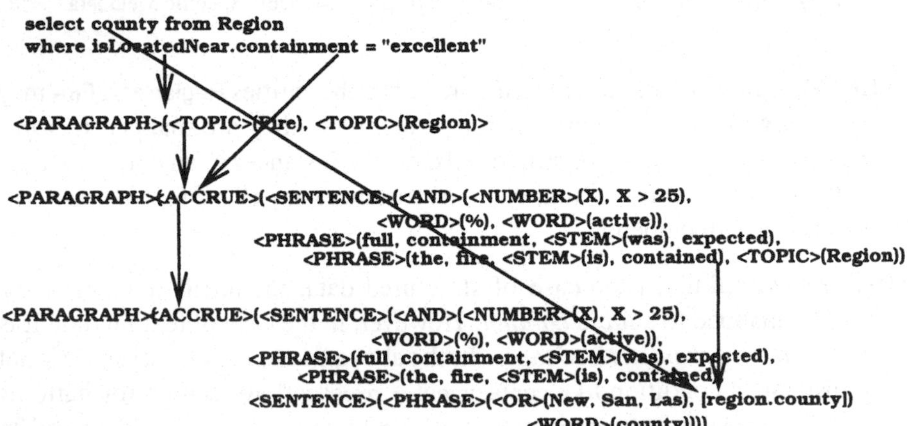

Figure 4.12. Translating Information Requests into Information Retrieval Operations

Metadata-based specification The information request uses the metadata Region, isLocatedNear, county and containment to specify that regions located near fires having excellent containment need to be identified and retrieved. This specification is independent of the underlying media in which the information may be stored (in this case in semi-structured text documents).

Mappings composition The text agent maintains mappings from the metadata discussed above, to patterns in the underlying text document. These patterns are specified using media specific metadata discussed earlier. The mappings corresponding to each of the metadata specified in the information request are composed. This functionality is found in the mappings composer subcomponent of the metadata brokering component.

- The relationship isLocatedNear is mapped to

  <PARAGRAPH>(<TOPIC>(Fire),<TOPIC>(Region))

  This results in replacement of the topic definitions corresponding to Fire and Region.

- The condition containment = "excellent" is substituted by the topic expression

  <ACCRUE>(<AND>(<NUMBER>(X), X >25),
  <PHRASE>(the, fire, is, contained), ..)

- We are looking for counties that are located near fires. This results in the modification of the topic expression corresponding to Region as <SENTENCE>(<OR>(San,Los,New),[Region.county], <WORD>(county)). The parts of the topic expression corresponding to state and block are removed.

- The resultant topic expression that is constructed, is a parameterized expression and contains [Region.county] as a parameter.

Execution of Information Retrieval Operations The media specific expression generated as a result of mapping composition typically needs to be translated to native information retrieval expressions supported by the indexing engine. This functionality is found in the translator/wrapper subcomponent of metadata brokering component. In this case, the Verity indexing engine supports evaluation of topic expressions, and the translation capability is not required. However, parameterized topic expressions are not supported, and the text agent needs to remove the parameter [Region.county] before evaluating the topic expression *wrt* the Verity index.

Post Processing When the topic expressions are evaluated, the relevant documents are identified and those with a high relevance score are chosen.

However, patterns corresponding to the topic expression are also highlighted in the given documents. The text agent keeps track of the **position** in which the parameter Region.county, appears and extracts the values from the highlighted patterns.

The counties that are located near fires of excellent containment are, thus, identified and returned to the MIDAS system which then correlates this information with that stored in image and structured data. This is the subject of discussion of the next section.

5. METADATA-BASED CORRELATION IN THE MIDAS SYSTEM

The MIDAS system enables metadata-based correlation across the information sources storing data, using different media types. In the overall approach for the example information request (Figure 4.2), the MIDAS system correlates the following information:

1. It correlates information across census objects stored as structured data, and map objects stored as image data, to determine regions that satisfy the specified area, population, and land cover constraints.

2. It correlates information across fire and region objects stored as textual data, and region objects obtained from Step 1 to determine regions which satisfy the given area, population, and land cover constraints, and are located near a fire with excellent containment.

We now discuss in detail, aspects related to strategies of metadata-based correlation, and their impact on "SEA" properties of the metadata-based architecture. The discussion is in the context of the first correlation described earlier.

5.1 SCALABILITY V/S EXTENSIBILITY: SPACE/TIME TRADE-OFFS

Approaches for evaluation of space-time trade-offs discussed earlier, are an instance of the scalability versus extensibility trade-off in information brokering. We present and discuss various (disk) caching strategies for varying sizes of the cache.

5.1.1 THE (MODIFIED) VIEW MATERIALIZATION PROBLEM

The View Materialization problem has been studied extensively for structured databases. We now present the metadata correlation process from the perspective of the view materialization problem. We described the correlation as a query on the view

Metadata_Table(county, block, area, population, land-cover)

This view is defined on the base tables which belong to the various data repositories enumerated earlier in this chapter.

select county, block from Metadata_Table
where <minArea> ≤ area ≤ <maxArea>
and <minPop> ≤ population ≤ <maxPop>
and land-cover = <category>

Work discussed in (Stonebraker et al., 1990) uses object relational features such as rules and procedures to define views. Caching approaches have been used to support efficient query processing on these views in (Sellis, 1987; Hanson, 1988; Jhingran, 1988). Whereas the views have been defined on object-relational databases, and procedures for specifying the views have been SQL queries, we adapt these techniques (Sellis, 1987) for image data, and for image processing routines instead of SQL queries. In the MIDAS system, we compute the view in the following steps.

Join Correlation: The metadata corresponding to structured data is stored in the Parameterized_Routine table (Table 4.7). These routines encode mappings between the metadata area and population and the schema of **Census DB**, and are invoked by the MIDAS server. We do not cache these metadata as they are computed efficiently by issuing SQL queries against structured data. This is called join correlation and is computed as follows. Let Obj_{area} and $\text{Obj}_{population}$ be the objects returned by the parameterized routines compute_area(minArea, maxArea) and compute_population(minPop, maxPop) after evaluation of constraints on the metadata area and population respectively. The final set of objects are computed by the MIDAS server as:

$$\text{Objects} = \text{Obj}_{area} \cap \text{Obj}_{population}.$$ [1]

Selection Correlation: The metadata for image data are stored as procedural fields as illustrated in Figure 4.9. These routines compute metadata from image data and are expensive to compute. The steps required by the stored procedure compute_land_cover (Appendix 4.C) to compute the land cover of a region are:

- Connect to **TIGER DB** and compute the boundaries.
- Connect to **Image DB** and determine the image (map) in which the region is contained. Execute a polygon filling routine to determine the pixels within the region.

[1]These two mappings could be composed and computed at **Census DB**, but in our implementation this is not possible as they are hard-coded in the parameterized routines. Composition of mappings is implemented in the OBSERVER project discussed in a later chapter.

- Execute an image processing routine to determine the land cover of region.

As noted earlier, it is very expensive to compute image metadata. Hence, these metadata can be cached, and the space-time trade-offs evaluated, based on the resource and time constraints on an information brokering system.

5.1.2 CACHING STRATEGIES FOR PRE-COMPUTED METADATA IN MIDAS

We now discuss the issues involved in caching pre-computed metadata in the metadata repository. The basic idea is to keep in secondary storage, materialized objects that are frequently used in queries. Under that formulation, the caching problem is conceptually the same as the well known caching problem in operating systems. Sellis (Sellis, 1987) has discussed caching the results of QUEL+[2] queries in procedural fields in the POSTGRES (Stonebraker and Rowe, 1986) system. We subscribe to his formulation of the problem, and adapt it for the case of general parameterized routines, that perform computations on image data. We also assume that updates to the underlying data are not frequent. In our application, this is acceptable because the land cover of a region does not change often. The caching problem introduces the following sub-problems to be solved:

- *Which query results to cache?*
- *Which algorithm should be used for the replacement of cache entries?*

The MIDAS server first checks whether a metadata object is cached in the metadata repository before it spawns parameterized routines to compute metadata. It caches all objects the first time they are referenced by the server. If we make an *unbounded space* assumption, then pre-computation of metadata is a better alternative, since the underlying data is not updated that frequently. However the *bounded space* assumption, where the metadata cache is of a fixed size is a more realistic assumption.

Depending on the information known about the previously cached objects, the system can decide whether metadata computed for a new object should be cached or not. Metadata corresponding to some of the objects (for which there is a big performance gain) are stored in the cache such that, the metadata satisfy space constraints. Since it is not possible to predict the behavior of a brokering system ahead of time, it may not be possible to predict an optimal collection of objects. Hence, the objects stored in the cache may be prioritized based on last access, frequency of access, and performance gain. Criteria for replacement of these objects based on the above may be developed and cached objects may be replaced based on their estimated priority.

[2]QUEL+ is an earlier variant of SQL proposed in (Stonebraker et al., 1985).

5.2 SCALABILITY: THE STEPPING STONE TO ADAPTABILITY

One of the key features of the MIDAS system is the ability to support correlation of information at different levels of abstraction. We have discussed earlier how this enhances the scalability of the system and also results in increased adaptability within the application or subject domain. We refer to this as *intra-domain adaptability*.

In the previous section, we discussed caching techniques to exploit space-time trade offs in the MIDAS system. The caching strategies discussed in the previous section need to be enhanced to support querying at multiple levels of abstraction within an information domain. Questions of the following nature need to be answered.

- *Is it possible to compute metadata based on pre-computed metadata at other levels of abstraction?*

- *Is it better to compute metadata directly from underlying data or use pre-computed metadata at a different level of abstraction?*

- *At what level of abstraction should the metadata be pre-computed and stored?*

5.2.1 METADATA COMPUTATIONS ACROSS LEVELS OF ABSTRACTION

To support brokering at the level of information content, we have to investigate techniques to pre-compute metadata across all levels of abstraction within the information domain. One approach would be to blindly apply caching strategies discussed in the previous section, and not distinguish between metadata corresponding to different levels of abstraction. This, however, does not take advantage of the relationships between the vocabulary elements of an information domain. We now discuss an approach which does precisely that, and results in enhancing the adaptability of the system.

We assume that vocabulary elements of a domain are related to each other via *generalization* and *aggregation* relationships, and organized according to differing levels of abstraction in hierarchical/lattice structures. An example of such a hierarchy is illustrated in Figure 4.13. Based on these relationships, it may be possible to use pre-computed metadata at different levels of abstraction to achieve the following advantages:

- It obviates the need to compute metadata directly from the underlying data repositories as metadata can now be computed from pre-computed metadata already stored in the metadata repository.

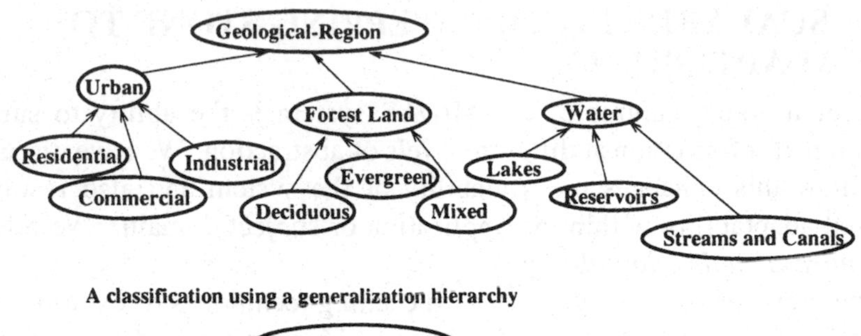

A classification using a generalization hierarchy

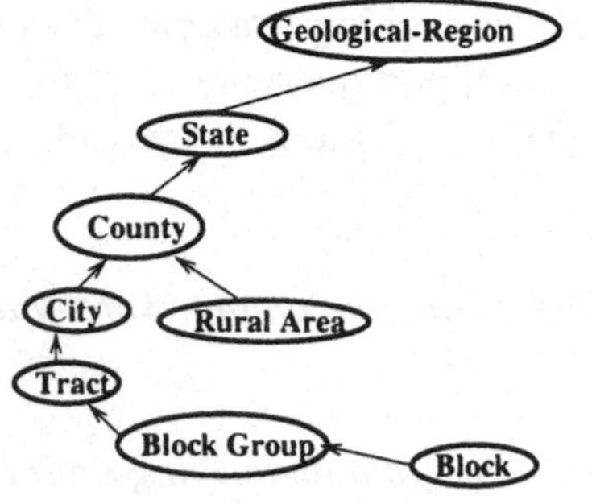

A classification using an aggregation hierarchy

Figure 4.13. Hierarchies Describing a Domain Vocabulary

- There is no need to store the metadata, as it is already implicitly cached in the metadata repository. This has been discussed in the context of caching DL expressions in (Goñi et al.,).

Consider the information correlation example chosen in the beginning of this section, that expresses constraints on regions. Also, consider the US Census Bureau classification illustrated in Figure 4.13. Consider two vocabulary elements **county** and **block** illustrated in the classification, and assume that all relevant metadata are stored in the metadata repository as illustrated in Table 4.6. SQL-like queries for the two elements are illustrated in Table 4.8.

Here, there is an aggregation relationship between the vocabulary item **county**, and the vocabulary item **block**. This is reflected in the query for the appropriate counties, where metadata corresponding to blocks (assumed to have been pre-computed) are aggregated to compute corresponding metadata for counties. The aggregation of metadata corresponding to structured data is implemented as a simple summation. We now discuss the trade-offs involved in aggregation of image metadata.

5.2.2 TRADE-OFFS IN METADATA COMPUTATION

We have discussed how pre-computed metadata stored in the metadata repository can be used to compute metadata at other levels of abstraction. However,

Level of Abstraction	Metadata Query
region = 'block'	select county, block from Extracted_Metadata where area $\geq$ 50 and population $\geq$ 500 and land_cover = 'urban'
region = 'county'	select county from Extracted_Metadata group by county having sum(area) $\geq$ 50 and sum(population) $\geq$ 500 and aggregate(land_cover) = 'urban'

Table 4.8. Querying Metadata at Different Levels of Abstraction

there are cases where it might be more expensive to use pre-computed metadata, as opposed to directly computing metadata from the underlying data. Consider computation of the metadata land_cover discussed in the previous section. There are two possibilities for computing the land cover of a county: (a) computation of the land cover directly from underlying maps (compute_direct), and (b) using the pre-computed metadata for blocks in the county to compute the land cover (compute_aggregate). The processing which needs to be done for the routine compute_direct are:

1. Compute the county boundary from **TIGER DB**.
2. Execute a polygon filling routine to determine the region covered by the county boundary.
3. Compute the land cover by processing the appropriate region in the map containing the region in **Image DB**.

The processing which needs to be done for the routine compute_aggregate are:

1. Determine the set of blocks belonging to the county.
2. Execute polygon filling routines to determine the region covered by the pre-computed block boundaries. Compute the aggregation of the regions.
3. Compute the land cover by processing the appropriate region in the map containing the region in **Image DB**.

It is necessary to process the map to determine the land cover of the county as there is not enough information in the pre-computed metadata to accurately combine the land cover information of the individual blocks to compute the county land cover. However, the pre-computed metadata for the county and block boundaries can be re-utilized. It is not clear which of the two:

compute_direct or compute_aggregate is more appropriate. The trade-off can be characterized as follows. Let:
C_1 = cost of computing county boundary
C_2 = cost of computing region covered by county boundary
C_3 = cost of determining blocks belonging to the county
C_4 = cost of computing region covered by the block boundaries
. There are two possibilities:

1. $[C_1 + C_2] < [C_3 + C_4]$
   In this case, it is cheaper to compute the metadata for county directly from the underlying data. One reason for this is that it takes lesser time to determine the region determined by a county even though it is bigger in size. Determining the region covered by a boundary involves some kind of polygon filling, and a smaller polygon with a complicated boundary may take more time to fill then a bigger polygon with a relatively simple boundary.

2. $[C_1 + C_2] > [C_3 + C_4]$
   In this case, it is cheaper to compute the metadata from the county based on the metadata of the blocks already stored in the (disk) cache.

In general, it may be advantageous to re-use some of the pre-computed metadata to compute other metadata at higher (or lower) levels of abstraction. However, there are cases where it may be cheaper to compute metadata directly from the underlying data. A critical task in enabling the scalability of metadata computation may be the characterization and structuring the terms in a domain, possibly as hierarchies, and reformulation of metadata expressions within a domain of information. Thus, our quest to enhance the scalability of a brokering system leads us to issues of adaptability within a domain of information.

6. SUMMARY: METADATA AS SCHEMA FOR DIGITAL DATA

In this chapter, we discussed with the help of an example, how related information represented in different digital media can be combined by making use of domain specific metadata. These metadata can be considered as an *elementary schema* for the underlying information. Based on the example information request, the text and image databases can be considered to have the following schemas:

Image Database Schema The domain specific metadata help view maps in the underlying image database as a collection of regions having certain land-cover characteristics.

Region(county, block, land-cover)

Text Database Schema The domain specific metadata help view fire reports in the underlying text database as a collection of fires with a level of containment, located near geographical regions.

Fire(name, containment)
Region(state, county, block)
IsLocatedNear(Fire, Region)

Given the assumption that multimedia data can be described in a manner similar to structured data using database schemas, we now turn our attention to schemas as a special kind of metadata used to capture information content. This is the focus of discussion of the next chapter.

APPENDIX 4.A: A Media and Domain Specific Extractor for Image Data

```
function extract_land_cover(Census_DB, Image_DB) {
    connection1 = openDatabase(Census_DB, 0, 0); // Open Database connection
    query = "select distinct county, block
             from Census_Table;"
    execute(connection1, query, 0);
    WHILE getResult(connection1) DO {
       curr_county = tuple.field1;
       curr_block = tuple.field2;
       /* Compute the region boundaries  from TIGER/Line Data */
       edgeList = compute_region_boundary(curr_county, curr_block, TIGER_DB);
       edgeListPlanar = convertSphericalPlanar(edgeList, projectionParameters);
       BoundingBox = getBoundingBox(edgeListPlanar);
       connection2 = openDatabase(Image_DB, 0, 0) // Image Database connection
       query = "select origin, scale, map from Image_Table
              where containedInMap(BoundingBox, origin, scale, width, height)
              and map_type = 'LULC';"
       execute(query, connection2, 0);
       IF getResult(connection2) THEN {
           origin = tuple.field1;
           scale = tuple.field2;
           map = tuple.field3;
           /* Convert from Planar Coordinates to pixel positions */
           edgeListImage = convertPlanarImage(edgeListPlanar, scale, origin);
           pixelSet = fillPolygon(edgeListImage); // compute pixels in a region
           (land_cover_type, percentage) = compute_cover(map, pixelSet); //compute land cove
           connection3 = openDatabase(MetadataDB, 0, 0);
           FOR EACH land_cover_type DO {
               query = "update Extracted_Metadata
                        set land_cover = land_cover UNION {(land_cover_type, percentage)};"
               execute(query, connection, 0);
           } /* ENDFOR */
           close(connection3)
        } /* ENDIF */
        close(connection2)
    } /* ENDWHILE */
    close(connection1)
} /* ENDEXTRACTOR */
```

APPENDIX 4.B: Routine to Compute Population

```
function compute_population(minPopulation, maxPopulation) {
   connection = openDatabase(Census_DB, 0, 0) // Open Connection
   // Get population from the Census Database
   query = "select county, block from Census_Table
            where population >= minPopulation
            and population <= maxPopulation;"
   execute(query, connection, 0)
   WHILE getResult(connection) DO
       insert <county, block> into Result
   return(Result)
// Note: Location of DB, Mappings and Query Language are
// Hard-coded in this routine
}
```

APPENDIX 4.C: Routine to Compute Land Cover

```
function compute_land_cover(input_county, input_block) {
    edgeList = compute_region_boundary(input_county, input_block, TIGER_DB)
    edgeListPlanar = convertSphericalPlanar(edgeList, projectionParameters)
    BoundingBox = getBoundingBox(edgeListPlanar)
    /* => Location, Query language, Coordinate mappings and functions Hard-Coded */
    connection = openDatabase(Image_DB, 0, 0) // Open Connection to Database
    query = "select origin, scale, map from Image_Table
             where containedInMap(BoundingBox, origin, scale, width, height)
             and map_type = 'LULC';"
    execute(query, connection2, 0)
    IF getResult(connection) {
        origin = tuple.field1
        scale = tuple.field2
        map = tuple.field3
        /* Convert from Planar Coordinates to Pixel Positions      */
        /* and compute land-cover-types over all pixels in region */
        /* => Domain knowledge of land-cover-types and coordinate  */
        /*    mappings are hard-coded                              */
        edgeListImage = convertPlanarImage(edgeListPlanar, scale, origin)
        pixelSet = fillPolygon(edgeListImage)
        (land_cover_type, percentage) = compute_cover(map, pixelSet)
        land_cover_type = get_max({(land_cover_type, percentage)})
        return(<land_cover_type>)
    } /* ENDIF */
    close(connection)
}
```

Chapter 5

CAPTURING INFORMATION CONTENT IN STRUCTURED DATA

The use of metadata (especially domain specific) as a *schema* over underlying data was a key feature in the techniques used for brokering over heterogeneous digital data. We now focus on structured data, which typically has an intensional schema describing its contents. The schema may or may not describe information content in a manner specific to a particular application or subject domain. In this chapter, we present techniques to capture application and domain specific information content in structured data.

The ability to reconcile schematic/representational heterogeneities when different databases use different schemas to describe similar information, is a critical pre-requisite to capturing information content in structured data. The various representational heterogeneities are first identified and organized in a taxonomy. A common object model is assumed, where "object" refers to a representation or intensional definition, e.g., an object class definition in object oriented models, or a table in the relational model. Information may be modeled at either the entity or the attribute level. Resolution of schematic heterogeneities by mapping underlying data to semantic metadata expressions constructed from terms in domain specific ontologies, is then discussed. This may be viewed as a process of abstracting out representational details from the data.

A *semantic proximity* model, of which the semantic metadata expression or c-context is a key component, is used for capturing information content of objects independent of their representation. A partial representation of c-contexts is also presented. These c-contexts provide an intermediate language to map underlying data to terms in domain specific ontologies. A set of operations are defined, that enable inferences on c-contexts, and map c-contexts to underlying schemas describing structured data. Examples illustrating the advantages of such an approach are presented. Issues related to the use of domain specific ontologies to construct c-contexts are also discussed. Capture of information content in structured data is thus enabled by:

- Abstraction of representational details in the underlying structured data by mapping schema elements to terms, and c-contexts constructed from terms in domain specific ontologies.

- Use of c-contexts to capture extra information not represented in underlying schemas, and the use of inference operations to reason about information content.

1. SCHEMATIC HETEROGENEITIES ACROSS MULTIPLE DATABASES

We now discuss a broad class of schematic differences between objects having some semantic similarity: *domain incompatibility, entity definition incompatibility, data value incompatibility, abstraction level incompatibility* and *schematic discrepancies* (Figure 5.1).

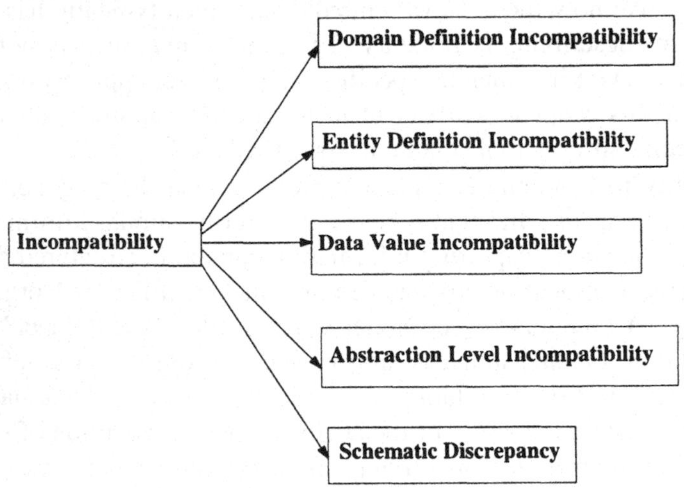

Figure 5.1. Schematic Heterogeneities Across Data in Multiple Databases

The issue of schematic/representational/structural heterogeneity has been addressed by a number of researchers (Dayal and Hwang, 1984; Breitbart et al., 1986; Czejdo et al., 1987; Krishnamurthy et al., 1991; Kim and Seo, 1991). However, we emphasize the use of terms, and c-contexts constructed from terms in domain specific ontologies, to abstract out schematic differences (Kashyap and Sheth, 1996). In the following sections, for each schematic difference, we discuss approaches to abstract out representational details, and map schema elements to terms, or c-contexts constructed from terms in domain specific ontologies.

1.1 DOMAIN DEFINITION INCOMPATIBILITY

In this section, we discuss incompatibilities that arise (Figure 5.2) when domains of two different types are used to define domains of semantically similar attributes. The broad definition of this incompatibility given in (Czejdo et al., 1987) is refined. For each incompatibility, possible ways of mapping schema elements to terms, or c-contexts constructed from terms in appropriate domain specific ontologies, are discussed. In some cases, *transformer functions* (Mena et al., 1996b) that map instances from one domain type to a corresponding instance in another are used. This approach is similar to that of dynamic attributes (Litwin and Abdellatif, 1986) and abstract data types (ADTs) used in (Czejdo et al., 1987). Transformer functions are formally discussed later in this chapter.

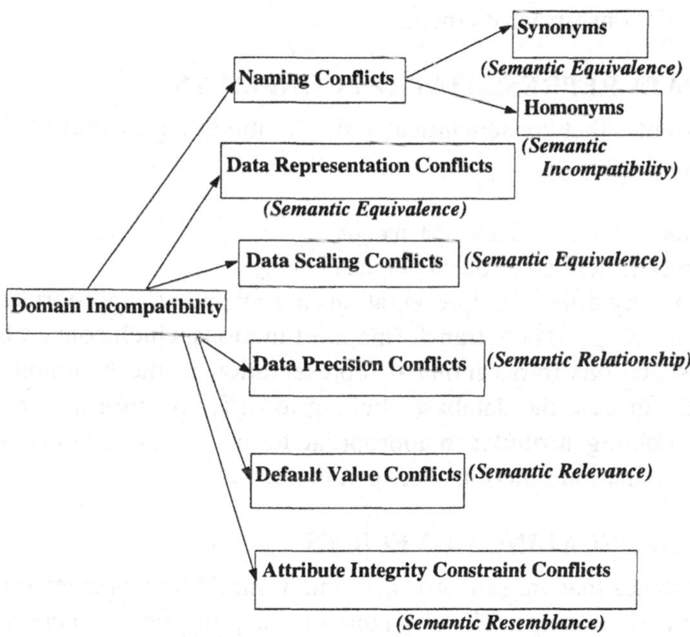

Figure 5.2. Heterogeneities Arising Out of Domain Incompatibility

1.1.1 ATTRIBUTE NAMING CONFLICTS

Two attributes are termed *synonyms* if they are semantically alike and have different names.

Example: Consider two databases having the following tables.

STUDENT(Id#, Name, Address)
TEACHER(SS#, Name, Address)
Id# of STUDENT and SS# of TEACHER are synonyms.

In our approach, synonym attributes are mapped to the same term in a common ontology. In case the databases belong to different information domains, we map them to synonymous terms in their respective ontologies. On the other hand, two attributes that are semantically unrelated might have the same names. They are known as *homonyms*.

Example: Consider two databases having the following tables.

STUDENT(Id#, Name, Address)
BOOK(Id#, Name, Author)
Id# of STUDENT and BOOK are homonyms.

The homonym attributes are mapped to different terms in a common ontology. In case the databases belong to different information domains, and we have to map them to the same (lexical) term in different ontologies, we establish a homonym relationship across them.

1.1.2 DATA REPRESENTATION CONFLICTS

Two attributes that are semantically similar might have different data types or representations.

Example:

STUDENT.Id# is defined as a 9 digit integer.

TEACHER.SS# is defined as an 11 character string.

Attributes having different representations are mapped to appropriate terms in a common ontology. Then, transformation functions which convert data from both representations to a canonical representation in the common ontology are defined. In case the databases belong to different information domains, we map conflicting attributes to appropriate terms in different ontologies, and define transformation functions between them.

1.1.3 DATA SCALING CONFLICTS

Two attributes that are semantically similar might be represented using different units and measures. There is a one-one mapping between domain values of the two attributes. For instance, the salary attribute might have values in \$ and £.

Attributes having different scales of measurement are mapped to appropriate terms in a common ontology. Then, transformer functions which convert data from different scales to a common scale registered with the common ontology, are defined. In case the databases belong to different information domains, the conflicting attributes are mapped to appropriate terms in different ontologies, and transformation functions between them are defined.

1.1.4 DATA PRECISION CONFLICTS

Two attributes that are semantically similar might be represented using different precisions. This case differs from the previous one, as there may not be a one-one mapping between values of the domains. There may be a many-one mapping from the domain of the precise attribute to the domain of the coarser attribute.

Example:
Let the attribute Marks have an integer value from 1 to 100.
Let the attribute Grades have the values $\{A, B, C, D, F\}$.

Marks	Grades
81-100	A
61-80	B
41-60	C
21-40	D
1-20	F

Table 5.1. Mapping Between Marks and Grades

Attributes having differing precision in their measurements are mapped to appropriate terms in a common ontology. Then, transformer functions that convert data to the precision of measurement used by the ontology are defined. In this case, the functions may have to do a table lookup. In case measurements in the ontology have a coarser precision, we may have to define a new term having finer precision. In case the databases belong to different information domains, conflicting attributes are mapped to appropriate terms in different ontologies. Transformation functions between terms across the two ontologies are defined, while taking care of differences in precisions of measurements in the two ontologies.

1.1.5 DEFAULT VALUE CONFLICTS

This type of conflict depends on the domain definition of the concerned attributes. The *default value* of an attribute is that which it is defined to have in the absence of more information about the real world. For instance, the default value for Age of an adult might be defined as 18 years in one database, and as 21 years in another.

Attributes having different default values are mapped to the same term in a common ontology describing the appropriate information domain. However, since the default value of an attribute is an intrinsic property of the database, we use c-contexts to capture the "default value" information. Thus, the default value is evaluated differently with respect to different databases.

1.1.6 ATTRIBUTE INTEGRITY CONSTRAINT CONFLICTS

Two semantically similar attributes might be restricted by constraints that are not consistent with each other. For instance, in different databases, the attribute Age might follow these constraints:

Example:

C1 : $Age_1 \leq 18$

C2 : $Age_2 > 21$

C1 and C2 are inconsistent, and hence integrity constraints on the attribute Age are said to conflict. One way of resolving this conflict is to map attributes having conflicting constraints to *disjoint* terms in the ontology. Another approach is to ignore the inconsistency altogether (this might be possible depending on the application domain), and capture *roles* played by the attributes in the domain ontology. Similarity of roles would help establish similarity at a very abstract level, and can be useful as an aid to browsing various databases on the GII.

1.2 ENTITY DEFINITION INCOMPATIBILITY

In this section, we discuss incompatibilities that arise between two objects (Figure 5.3) when partially compatible entity descriptors are used, even when the same type of entity is being modeled. The broad definition of this class of conflicts given in (Czejdo et al., 1987) is refined. For each incompatibility, possible ways of mapping schema elements to terms or c-contexts constructed from terms in appropriate domain specific ontologies, are discussed. In some cases, the use of transformer functions to transform instances from one type domain to another are also discussed.

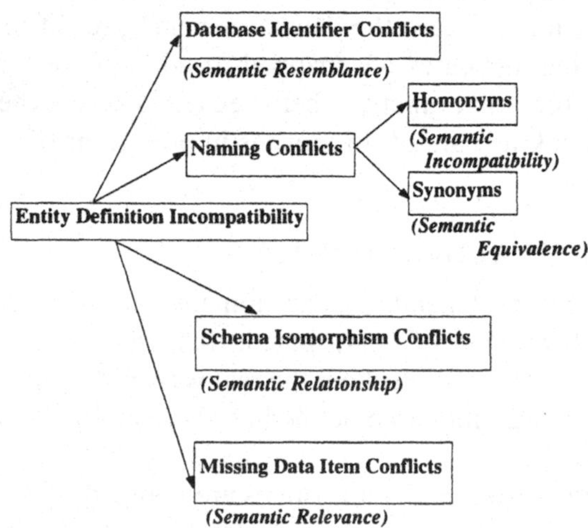

Figure 5.3. Heterogeneities Arising Out of Incompatible Entity Descriptions

1.2.1 DATABASE IDENTIFIER CONFLICTS

In this case, entity descriptions in two databases are incompatible because they use identifier records that are semantically different.

Example: Consider two databases modeling the same entity as follows:

STUDENT1(SS#, Course, Grades)
STUDENT2(Name, Course, Grades)
STUDENT1.SS# and STUDENT2.Name are semantically different keys.

We adopt an approach similar to that in the previous section, where conflicting attributes are mapped to the same term in a common ontology. An appropriate transformer function is defined to translate across the identifiers' domains. In this case, the transformer function is most likely to be a table lookup. Another approach, identified in the previous section, is to capture *roles* played by the attributes in the domain ontology. Similarity of roles (e.g., identifier) helps to establish similarity at a very abstract level, and might be useful as an aid to browsing various databases on the GII.

1.2.2 ENTITY NAMING CONFLICTS

Semantically alike entities might be named differently in different databases. For instance, EMPLOYEE and WORKERS might be two objects describing the same set of entities. They are known as *synonyms*. Objects that are synonyms are mapped to the same term in a common ontology. In case the databases belong to different information domains, the objects are mapped to synonymous terms in their respective ontologies.

On the other hand, semantically unrelated entities might have the same name in different databases. For instance, TICKETS might be the name of a relation which models movie tickets in one database, whereas it might model traffic violation tickets in another database. They are known as *homonyms* of each other. Objects that are homonyms are mapped to different terms in a common ontology. In case the databases belong to different information domains, and we need to map them to the same (lexical) term, we establish a homonym relationship between the terms.

1.2.3 SCHEMA ISOMORPHISM CONFLICTS

Semantically similar entities may have a different number of attributes, giving rise to schema isomorphism conflicts.

Example: Consider two databases modeling two entities as follows:

INSTRUCTOR1(SS#, HomePhone, OffPhone)
INSTRUCTOR2(SS#, Phone)
This is an example of schema non-isomorphism.

Note that this can be considered an artifact of the *Data Precision Conflicts* identified in the previous section. The phone number of INSTRUCTOR1 can be considered to be represented in a more precise manner than the phone number of INSTRUCTOR2. However, conflicts discussed in the previous section are due to differences in the attribute domains representing the same information, and hence are *attribute level conflicts.* Conflicts in this section arise due to differences in the way the entities INSTRUCTOR1 and INSTRUCTOR2 are defined, and hence are *entity level conflicts.*

In our approach, both of these objects would be mapped to the same term in a common ontology (or synonym terms in different ontologies) describing the appropriate information domain(s). Attributes of different objects are mapped to appropriate properties of terms in the ontologies. It is possible that two or more attributes are mapped to the same property. Relational algebra-like expressions may be used for expressing this mapping.

1.2.4 MISSING DATA ITEM CONFLICTS

This conflict arises when one of the entity descriptors modeling semantically similar entities has a missing attribute. This conflict is subsumed by the one discussed in the previous section. A special case of the missing data item conflict satisfies the following conditions:

- The missing attribute is compatible with the entity
- There exists an inference mechanism to deduce the value of the attribute.

Example: Consider two databases modeling related entities.

STUDENT(SS#, Name, Type)
GRAD-STUDENT(SS#, Name)
STUDENT.Type can have values UG or Grad
GRAD-STUDENT can be implicitly deduced to have an attribute Type with value Grad

In the above example, GRAD-STUDENT can be thought to have a Type attribute whose default value is "Grad". The conflict discussed in this section is different from the *default value* conflict in the previous section. The default value conflict is an *attribute level conflict*, whereas the missing data item conflict is an *entity level conflict*.

Objects and attributes are mapped to different but related terms in a common ontology describing information in the appropriate domain. The value of the attribute can be inferred from the relationship specified between the two terms. Alternatively, one might design c-contexts for each of the objects in a way that they reflect relationships between them. The constraints specified by the relationships in turn, are propagated to mappings between c-contexts and the underlying data, so that the appropriate data is automatically retrieved. This is called "conditioning" and is discussed in greater detail in the next section.

1.3 DATA VALUE INCOMPATIBILITY

This class of conflicts covers incompatibilities that arise due to the values of data present in different databases (Breitbart et al., 1986). These conflicts are different from default value conflicts and attribute integrity constraint conflicts (Section 1.1), in that the latter are due to differences in the definitions of the attribute domain types. Here, we refer to data values already existing in the database. Thus, the conflicts here depend on the database state. Since we are dealing with independent databases, it is not necessary that data values for the same entities in two different databases be consistent with each other. We now discuss various types of inconsistencies (Figure 5.4), and our approach to resolving these inconsistencies by mapping schema elements to terms or c-contexts constructed from terms in appropriate domain specific ontologies.

Example: Consider two databases modeling the entity Ship

SHIP1(Id#, Name, Weight)
SHIP2(Id#, Name, Weight)

Consider an entity represented in both databases as follows:

SHIP1(123, USSEnterprise, 100)
SHIP2(123, USSEnterprise, 200)

Thus, we have the same entity, for which SHIP1.Weight is not the same as SHIP2.Weight, i.e., it has inconsistent values in the database.

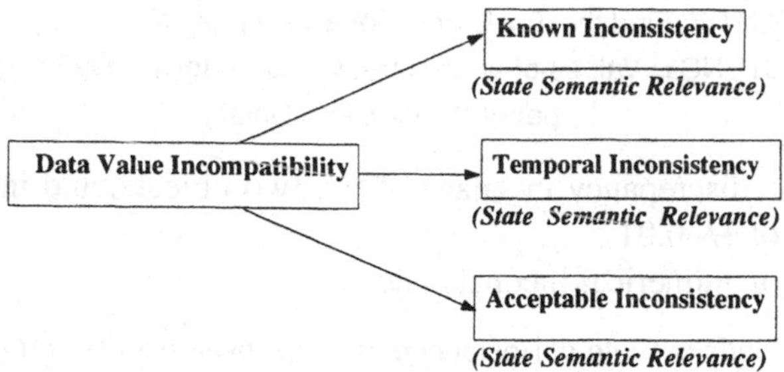

Figure 5.4. Heterogeneities Arising Out of Inconsistencies in Data Values

1.3.1 KNOWN INCONSISTENCY

In this case, the cause of inconsistency in the data values is known ahead of time and measures can be initiated to resolve it. For instance, it might be known ahead of time that one database is more reliable than the other. Since information describing reliability of information sources is application-specific, it is represented in c-contexts constructed from terms in ontology(ies), and may be used to compute answers at run-time in response to a user request for information.

1.3.2 TEMPORARY INCONSISTENCY

In this type of conflict, the inconsistency is of a temporary nature. It has been expressed as a *temporal consistency predicate*[1] (Rusinkiewicz et al., 1991). The database which has conflicting values might have obsolete information. This means that information stored in the databases is time-dependent. The time lag information (Δt) can be represented as a function associated with the appropriate term(s):

$$\text{Weight}(t + \Delta t) = \text{Weight}(t)$$

Since, this information is application-specific, it is represented in c-contexts constructed from terms in ontology(ies).

1.3.3 ACCEPTABLE INCONSISTENCY

In this type of conflict, inconsistencies between values from different databases might be within an acceptable range. Thus, depending on the type of query being answered, the error in values of two inconsistent databases might be considered tolerable. The *tolerance* of inconsistency can be of a numerical or a non-numerical nature. Since tolerance level is application specific, it is represented in c-contexts constructed from terms in ontology(ies), and may be used to compute answers to a user information request at run time.
Example: Numerical Inconsistency

QUERY: Find the Tax Bracket of an Employee.
INCONSISTENCY: Values of up to a fraction of a dollar may be ignored.

$$\text{peturb}(\text{Salary}, \epsilon) = \text{Salary}$$

where ϵ is the discrepancy in salary of the two objects, and in this case may have a value of +/- 0.01
Example: Non numerical Inconsistency

QUERY: Find the State of Residence of an Employee for tax purposes.
INCONSISTENCY: Inconsistency of residences within the same state may be ignored.

$$\text{peturb}(\text{Residence}, \epsilon) = \text{state}(\text{Residence})$$

where ϵ is the discrepancy in residence of the two objects, and in this case may represent a generalization from the town to state.

1.4 ABSTRACTION LEVEL INCOMPATIBILITY

An early discussion of this class of conflicts was presented in (Dayal and Hwang, 1984) for schemas represented using the functional data model. These

[1] Additional information on weaker criteria for consistency can be found in the literature on transaction models [e.g., see (Sheth et al., 1992)].

incompatibilities arise when two semantically similar entities are represented at differing levels of abstraction. Differences in abstraction can arise due to differing levels of generality and aggregation at which an entity (or attribute) is represented in the database. We now discuss various types of incompatibilities arising out of differing abstraction levels (Figure 5.5). Also discussed, is our approach for resolving incompatibilities by mapping schema elements to terms in domain specific ontologies describing the appropriate information domain.

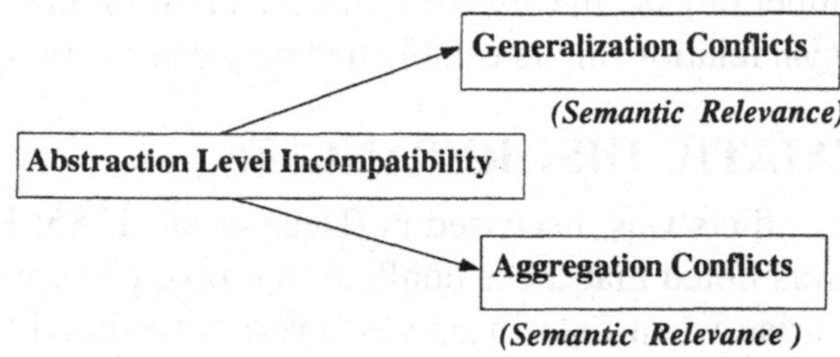

Figure 5.5. Heterogeneities Arising Out of Differing Levels of Abstraction

1.4.1 GENERALIZATION CONFLICTS

These conflicts arise when two entities are represented at different levels of generalization in two different databases.

Example: Consider the entity Graduate Students, which may be represented in two different databases as follows:

STUDENT(Id#, Name, Major, Type)
GRAD-STUDENT(Id#, Name, Major)

Thus, we have the same entity set being defined at a more general level in the first database. In our approach, objects in the database are mapped to terms at the appropriate level of abstraction in a common ontology. In the above example, the term associated with the more general object *subsumes* the term associated with the more specific object. In case the terms are in different ontologies, then a *hyponym/hypernym* relationship is established between the two terms.

1.4.2 AGGREGATION CONFLICTS

These conflicts arise when an aggregation is used in one database to identify a set of entities in another database. Also, properties of the aggregate entity can be an aggregate of the corresponding property of the entities being aggregated.

Example: Consider the aggregation SET-OF which is used to define an entity in the first database and the set of entities in another database as follows:

CONVOY(Id#, AvgWeight, Location)

SHIP(Id#, Weight, Location, Captain)

CONVOY in the first database is a SET-OF SHIPs in the second database. Also, CONVOY.AvgWeight is the average (aggregate function) weight (SHIP.Weight) of ships that are members of the convoy. In our approach, objects in the database are mapped to terms at the appropriate level of abstraction in a common ontology. In the above example, the term associated with the collection/aggregate object is related by a *holonym* relationship with the term associated with the member object. In case the terms are in different ontologies, then a *holonym/meronym* relationship is established between the two terms.

1.5 SCHEMATIC DISCREPANCIES

This class of conflicts was discussed in (Deen et al., 1985; Krishnamurthy et al., 1991). It was noted that these conflicts can take place within the same data model, and arise when data in one database correspond to metadata of another database. We now analyze the problem and identify three aspects with help of an example given in (Krishnamurthy et al., 1991). We discuss various types of inconsistencies (Figure 5.6) and our approach to resolving them. These inconsistencies are resolved by mapping schema elements to terms or c-contexts constructed from terms in appropriate domain specific ontologies.

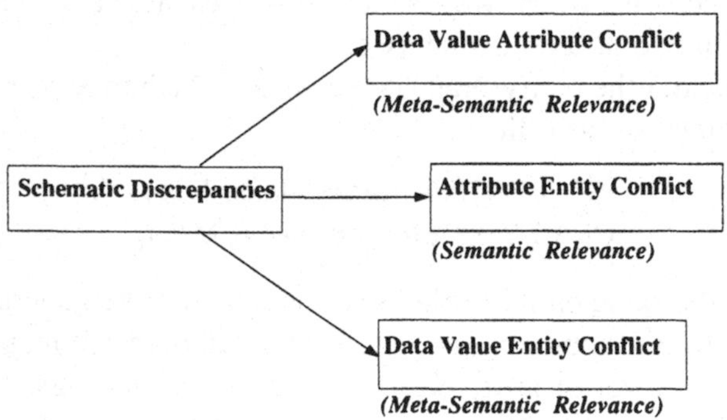

Figure 5.6. Heterogeneities Arising Out of Schematic Discrepancies

Example:
Consider three stock market databases. All contain the closing price for each day of each stock in the stock market. The schema for the three databases are as follows:

- **Database DB1:**
  relation r : {(date, stkCode, clsPrice) . . . }
- **Database DB2:**
  relation r : {(date, Stk_1, Stk_2, . . .) . . . }

- **Database DB3:**
  relation Stk_1 : {(date, clsPrice) ... },
  relation Stk_2 : {(date, clsPrice) ... },
  ⋮

DB1 consists of a single relation that has a tuple per day per stock with its closing price. DB2 also has a single relation, but with one attribute per stock, and one tuple per day, where the value of the attribute is the closing price of the stock. In contrast, DB3 has one relation per stock that has a tuple per day with its closing price. Let us consider that the stkCode values in DB1 are the names of the attributes, and in the other databases they are the names of relations (e.g., Stk_1, Stk_2).

1.5.1 DATA VALUE ATTRIBUTE CONFLICT

This conflict arises when the value of an attribute in one database corresponds to an attribute in another database. Thus, this kind of conflict depends on the *database state*. Referring to the above example, values of the attribute *stkCode* in the database **DB1** correspond to the attributes Stk_1, Stk_2, ... in the database **DB2**.

For resolving this type of incompatibility, we need terms in a *meta-model*, of which terms in an ontology would be an instantiation. In the case of the above example, the attributes Stk_i would be instantiations of the term *Attribute* in a meta-model describing the database. The attribute *stkCode* would be mapped to a term in an ontology. An appropriate transformer function (possibly idempotent) would be then defined between the domain of the term in the ontology and the term in the meta-model.

1.5.2 ATTRIBUTE ENTITY CONFLICT

This conflict arises when the same entity is modeled as an attribute in one database, and as an entity in another database. This kind of conflict is different from other conflicts defined in this section, because it depends on the *database schema*, and not on the *database state*. This conflict can also be considered as an entity definition incompatibility (Section 1.2). Referring to the example described in the beginning of this section, the attributes Stk_1, Stk_2 in the database **DB2** correspond to entities of the same name in the database **DB3**.

In our approach, entities and attributes are mapped to appropriate terms in a common ontology. In case the databases belong to different information domains, entities and attributes are mapped to appropriate synonym terms in their respective ontologies.

1.5.3 ENTITY DATA VALUE CONFLICT

This conflict arises when the value of an attribute in one database corresponds to an entity in another. Thus, this kind of conflict depends on the *database state*. Referring to the example described in the beginning of this section, the values of the attribute stkCode in the database **DB1** correspond to the entities Stk_1, Stk_2 in the database **DB3**.

For resolving this type of incompatibility, we need terms in a *meta-model*, of which terms in an ontology, would be an instantiation. In the case of the above example, entities Stk_i would be instantiations of the term *Entity* in a meta-model describing the database. The attribute *stkCode* would be mapped to a term in an ontology. An appropriate transformer function (possibly idempotent) would then be defined between the term domain in the ontology, to the term in the meta-model.

2. CAPTURING THE INFORMATION CONTENT OF DATABASE OBJECTS

In the previous section, schematic heterogeneities across data in multiple databases were discussed, and approaches for abstracting schematic details using terms or c-contexts constructed from terms in appropriate domain specific ontologies were presented. We now discuss the *semantic proximity* model (with c-contexts as its central components), and demonstrate its use for capturing information content, especially information that may not be modeled in the schema metadata.

We distinguish between the *real world*, and the *model world*, which is a representation of the real world. Attempts have been made to capture similarity of objects in the model world by using mathematical tools like value mappings between domains, and abstractions like generalization, aggregation, etc. We need to understand and represent more knowledge to capture the semantics of relationships between objects. This knowledge should be able to capture the **context** of the objects, and **abstractions** relating the object domains. We attempt to capture and reason with this knowledge in the semantic proximity model.

We first discuss the semantic proximity model and relate it to other attempts made by various practitioners. A partial representation of c-contexts is proposed, and operations that enable inferences on them are defined. An algebra of mapping operations, dependent on c-context based inferences, is used to map c-contexts to underlying database objects. Finally, the advantages of representing c-contexts are discussed. Examples are used to illustrate how information content not modeled in the schema, can be captured using the semantic proximity model.

2.1 SEMANTIC PROXIMITY: CAPTURING INFORMATION CONTENT

We now present a modified version of the semantic proximity given in (Sheth and Kashyap, 1992), to capture information content of a database object **O** with the help of a *c-context* $C_{def}(O)$, The c-context captures the context in which the object is defined. The semantic view of the object exported to the GII is denoted as $\mathbf{O_G}$ (Figure 5.7). The 4-tuple defining the *semantic proximity* is given by:

semPro(O_G, O)=<C_{def}(O), Abstraction, (D_{O_G}, D_O), (S_{O_G}, S_O)>

where D_O is the defined domain of O and S_O is the state of O in the database in which it is defined.

- The first component denotes the **context** in which O is exported to the GII. C_{def}(O) is a c-context constructed from terms in a domain specific ontology describing the appropriate information domain.
- The second component identifies the abstraction/mapping used to map the exported object O_G to the underlying database object O.
- The third component enumerates domain definitions of the objects, O_G and O. The domains may be defined by either enumerating values as a set, or by using existing type definitions in the database.
- The fourth component enumerates states of the objects, which are extensions of the objects recorded in their respective databases at a particular time.

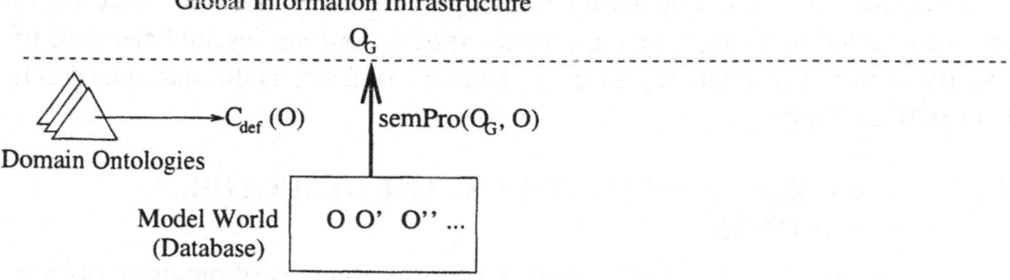

Figure 5.7. Capturing Information Content Using Semantic Proximity

2.1.1 CONTEXT: THE SEMANTIC COMPONENT

The context is the key component that captures semantics related to an object's definition, and its relationships to other objects. Alternatives discussed in multidatabase literature for representing context are as follows.

- In (Ouksel and Naiman, 1993), context is defined as the knowledge that is needed to reason about another system, for the purpose of answering a query. It is specified as a set of assertions identifying correspondences between various schema elements.

- In (Sciore et al., 1992), context is defined as the meaning, content, organization and properties of data. It is modeled using metadata associated with the data.
- In (Yu et al., 1991), *common concepts* are proposed to characterize similarities between attributes in multiple databases.
- When using a well defined ontology, such as Cyc (Guha, 1990), a well defined partition (called *Microtheory*) of the ontology is assigned a context.
- A context may be identified or represented using the following (Sheth and Kashyap, 1992):
  - By association with a database or a group of databases.
  - As the *relationship* in which an entity participates.
  - From a schema architecture (e.g., the multidatabase or federated schema architecture of (Sheth and Larson, 1990)), a context can be specified in terms of an *export schema* (a context that is closer to the database) or an *external schema* (a context that is closer to the application).
  - At a very elementary level, as a *named collection* of object domains.

A context may be used in several ways to capture relevant semantics. The context may be associated with an object, to specify the assumptions used in designing the object and its relationships with other objects. C-contexts are constructed by using terms in domain specific ontologies, and are used to specify information content present in database objects, as discussed in detail later in this chapter.

2.1.2 ABSTRACTIONS/MAPPINGS: THE STRUCTURAL COMPONENT

Abstraction refers to the relation between the domains of database objects and the semantic view exported to the GII. Mapping between domains of objects is the mathematical expression to denote the abstractions. However, since abstractions by themselves cannot capture semantic similarity they have to be associated either with the context (Kashyap and Sheth, 1996), or with extra knowledge in order to capture real world semantics. Some proposals for expressing abstractions are as follows.

- In (Sheth and Kashyap, 1992), abstractions are defined in terms of value mappings between domains of objects, and are associated with the context as a part of the semantic proximity.

- In (Ouksel and Naiman, 1993), mappings are defined between schema elements called *inter schema correspondence assertions* or ISCAs. A set of ISCAs under consideration define the context for integration of the schemas.
- In (Sciore et al., 1992), mappings called *conversion functions* are associated with the meta-attributes which define the context.
- In (Yu et al., 1991), the attributes are associated with "common concepts". Thus, mappings (relationship) between the attributes are determined through the extra knowledge associated with the concepts.

We utilize a formalism called *schema correspondences* (Kashyap and Sheth, 1996) to represent abstraction/mappings from the exported object O_G to the corresponding object O in the database. The schema correspondence can be represented as:
schCor(O_G, O) = <O_G, attr(O_G), O, attr(O), M>

- O_G is the object exported to the GII. It is obtained by applying constraints specified in C_{def}(O) to the object O in the database.
- *attr(O)* denotes the attributes associated with an object. *attr(O_G)* depends on the representation of C_{def}(O) and is discussed in detail in a later section.
- M is a mapping (possibly higher-order) expressing correspondences between objects, their attributes, and values of the objects/attributes.

In later sections, we discuss how mappings associated with the c-context in a semPro descriptor are used to map c-contexts to the underlying data. At the intensional level, these mappings may specify associations between terms in domain specific ontologies and objects in various databases. This enables abstraction of schematic details at the intensional level. At the extensional level, the mappings may be expressed as transformer functions across the domain definitions of various attributes and objects.

2.1.3 DOMAINS OF THE OBJECTS

The concept of an object domain here refers to the set from which objects can take their values. When using an object-oriented model, the domains of objects can be thought of as types, whereas collections of objects might themselves be thought of as classes. A domain can be either **atomic** (i.e., cannot be decomposed any further), or composed of other atomic or composite domains. The domain of an object can be thought of as a subset of the cross-product of the object property domains (Figure 5.8). Analogously, we can have other combinations, such as union and intersection of domains.

An important distinction between a context or a knowledge domain (in the sense it is used in "domain specific ontologies") and an object domain should

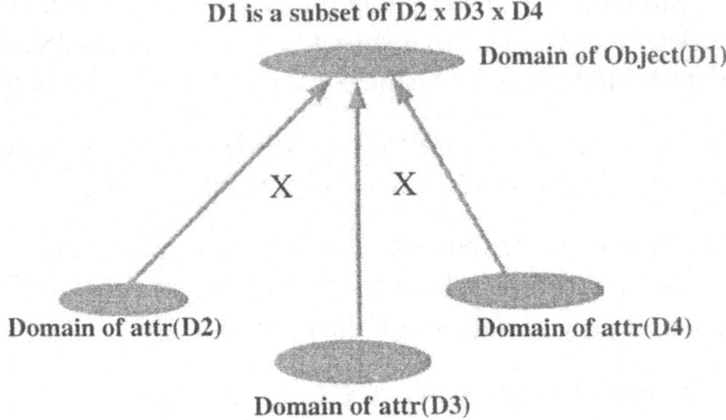

Figure 5.8. Attribute and Object Domains in a Database

be noted. A context may be specified as a named collection of object domains, i.e., it is associated with a group of objects. On the other hand, a domain is the property of an object, and is associated with the description of that object.

2.1.4 STATES (EXTENSIONS) OF THE OBJECTS

The state of an object can be thought of as an extension of an object recorded in a database. However, this extension must not be confused with the actual state of the entity being modeled according to the real world semantics. Two objects having different extensions can have the same state real world semantics (and hence be semantically equivalent).

2.1.5 USING C-CONTEXTS TO ABSTRACT OUT SCHEMATIC DETAILS

Having discussed various schematic heterogeneities in the previous section, we now discuss, how c-contexts associated with mapping expressions can be instrumental in abstraction of schematic details and heterogeneities. The various schematic heterogeneities have been broadly classified as follows.

Domain Definition Incompatibility In this case heterogeneities arise due to differences in definition of semantically similar attributes (Section 1.1). The various types of heterogeneity in this category are both intensional and extensional in nature. The heterogeneities that are extensional in nature, viz., those pertaining to differences in representation, scales, and precision of data, can be resolved by mapping attribute domains to concept domains, or abstract data types in a domain specific ontology. Transformer functions can be used to map instances of one domain or abstract data type into another. This approach has been used in (Czejdo et al., 1987; Mena et al., 1996b). The heterogeneities that are intensional in nature, viz., conflicts stemming from naming, defaults and inconsistent constraints, can be resolved by mapping attributes to common or different concepts in the domain ontology. In some cases, it might be necessary to map them to c-contexts constructed from concepts in domain ontologies.

Entity Definition Incompatibility In this case, heterogeneities arise due to the use of partially compatible entity descriptors (Section 1.2). Most of the conflicts here are intensional in nature and can be resolved by mapping the entities to common or different concepts in the domain ontology. In some cases, it might be necessary to map them to c-contexts constructed from concepts in domain ontologies. An exception is the *database identifier conflict*, where heterogeneous identifiers for the entities may be mapped to appropriate concepts or abstract data types. Transformer functions can be used to map an identifier in one database to an equivalent identifier in another database.

Data Value Incompatibility In this case, heterogeneities arise due to differences in data values already existing in the database (Section 1.3). The heterogeneities are extensional in nature, and a naive approach would be to map conflicting attributes to appropriate concepts or abstract data types, and use appropriate transformer functions. However, for different applications there might be different definitions of inconsistency and different functions would need to be defined. A better approach would be to construct c-contexts and attach appropriate functions as illustrated in Section 1.3.

Abstraction Level Incompatibility In this case, heterogeneities arise due to differing levels of abstraction at which the entities may be represented (Section 1.4). These heterogeneities can be resolved by mapping the entities to concepts at appropriate levels of abstraction in the domain ontology. In case there do not exist appropriate concepts, one may have to construct c-context from concepts in the domain ontology. In case the concepts are from different ontologies, one may have to define terminological relationships across them. Examples of terminological relationships are *hyponyms/hypernyms* in the case of generalization/specialization and *holonyms/meronyms* in the case of aggregations.

Schematic Discrepancies In this case, heterogeneities arise when data in one database corresponds to metadata in another (Section 1.5). One form of this heterogeneity is the *attribute entity conflict*. It can be resolved by mapping corresponding entities and attributes to appropriate c-contexts. For other forms of this heterogeneity, it is necessary to have a mechanism to specify correspondences between data in one database and metadata in another, and is beyond the scope of this book.

We have discussed above how schematic details and heterogeneities can be abstracted out by using c-contexts associated with mapping expressions and transformer functions. The c-contexts so constructed are also used to capture the information content. From the perspective of information brokering, they may also be viewed as an *intermediate language* in which information content of the underlying databases is represented. The two perspectives based on which the c-contexts may be constructed are as follows.

Bottom-Up Perspective In this case, the focus is on abstracting out the representational and schematic details. Thus, c-contexts are used as views on objects in the underlying databases, and the set of instances exported to the information broker on the GII obeys the view constraints. This is the perspective primarily followed in (Kashyap and Sheth, 1996).

Top-Down Perspective In this case, the focus is on modeling and specifying information in an application or domain specific manner. Thus, it is assumed that there exist underlying objects in the databases for concepts in the ontologies. Mappings are then appropriately combined to determine the object instances in the underlying databases that satisfy the constraints specified in the c-contexts. This perspective is taken in (Mena et al., 1996b). A similar perspective has been taken in (Borgida and Brachman, 1993) for populating description logic (DL) expressions.

2.2 C-CONTEXTS: A PARTIAL REPRESENTATION

Several efforts attempt to represent the similarity between two objects in databases. In (Larson et al., 1989), a fixed set of descriptors define essential characteristics of attributes, and are used to generate mappings between them. We have discussed in (Kashyap and Sheth, 1996), how the descriptors do not guarantee semantic similarity. Thus, any representation of c-context which can be described by a fixed set of descriptors is not appropriate.

In our approach, the descriptors (or meta-attributes) are chosen dynamically to model characteristics of the application domain. It is not possible a priori to determine all possible meta-attributes that would completely characterize the semantics of an application domain. This leads to a *partial* representation of c-contexts. We represent a c-context as a collection of contextual coordinates (meta-attributes) as follows:

Context = $<(\mathbf{C_1}, \mathbf{Expr_1})\ (\mathbf{C_2}, \mathbf{Expr_2}) \ldots (\mathbf{C_k}, \mathbf{Expr_k})>$ where

- C_i, $1 \leq i \leq k$, is a contextual coordinate denoting an aspect of a c-context

- C_i may model some characteristic of the subject domain and may be obtained from a domain specific ontology (discussed later in this section)

- C_i may model an implicit assumption in the design of a database.

Now, we explain the meaning of the symbols C_i and $Expr_i$ by using examples and by enumerating the corresponding DL expressions. When using DL expressions, it is possible to define primitive classes and in addition, specify classes using intensional descriptions phrased in terms of necessary and sufficient properties that must be satisfied by their instances. The intensional descriptions may be used to express collection of constraints that make up a c-context. Using the terminology of DL systems, each term may be modeled as either a **concept** or a **role**. Also, each C_i roughly corresponds to a role, and each $Expr_i$ roughly corresponds to fillers for that role. $Expr_i$ might be a term, c-context, or a term associated with a c-context. Heuristics for modeling terms as contextual coordinates or their values are discussed later in this section. The DL expressions corresponding to c-contexts are summarized in Appendix 5.A. We use the following example and terminology to explain how c-contexts capture information in the databases using terms from a domain ontology. Consider the following database objects:

EMPLOYEE(SS#, Name, SalaryType, Dept, Affiliation)
PUBLICATION(Id, Title, Journal)
POSITION(Id, Title, Dept, Type)
HAS-PUBLICATION(SS#, Id)
HOLDS-POSITION(SS#, Id)

Let us now illustrate with examples how information content in these database objects can be captured with the help of terms organized as c-contexts in a domain specific ontology. Some relevant terminology is as follows.

- term(O)[2] and term(A) are terms corresponding to the database object O and attribute A at the intensional level. We assume the existence of transformer functions between the domains of the terms (also referred to as the extension of the term) in the ontology, and the domains of the appropriate object or attribute in the database.

- instance(V) is the instance corresponding to the data value V in the database. The data value might be a key or an object identifier. This might be implemented using a transformer function between the domains of the term to which the instance belongs in the ontology, and the domain of the appropriate object or attribute in the database.

- Ext(Term) denotes the set of instances corresponding to the term in the ontology.

[2]The predicate term should have one more argument identifying the ontology which is being used, as a database might contain information in more than one information domain. However, we can assume without loss of generality that one ontology is being used to capture the information in this database.

- $C_{def}(O)$ is the definition context of a database object O and is typically used to specify assumptions in the design of the object. It may also be used to share a pre-determined extension of the object with the GII (denoted as O_G).

- $O_1 \circ C_{ass}(O_1, O_2)$ denotes the association of an object O_1 with an association context. This may be used to represent relationships between the objects O_1 and O_2 with reference to an aspect of the application domain.

- C_q denotes the context associated with a query Q posed to an information broker on the GII. The context makes explicit (partially) the semantics of the query. A user can consult concepts in ontologies and objects in a database to construct the query context[3].

We can identify the following associations:
term(EMPLOYEE) = EmplConcept,
term(EMPLOYEE.SS#) = EmplConcept.self,
term(EMPLOYEE.Name) = name,
term(EMPLOYEE.Dept) = hasEmployer,
term(EMPLOYEE.Affiliation) = hasAffiliation,
term(PUBLICATION) = PublConcept,
term(PUBLICATION.Id) = { hasArticle, PublConcept.self }
term(PUBLICATION.Title) = hasTitle,
term(POSITION) = PostConcept,
term(POSITION.Id) = { hasPosition, PostConcept.self }
term(HAS-PUBLICATION) = HasPublConcept,
term(HAS-PUBLICATION.Id) = { hasArticle, isAuthorOf }
term(HAS-PUBLICATION.SS#) = hasAuthor,
term(HOLDS-POSITION) = HoldsPostConcept,
term(HOLDS-POSITION.SS#) = hasDesignee,
term(HOLDS-POSITION.Id) = { hasPosition, isDesigneeOf }
The value $Expr_i$ of a contextual coordinate C_i can be represented in the following manner.

- $Expr_i$ can be a variable. It is used as a place holder to elicit answers from the databases and impose constraints on them.

  Example:
  Suppose, we are interested in people who are authors and who hold a position (designee). We can represent the query context C_q as follows:

  C_q = <(isAuthorOf, X) (isDesigneeOf, Y)>

[3] For a detailed exposition about the various types of context see (Kashyap, 1997).

The same thing can be expressed in a DL as follows:

C_q = (AND Anything (ATLEAST 1 isAuthorOf) (ATLEAST 1 isDesigneeOf)).

The terms isAuthorOf and isDesigneeOf are obtained from a domain specific ontology. From a modeling perspective, the above query expresses the users' interest in all employees that hold a position and have authored a published article. In this particular case, it can be seen intuitively that objects that are instances of EmplConcept are the right candidates. This can be expressed in the following manner.

C_q = (AND EmplConcept (ATLEAST 1 isAuthorOf) (ATLEAST 1 isDesigneeOf))

It may be noted here that we use variables in a very restricted manner for the specific purpose of retrieving relevant properties of the selected objects. They are used only at the highest level of nesting though the c-contexts can have an arbitrary level of nesting (since each $Expr_i$ can be a c-context or a term associated with a c-context), and hence we do not need to perform complex nested unifications.

- $Expr_i$ can be a set.
  - The set may be an enumeration of terms from a domain specific ontology.
  - The set may be defined as the extension of an object or as elements from the domain of a type defined in the database.
  - The set may be defined by posing constraints on pre-existing sets.

Example:
Suppose we want to represent assumptions implicit in the design of the object EMPLOYEE in a database. Let all employees in the database either be researchers or employed in a particular department. Furthermore, let all publications of an employee be represented in the object PUBLICATION in the database. These assumptions can be represented in the definition context of EMPLOYEE as follows:

C_{def}(EMPLOYEE) = <(hasEmployer, [**Deptypes**∪{restypes}])
(isAuthorOf, PUBLICATION)>

Deptypes is a type defined in the database, and along with the data value restypes defines the domain of the attribute EMPLOYEE.Dept.
Let term(**Deptypes**) = DeptConcept and instance(restypes) = researcher ⇒

C_{def}(EMPLOYEE) = <(hasEmployer, [Ext(DeptConcept)∪{restypes}])
(isAuthorOf, PublConcept)>

The same thing can be expressed in a DL as follows:

C_{def}(EMPLOYEE) = (**AND** EmplConcept (**ALL** isAuthorOf PublConcept)
(**ALL** hasEmployer
(**OR** DeptConcept (**ONE-OF** researcher))))

- $Expr_i$ can be a variable associated with a c-context. This can be used to express constraints, that the result of the query should obey.
  Example:
  Suppose we want all articles whose titles contain the substring "abortion" in them. This can be expressed in the following query context:

  C_q = <(hasArticle, X∘ <(hasTitle, {y|substring(y) = "abortion"})>)>
  = <(hasArticle, X∘Context)>

  where ∘ denotes association of a c-context with a variable X.
  Let us assume that there is a concept AbortionString in the ontology which is subsumed by the concept String where

  Ext(AbortionString) = {y|substring(y) = "abortion"}
  Context = <(hasTitle, AbortionString)>

  Association of a variable and a c-context ensures that the answer satisfies constraints expressed in the c-context. From a modeling perspective, it may be noted that the query expresses a user's interest in any concept, having values of hasArticle as described in the query context. The relevant concept may be identified after reasoning has been performed on the c-contexts, and is illustrated later in this section. The same query can be expressed in a DL as follows:

  C_q = [rf(hasArticle)] for (**ALL** hasArticle (**ALL** hasTitle AbortionString))

- $Expr_i$ can be a set, type or an object associated with a c-context. This is called an association context and is used to express semantic dependencies between objects that may not be modeled in the database.
  Example:
  Suppose we want to represent information relating publications to employees in a database. Let PUBLICATION and EMPLOYEE be objects in a database. Let the object HAS-PUBLICATION in the database contain information about publications written by employees who are researchers. The definition context of HAS-PUBLICATION can be defined as follows.

C_{def}(HAS-PUBLICATION) = <(hasArticle, PUBLICATION)
(hasAuthor, EMPLOYEE∘ <(hasAffiliation, {research})>)>

where research is a term from the ontology, and corresponds to a data value in the domain of the attribute EMPLOYEE.Affiliation in the database ⇒

C_{def}(HAS-PUBLICATION) = <(hasArticle, PublConcept)
(hasAuthor, EmplConcept ∘ Context)>

where ∘ denotes association of a c-context with an object EMPLOYEE, and Context = <(hasAffiliation, {research})>
Association of a c-context with an object is similar to defining a view on object extensions such that only those instances satisfying the constraints defined in the c-context are exported to the federation. The expanded version of the above c-context can be expressed in a DL as follows:

C_{def}(HAS-PUBLICATION) = (**AND** HasPublConcept
(**ALL** hasArticle PublConcept)
(**ALL** hasAuthor (**AND** EmplConcept
(**ALL** hasAffiliation (**ONE-OF** {research})))))

Note that the relationships between EMPLOYEE, PUBLICATION, and HAS-PUBLICATION is information represented in the c-context, that has not been modeled in the database schema.

Heuristics to construct C-Contexts

The contextual coordinates and values are taken from the concepts in the ontology. A key issue in constructing intensional descriptions is how to assign concepts to contextual coordinates and their values. We view contextual coordinates as two-place predicates p(x,y), and their values as one-place predicates q(x).

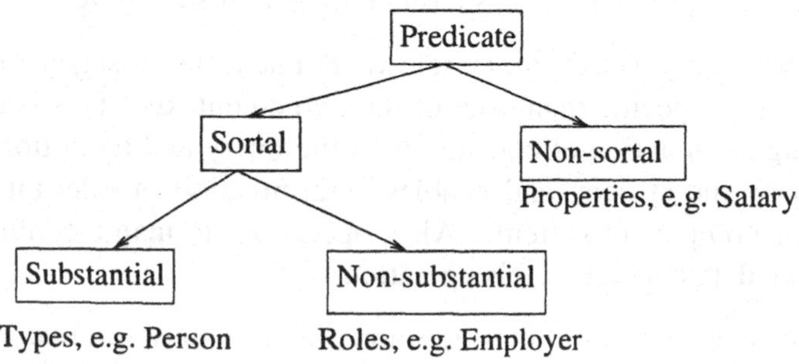

Figure 5.9. A Classification of Predicates and Concepts

Consider a classification of predicates proposed in (Guarino, 1993) (Figure 5.9). Based on the classification of predicates in Figure 5.9, we propose two criteria for the construction of intensional descriptions:

- If a concept in the ontology is associated with a non-sortal or non-substantial sortal predicate type, i.e., it denotes the role or a property of a concept, then it may be assigned as a meta-attribute.
- If a concept in the ontology is associated with a substantial sortal predicate type, i.e., something which can be identified by itself (and not due to its association with another concept), then it may be assigned as the value of a meta-attribute.

2.2.1 INFERENCES AND REASONING WITH C-CONTEXTS

We have proposed a partial representation of c-contexts in the previous section. Earlier, we discussed how inferences may be performed on c-contexts before they are mapped to the underlying data. Since objects corresponding to c-contexts are also exported to the GII, the proposed representation can be used in a meaningful manner to determine relevant information. To reason with information on the GII, the following need to be precisely defined.

- The most common relationship between c-contexts is the "specificity" relationship. Given two c-contexts C_1 and C_2, $C_1 \leq C_2$ iff C_1 is at least as specific as C_2. This is useful when objects defined in a particular context have to transcend (McCarthy, 1993) to a more specific or general c-context. This is discussed in detail with examples in (Kashyap and Sheth, 1995).
- It is also the case that two c-contexts may not be comparable to each other, i.e., it may not be possible to decide whether one is more general than the other or not. Thus, the specificity relationship gives us a partial order, enabling the organization of a set of c-contexts as a lattice structure. Before mapping a c-context to underlying data, inferences can be performed to determine its position in the lattice. This leads to a decrease in the computation required as well as a semantically closer answer.
- For any two c-contexts, the greatest lower bound is the most general context, which is more specific than each of the two c-contexts. This is useful for computing conjunction of constraints in the query and definition contexts exported by the system, and enables determination of relevant information in the component systems. Also, operations to map c-contexts to the underlying data depend on this operation.

We now discuss with examples, the notions of *context coherency* and *glb*. A detailed presentation of context-based inferences is presented in (Kashyap, 1997).

Coherence of two contexts

This operator determines whether constraints captured by two c-contexts are consistent with each other, and enables inference of relevant information in the underlying systems. It may involve inferences *wrt* to a domain specific ontology to determine whether two terms contradict each other. If two terms are inconsistent with each other, then their underlying extensions must necessarily be disjoint.

Example:

Suppose we are interested in employees earning more than $10000 (represented by $Cntxt_2$). However if the database contains information only about employees earning less than $10000 (represented by $Cntxt_1$), then the coherence of contexts is instrumental in determining relevance of information in the database.

$$\text{Let } Cntxt_1 = <(salary, \{x \mid x \leq 10000\})>$$
$$Cntxt_2 = <(salary, \{x \mid x > 10000\})>$$
$$\text{Thus, } coherent(Cntxt_1, Cntxt_2) = FALSE$$

The glb of two c-contexts

As observed earlier, the specificity relationship between c-contexts induces a partial order among them. Thus, the context can be organized as a meet semi-lattice where every pair of contexts has the greatest lower bound. We now define the *glb* operation. The rules determining **glb($Expr_1$, $Expr_2$)** are as follows.

Variable: $glb(Expr_1, X) = Expr_1$

Sets: $glb(Set_1, Set_2) = Set_1 \cap Set_2$

Terms: $glb(Term_1, Term_2)$ can be determined by the subsumption relationships in the domain specific ontology. It is the most specific term in the ontology which is subsumed by both $Term_1$ and $Term_2$.

Association Contexts: These are rules concerning the glb of values of contextual coordinates when an association context is involved.

- $glb(Expr_1 \circ Context_1, Expr_2) = glb(Expr_1, Expr_2) \circ Context_1$
- $glb(Expr_1 \circ Context_1, Expr_2 \circ Context_2)$
  $= glb(Expr_1, Expr_2) \circ glb(Context_1, Context_2)$

The greatest lower bound of the contexts **glb($Context_1$, $Context_2$)** can now be defined as:

- $glb(Cntxt_1, <>) = Cntxt_1$, *[Empty Context]*
- $glb(glb(<(C_i, Expr_i)>, Context_1), Context_2)$
  $= glb(<(C_i, Expr_i)>, glb(Context_1, Context_2))$ if $C_i \notin Context_2$

- glb(glb(<(C'$_i$, Expr'$_i$)>, Context$_2$), Context$_1$)
  = glb(<(C'$_i$, Expr'$_i$)>, glb(Context$_2$, Context$_1$)) if C'$_i$ $\notin$ Context$_1$
- glb(glb(<(C$_i$, Expr$_i$)>, Context$_1$), glb(<(C$_i$, Expr'$_i$)>, Context$_2$))
  = glb(<(C$_i$, glb(Expr$_i$, Expr'$_i$))>, glb(Context$_1$, Context$_2$))

An alternative and equivalent representation of a c-context (expressed using the glb operation) is very useful when there is a need to carry out inferences on the context and information associated with it.

Cntxt = <(C$_1$, Expr$_1$)(C$_2$, Expr$_2$) ... (C$_k$, Expr$_k$)>
= glb(<(C$_1$, Expr$_1$)>, glb(<(C$_2$, Expr$_2$)>, ..., glb(<(C$_k$, Expr$_k$)>, <>) ...))

Example: Consider the following two c-contexts:

Context$_1$ = <(hasAuthor, EmplConcept$\circ$ <(hasAffiliation, {research})>)
(hasArticle, PublConcept)>
Context$_2$ = <(hasArticle, X$\circ$ <(hasTitle,{x| substring(x)="abortion"})>)>

It may be noted that Context$_2$ is actually a query context, and computation of the greatest lower bound helps identify objects of interest in the database and propagate the relevant constraints (Figure 5.11). The computation of the greatest lower bound of these two c-contexts is as follows:

glb(Context$_1$, Context$_2$)
= glb(glb(<(hasArticle, PublConcept)>, Context$_{1,2}$),
glb(<(hasArticle, X$\circ$ <(hasTitle,{x| substring(x)="abortion"})>)>, Context$_{2,2}$))
where Context$_{1,2}$ = <(hasAuthor, EmplConcept$\circ$ <(hasAffiliation, {research})>)>
and Context$_{2,2}$ = <>
= glb(<(hasArticle,
glb(PublConcept, X$\circ$ <(hasTitle,{x| substring(x)="abortion"})>))>,
glb(Context$_{1,2}$, Context$_{2,2}$))
= glb(<(hasArticle,
glb(PublConcept, X$\circ$ <(hasTitle,{x| substring(x)="abortion"})>))>,
Context$_{1,2}$)
= glb(<(hasArticle,
glb(PublConcept, X)$\circ$ <(hasTitle,{x| substring(x)="abortion"})>)>,
Context$_{1,2}$)
= <(hasArticle, PublConcept$\circ$ <(hasTitle,{x| substring(x)="abortion"})>)
(hasAuthor, EmplConcept$\circ$ <(hasAffiliation, {research})>)>

2.3 ASSOCIATION OF MAPPINGS WITH CONTEXTS: AN ALGEBRA

We have discussed earlier in this section, the construction of c-contexts to capture the semantics of information. However, for any meaningful operation to be performed on the computer, the semPro descriptor between two objects has to be mapped to a mathematical expression which would essentially express the structural correspondence between two objects. Our approach consists of the following three aspects:

The Semantic aspect: The semPro descriptor captures real world semantics of data in the database through context and includes intensional descriptions of:

- objects and their attributes,
- relationships between various objects,
- implicit assumptions in the design of the objects, and
- constraints which the objects and attributes satisfy.

The GII objects are objects obtained by applying constraints in the intensional descriptions to the database objects.

The Data Organization aspect: This refers to the actual organization of data in the databases, e.g., the tables and views in a relational database, or the class hierarchy in object-oriented databases.

The Mapping/Abstraction aspect: The schema correspondence (discussed later in this chapter) descriptor captures the association between objects on the GII and database objects. The association uses object algebraic operations to express correspondences between objects exported to the GII and the database objects. The evaluation of these associations results in the retrieval of database objects which satisfy constraints specified in the context.

The mapping aspect can be succinctly expressed as:
schCor(O_G,O) = $\Pi_{Context}$[semPro(O_G,O)]
In the rest of this section, we explain the mapping aspect with the help of examples. We discuss the terminology, operations, and projection rules, used to specify semantics of associations between objects exported to the GII, and the underlying database objects.

2.3.1 STRUCTURAL MAPPINGS FOR EXPRESSING ABSTRACTION

We discuss formalisms to represent structural mappings between schematic elements in databases, and c-contexts constructed from terms in a domain specific ontology. As discussed earlier in this chapter, there are two types of conflicts across databases: *extensional* and *intensional*. We use *transformer functions* for resolving conflicts at the extensional level. At the intensional level, we construct c-contexts associated with mappings to database objects. A uniform formalism called *schema correspondences* is used to represent these mappings. The schema correspondences are a component of semantic proximity discussed in Section 2.1, and are dependent on the c-context in which the semantic proximity is defined.

Transformer Functions

Transformer functions are functions between the domains/extensions of two terms in the same or different domain ontologies. They are useful in resolving conflicts at the extensional level. Entities and attributes with conflicting domain definitions are mapped to appropriate concepts, and it is the responsibility of the transformer function to map an instance or value in that domain to one in another. The transformer functions are defined in the following manner:

<function-name, domain, range>

where *domain* and *range* are sets of pairs of the format <term, ont>, *term* is defined in ontology *ont* and *function-name* is the name of the function that translates values or instances in *domain* into equivalent values or instances of *range*. The implementations of such functions in the worst case might be a table lookup.

Example: The following example shows a transformer function from a database type to an associated term in the ontology. All the terms in the ontology describing the database are represented in capital letters. We need to transform instances of departments in the database to conform to values in the ontology.

FUNCTION: capitalize

DOMAIN: <EMPLOYEE.Dept, Database>

RANGE: <DeptConcept, Ontology>

It may be noted that the domain and range of the transformer function is specified as a set of pairs. This is to facilitate re-use of the function, as similar transformations may be required between multiple database types/objects and concepts in the ontology.

A special case of transformer functions is used in the OBSERVER project discussed in Chapter 7. In that case, transformer functions are defined across terms in different ontologies. We use the same format as above to represent those transformer functions.

2.3.2 SCHEMA CORRESPONDENCES AND CONTEXT

We now describe in detail, schema correspondences used to capture associations from c-contexts to objects in the database schema. As discussed earlier, each database system exports global objects O_G, to the GII corresponding to the objects O, it manages. The user at the level of the GII sees only the global objects. The contextual coordinates C_i of the $C_{def}(O)$ act as attributes of O_G. We use schema correspondences to express these associations (Figure 5.10)

$$\mathbf{schCor}(\mathbf{O}_G, \mathbf{O}) = <\mathbf{O}_G, \{\mathbf{C}_i | \mathbf{C}_i \in \mathbf{C}_{def}(\mathbf{O})\}, \mathbf{O}, \{\mathbf{map}_O(\mathbf{C}_i) | \mathbf{C}_i \in \mathbf{C}_{def}(\mathbf{O})\}, \mathbf{M}> \text{ where}$$

- O_G is the exported global object of a database object O.
- The attributes of object O_G are contextual coordinates of the definition context $C_{def}(O)$. We also assume a special contextual coordinate called **self** which identifies the instances of O_G.
- The mapping operation $\mathbf{map}_O(\mathbf{C}_i)$ stores information about object attributes, the query required to compute their values, and associated transformer function(s) required to transform values/instances of attributes to those corresponding to the contextual coordinate.
- The mapping M between O_G and O can be evaluated using the projection rules discussed later in this section.

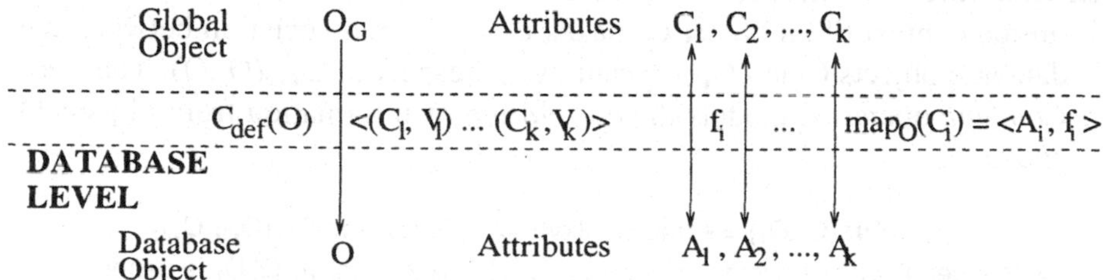

Figure 5.10. Association Between Global and Database Objects

Relevant Terminology and Projection Rules

We now enumerate and explain operations used to specify associations between c-contexts and the underlying database objects. The detailed specifications and descriptions of the operations and projection rules are found in (Kashyap, 1997). The exported global object O_G, is obtained by iteratively applying constraints in $C_{def}(O)$ to the database object O. In the following, we shall use Cntxt, $Cntxt_1$, ..., to refer to c-contexts and C, C_1, ..., to refer to contextual coordinates. O_1, O_2, ..., shall be used to refer to actual database objects whereas O_{1G}, O_{2G}, ..., shall be used to denote their counterparts exported to the GII. O', O", ..., shall be used to denote temporary objects obtained by applying some constraints to O.

$\mathbf{map}_O(\mathbf{C}_i)$ This operation stores the association between contextual coordinate C_i to attribute(s) of object O in the database and appropriate transformer function(s) between attribute domains and the domain of C_i in the ontology.

semConstrain(<$(C_i, Expr_i)$>, semPro(O', O)) This operation models the application of one constraint in C_{def}(O) to the database object O and is expressed as follows:

semPro(O_G,O) = semConstrain(<$(C_i, Expr_i)$>, semPro(O',O))
where C_{def}(O) = glb(<$(C_i, Expr_i)$>, Cntxt) and
semPro(O_G,O) is defined *wrt* to C_{def}(O) and semPro(O',O) is defined *wrt* Cntxt

semCondition(Cntxt, semPro(O_G, O)) In some cases, a database object O may be associated with another database object with respect to a c-context *Cntxt*. The *semCondition* operation modifies the semantic proximity descriptor by *lifting* (Guha, 1991) it into a context *(Cntxt)* different from the one *($C_{def}(O)$)* in which it is defined.

semCondition(Cntxt, semPro(O_G,O)) = semPro(O', O)
where semPro(O', O) is defined *wrt* glb(Cntxt, C_{def}(O))

semCombine(C_i, semPro(O', O), semPro(O", O_i)) In some cases, the definition context of an object O makes explicit, an association between the database objects O and O_i, typically with respect to $C_{ass}(O_i$,O). The *semCombine* operation models the *correlation* of information from objects O and O_i.

semPro(O",O_i) = semCondition($C_{ass}(O_i$,O), semPro(O_{iG},O_i))
where semPro(O_G,O) is defined *wrt* to C_{def}(O) and semPro(O',O) is defined *wrt*
Cntxt and C_{def}(O) = glb(<(C_i, term(O_i)o$C_{ass}(O_i$,O))>, Cntxt)

A set of *projection rules* helps describe in detail, the algebra of the operations discussed above. They help map a contextual expression to the underlying database objects. A detailed and formal specification of the rules is presented in (Kashyap, 1997).

2.4 ADVANTAGES OF CONTEXT REPRESENTATION: SOME ILLUSTRATIVE EXAMPLES

We have discussed a set of operations and projection rules, that enable us to map c-contexts constructed from concepts in domain specific ontologies to underlying database objects. We now discuss advantages of representing c-contexts with the help of illustrative examples.

2.4.1 REPRESENTING RELATIONSHIPS BETWEEN OBJECTS

We illustrate a case where the definition context of the object HAS-PUBLICATION captures its relationships with another database object EMPLOYEE in an intensional manner. These relationships are *not stored* in the database schema, and mapping the contextual description results in *extra information* being associated with the GII object HAS-PUBLICATION$_G$. A naive user will ordinarily not be aware of this relationship. The detailed mapping of this relationship is computed by using the projection rules described in the previous section. The detailed computation is illustrated in (Kashyap, 1997).

Example: Consider the objects EMPLOYEE, PUBLICATION and HAS-PUBLICATION defined earlier. The definition context of HAS-PUBLICATION (C_{def}(HAS-PUBLICATION)) as defined earlier is:

<(author, EMPLOYEE∘ <(affiliation,{research})>)(article, PUBLICATION)>

This represents a semantic relationship between the objects which is stated as: Only employees affiliated as researchers have publications and they are stored in the object PUBLICATION. This relationship is reflected in the HAS-PUBLICATION object when it is exported to the GII. The instances of HAS-PUBLICATION that are exported to the GII are given by the following SQL-like expression:

Join((SS# = SS#), Select(Affiliation ∈ {research}, EMPLOYEE),
Join((Id = Id), PUBLICATION, HAS-PUBLICATION))

Thus, instances that satisfy constraints in the contextual descriptions are exported to the GII.

2.4.2 USING TERMINOLOGICAL RELATIONSHIPS IN ONTOLOGY TO REPRESENT EXTRA INFORMATION

In this section, we illustrate an example in which terminological relationships obtained from an ontology are used to represent *extra information.* In the example illustrated below, the contextual coordinate researchInfo is a composition of two contextual coordinates (researchArea and journalTitle), and is obtained from the domain ontology. This is then used to correlate information between the objects PUBLICATION and JOURNAL. However, the contextual coordinate researchArea has not been modeled for the object PUBLICATION. Thus, this results in *extra information* about the relevant journals and research areas being associated with the object PUBLICATION, even though no information about research areas is modeled for it.

Example: Consider a database containing the following objects:
PUBLICATION(Id, Title, Journal), (as defined earlier) where
C_{def}(PUBLICATION)
= <(researchInfo,JOURNAL∘ <(researchArea,Deptypes)(journalTitle,JournalTypes)>)>
JOURNAL(Title, Area), where C_{def}(JOURNAL) = <>
The mapping expression is (see (Kashyap, 1997) for details):

PUBLICATION$_G$ = Join((researchArea=Area)∧(Title=Journal), PUBLICATION,
Select((Area∈Deptypes)∧(Title∈JournalTypes),JOURNAL))

- Only journals belonging to departmental research areas are selected (Select((Area∈ Deptypes)∧(Title∈JournalTypes),JOURNAL)).
- The join condition (Title = Journal) ensures that only those articles which are from departmental research areas, are exported to the GII (Join((researchArea=Area)∧(Title = Journal), PUBLICATION, Select(...))).
- The above is achieved even though the attribute Area is not modeled for PUBLICATION. Thus there is *extra information* in terms of association of Deptypes with PUBLICATION through the join condition.

2.4.3 INFORMATION FOCUSING BASED ON INFERENCES ON C-CONTEXTS

We have illustrated above with examples, how c-contexts may be used to capture information content in structured data. We now illustrate with the help of an example, how inferences on c-contexts can help determine information relevant to a user query within a database, without accessing the data. Consider the following query context which indicates that the user is looking for all articles related to abortion.

$$C_q = <(\text{hasArticle}, X\circ <(\text{hasTitle}, \text{AbortionString})>)>$$

Let the definition context of the database object (C_{def}(HAS-PUBLICATION)) be defined as follows.

<(hasAuthor, EmplConcept ∘ <(hasAffiliation, {research})>)
(hasArticle, PublConcept)>
where Ext(AbortionString) = {y | string(y) ∧ substring(y) = "abortion"},
term(EMPLOYEE) = EmplConcept and term(PUBLICATION) = PublConcept

Information focusing occurs when a constraint specified in the query context is applied to an object class. This results in selecting only those instances from the object class which satisfy these constraints. In Figure 5.11, the greatest lower bound of the query context C_q and C_{def}(HAS-PUBLICATION) is computed. Information is thus focused to only those publications that have the word "abortion" in their titles.

When the semantic proximity of the database object is *conditioned* with the query context, the *glb* is computed. This also results in the modification of schema correspondences associated with HAS-PUBLICATION, as appropriate constraints are incorporated from the query context. This results in the retrieval of only those instances of the database object PUBLICATION, which have the word "abortion" in their title. The incorporation of constraints is illustrated in Figure 5.12.

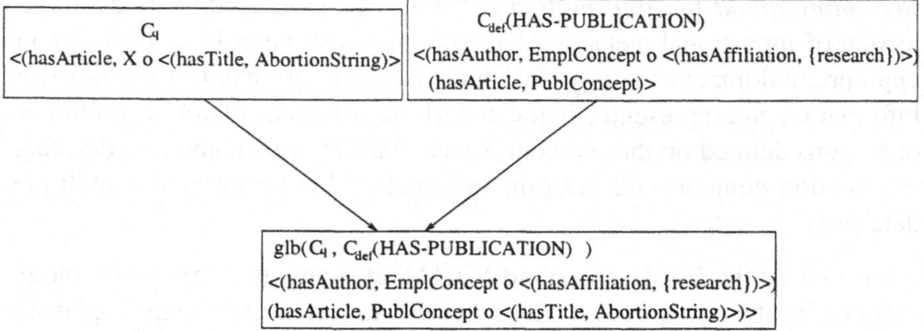

Figure 5.11. Information Focusing Based on Inferences on C-contexts

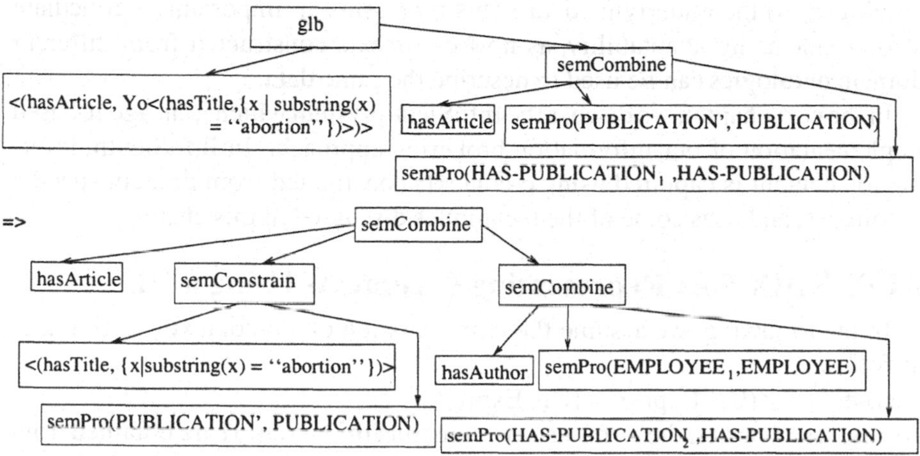

Figure 5.12. Incorporating Constraints from the Query

3. SUMMARY

In this chapter, we focused primarily on issues involved in capturing information content represented in structured data. Structured data are typically described and accessed using well-defined metadata known as the *schema* of the database. The critical issues involved in capturing and utilizing information content in structured data are as follows.

- *Abstracting out representational details.* We first characterized various schematic conflicts between schemas in different databases. For each conflict type, we proposed a resolution based on mapping respective schema elements to terms or c-contexts constructed from terms in a common domain ontology.

- *Reasoning about the information content.* We used c-contexts as a collection of intensional metadata descriptions constructed from terms in an appropriate domain ontology. We demonstrated with examples how extra information, not represented in the underlying schemas, is stored. Inference operations defined on these c-contexts are used to reason about underlying information content, and perform information brokering across multiple databases.

In the case of the InfoHarness and MIDAS systems, the domain ontology was implicit in the terms used to construct the metadata. The mappings from m-contexts to the underlying data were hard-coded in the routines to compute the metadata. In this chapter, we proposed techniques to explicitly store and utilize mappings from c-contexts, constructed from terms in appropriate domain ontologies, to the underlying data. This represents an important intermediate step in enhancing adaptability, as now c-contexts constructed from different domain ontologies can be used to describe the same data.

In the next chapter, we discuss the InfoSleuth system which is an agent-based implementation of our information brokering approach. In InfoSleuth, information content is captured using c-contexts constructed from domain specific ontologies, and uses some of the techniques discussed in this chapter.

APPENDIX 5.A: Representing C-contexts Using a DL

In the following, we assume the representation of a c-context (Section 2.2) as follows:
C-context = $<(C_1, Expr_1) \ldots (C_k, Expr_k)>$
As discussed earlier, the terms used to construct the c-context are obtained from domain specific ontologies. The terms C_i denoting the contextual coordinates are represented using *roles* in a DL. The values of the contextual coordinates are expressions which might consist of terms from ontologies associated with c-contexts. Both the c-contexts and values of the contextual coordinates are represented using *concept descriptions* in a DL. **Anything** and **Nothing** are special terms denoting the universal and empty concepts respectively.

The DL Expressions corresponding to C-contexts

Let the c-context be the definition context of an object O in the database.
$C_{def}(O) = <(C_1, Expr_1) \ldots (C_k, Expr_k)>$
$\Rightarrow$ (**AND** term(O) (**ALL** C_1 $Expr_1$) ... (**ALL** C_1 $Expr_1$))
The various possibilities corresponding to $Expr_i$ are as follows.

Variable $<(C_i, X)> \Rightarrow$ [rf(C_i)] for **Anything**
$<(C_i, X)\ (C_j, X)> \Rightarrow$ [rf(C_i)] for (**SAME-AS** C_i C_j)
rf(C_i) denotes the *role fillers* corresponding to C_i. Also, it should be noted here that since variables are used only for the specific purpose of retrieval,

they are not found at deeper levels of nesting in c-context expression. Hence, $[rf(C_i)]$ for **DL-expression** is not used as a concept forming expression.

Sets $C_{def}(O) = <(C_i, \{a_1, ..., a_n\})>$
$\Rightarrow$ (**AND** term(O) (**ALL** C_i (**ONE-OF** a_1 ... a_n)))

Terms $C_{def}(O) = <(C_i, term(O_1)> \Rightarrow$ (**AND** term(O) (**ALL** C_1 term(O_1)))

Term $\circ$ c-context $C_{def}(O) = <(C_i\ term(O_i) \circ c\text{-}context)>$
$\Rightarrow$ (**AND** term(O) (**ALL** C_i (**AND** term(O_i) Expr(c-context))))
where Expr(c-context) denotes the DL expression corresponding to the c-context. The c-context in this case is an association context and an association is expressed using the **AND** operator in a DL.

Variable $\circ$ c-context $<(C_i, X \circ c\text{-}context)>$
$\Rightarrow$ $[rf(C_i)]$ for (**ALL** C_i Expr(c-context))

Inferences on C-contexts using DL Operators

Let $Cntxt_1 = <(C_{1,1}, Expr_{1,1})...(C_{1,k}, Expr_{1,k})>$
and $Cntxt_2 = <(C_{2,1}, Expr_{2,1})...(C_{2,k}, Expr_{2,k})>$

DL Subsumption for Implementing C-context Specificity
We now present an implementation for specificity of contexts based on the subsumption operator in DL.
$Cntxt_1 \leq Cntxt_2$ iff Expr($Cntxt_1$) *subsumedBy* Expr($Cntxt_2$)
We now enumerate the conditions for the specificity of $Expr_i$

Variable Specificity: As discussed earlier we used the variables in a very restricted sense. They may be thought of as the concept **Anything**.
$<(C_i, X)> \Rightarrow [rf(C_i)]$ for **Anything**
$<(C_i, X \circ c\text{-}context)>$
$\Rightarrow$ $[rf(C_i)]$ for (**ALL** C_i (**AND Anything** Expr(c-context)))
Thus AnyExpression $\leq$ X iff AnyExpression *subsumedBy* **Anything** which is always true.

Set Specificity: Let $S_1 = \{a_1, ..., a_k\}$ and $S_2 = \{a_1, ..., ak, ..., a_n\}$
$S_1 \leq S_2$ iff $S_1 \subseteq S_2$
if (**ONE-OF** a_1 ... a_k) *subsumedBy* (**ONE-OF** a_1 ... a_k ... a_n)
which is always true.

Term Subsumption: $Term_1 \leq Term_2$ iff $Term_1$ *subsumedBy* $Term_2$
This will be true if the subsumption between two terms in a domain specific ontology are reflected in the DL system.

Association Context Specificity: The rules concerning specificity of association contexts are:

- $A_1 \circ Cntxt_1 \leq A_2$ iff $A_1 \leq A_2$
  $\Rightarrow$ (**AND** A_1 Expr($Cntxt_1$)) *subsumedBy* A_2
  $\Rightarrow$ (**AND** A_1 Expr($Cntxt_1$)) *subsumedBy* (**AND** A_2 **Anything**)
  iff A_1 *subsumedBy* A_2 and Expr($Cntxt_1$) *subsumedBy* **Anything**
  iff A_1 *subsumedBy* A_2
- $A_1 \circ Cntxt_1 \leq A_2 \circ Cntxt_2$ iff $A_1 \leq A_2$ and $Cntxt_1 \leq Cntxt_2$
  $\Rightarrow$ (**AND** A_1 Expr($Cntxt_1$)) *subsumedBy* (**AND** A_2 Expr($Cntxt_2$))
  iff A_1 *subsumedBy* A_2 and Expr($Cntxt_1$) *subsumedBy* Expr($Cntxt_2$)
  This is a special case of subsumption of an **AND** expression in DLs.

$Cntxt_1 \leq Cntxt_2$ if the following conditions hold:

- $m \leq k \Rightarrow$ Expr($Cntxt_1$) has more conjuncts than Expr($Cntxt_2$) and hence is likely to be subsumed by Expr($Cntxt_2$).
- $\forall i, 1 \leq i \leq m, \exists j\ C_{1,j} \leq C_{2,i} \wedge Expr_{1,j} \leq Expr_{2,i}$
  $\Rightarrow$ For each conjunct (**ALL** $C_{2,i}$ $Expr_{2,i}$), there exists at least one conjunct (**ALL** $C_{1,j}$ $Expr_{1,j}$) such that
  $C_{1,j}$ is **subsumedBy** $C_{2,i}$ and $Expr_{1,j}$ is **subsumedBy** $Expr_{2,i}$.

Using the AND Operation in DLs for glb of C-contexts
We now describe an implementation of the *glb* of two c-contexts based on the **AND** operator in DLs. The operations for glb of two $Expr_i$'s are as follows:

Variable: glb($Expr_i$, X) = $Expr_i \Rightarrow$ (**AND** $Expr_i$ **Anything**) = $Expr_i$.

Sets: glb(S_1, S_2) = $S_1 \cap S_2$
$\Rightarrow$ (**AND** (**ONE-OF** {ii}) (**ONE-OF** {jj})) = (**ONE-OF** $\{ii\} \cap \{jj\}$)

Terms: glb($Term_1$, $Term_2$) = (**AND** $Term_1$ $Term_2$)
The **AND** operator defines a new concept which can be named and used.

Association Contexts: The rules concerning glb values of the contextual co-ordinates when an association context is involved, can be expressed in a DL as follows:

- glb($A_1 \circ Cntxt_1$, A_2) = glb(A_1, A_2)$\circ Cntxt_1$
  $\Rightarrow$ (**AND** (**AND** A_1 Expr($Cntxt_1$)) A_2))
  = (**AND** (**AND** A_1 A_2) Expr($Cntxt_1$))
- glb($A_1 \circ Cntxt_1$, $A_2 \circ Cntxt_2$) = glb(A_1, A_2)$\circ$glb($Cntxt_1$, $Cntxt_2$)
  $\Rightarrow$ (**AND** (**AND** A_1 Expr($Cntxt_1$)) (**AND** A_j Expr($Cntxt_2$)))
  = (**AND** (**AND** A_1 A_2) (**AND** Expr($Cntxt_1$) Expr($Cntxt_2$)))

The greatest lower bound of the contexts **glb($Cntxt_1$, $Cntxt_2$)** can now be defined as:

- $\text{glb}(\text{Cntxt}_1, \langle\rangle) = \text{Cntxt}_1$
  $\Rightarrow$ (**AND** $\text{Expr}(\text{Cntxt}_1)$ (**AND** ()))
  = (**AND** $\text{Expr}(\text{Cntxt}_1)$ **Anything**) = $\text{Expr}(\text{Cntxt}_1)$

- $\text{glb}(\text{glb}(\langle(C_{1,i}, \text{Expr}_{1,i})\rangle, \text{Cntxt}_1), \text{Cntxt}_2)$
  $= \text{glb}(\langle(C_{1,i}, \text{Expr}_{1,i})\rangle, \text{glb}(\text{Cntxt}_1, \text{Cntxt}_2))$ if $C_{1,i} \notin \text{Cntxt}_2$
  $\Rightarrow$ (**AND** (**AND** (**ALL** $C_{1,i}$ $\text{Expr}_{1,i}$) $\text{Expr}(\text{Cntxt}_1)$) $\text{Expr}(\text{Cntxt}_2)$)
  = (**AND** (**ALL** $C_{1,i}$ $\text{Expr}_{1,i}$) $\text{Expr}(\text{Cntxt}_1)$ $\text{Expr}(\text{Cntxt}_2)$)

- $\text{glb}(\text{glb}(\langle(C_{2,i}, \text{Expr}_{2,i})\rangle, \text{Cntxt}_2), \text{Cntxt}_1)$
  $= \text{glb}(\langle(C_{2,i}, \text{Expr}_{2,i})\rangle, \text{glb}(\text{Cntxt}_2, \text{Cntxt}_1))$ if $C_{2,i} \notin \text{Cntxt}_1$
  $\Rightarrow$ (**AND** (**AND** (**ALL** $C_{2,i}$ $\text{Expr}_{2,i}$) $\text{Expr}(\text{Cntxt}_2)$) $\text{Expr}(\text{Cntxt}_1)$)
  = (**AND** (**ALL** $C_{2,i}$ $\text{Expr}_{2,i}$) $\text{Expr}(\text{Cntxt}_2)$ $\text{Expr}(\text{Cntxt}_1)$)

- $\text{glb}(\text{glb}(\langle(C_i, \text{Expr}_{1,i})\rangle, \text{Cntxt}_1), \text{glb}(\langle(C_i, \text{Expr}_{2,i})\rangle, \text{Cntxt}_2))$
  $= \text{glb}(\langle(C_i, \text{glb}(\text{Expr}_{1,i}, \text{Expr}_{2,i}))\rangle, \text{glb}(\text{Cntxt}_1, \text{Cntxt}_2))$
  $\Rightarrow$ (**AND** (**AND** (**ALL** C_i $\text{Expr}_{1,i}$) $\text{Expr}(\text{Cntxt}_1)$)
  (**AND** (**ALL** C_i $\text{Expr}_{2,i}$) $\text{Expr}(\text{Cntxt}_2)$))
  = (**AND** (**ALL** C_i (**AND** $\text{Expr}_{1,i}$ $\text{Expr}_{2,i}$)) $\text{Expr}(\text{Cntxt}_1)$ $\text{Expr}(\text{Cntxt}_2)$)

Chapter 6

THE INFOSLEUTH SYSTEM

The InfoSleuth project at Micro-electronics and Computer Technology Corporation (MCC), is an agent-based system, that performs information gathering and analysis tasks over networks of autonomous information sources. It represents the next step in the series of information brokering prototypes (after InfoHarness and MIDAS), and has the following distinguishing features:

- Domain specific metadata (c-context) expressions are constructed from semantically rich domain specific ontologies capturing information in a wide variety of domains. Any information request requires identification of the domain ontology from which query contexts are constructed.
- Mappings that associate metadata terms from domain ontologies to the underlying data are explicitly stored. These mappings are combined to retrieve data corresponding to metadata expressions specified by the query contexts. Different sets of mappings are used to map terms from different domain ontologies, thus supporting multiple world views on the same underlying data.
- C-contexts capturing information content in a particular information resource are advertised and compared with query contexts in a matchmaking process, to determine the relevance of information sources.
- Agent technology is used to implement functionality to support information brokering, the different pieces of which may be found in specialized agents having narrow and focused capabilities.

We discuss in detail the architecture of the InfoSleuth system and compare it with the agent-based information brokering architecture illustrated in Figure 3.7. The different types of metadata-based brokering supported in InfoSleuth, and the corresponding "SEA" properties are discussed.

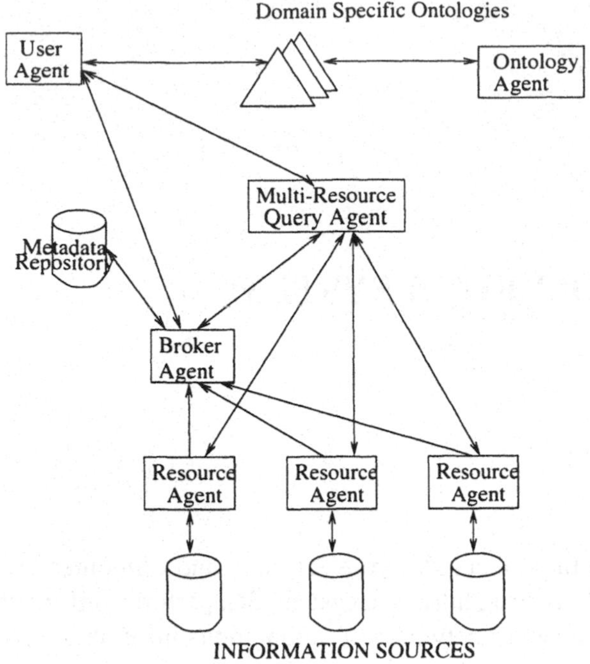

Figure 6.1. InfoSleuth's Agent Based Architecture

1. THE INFOSLEUTH AGENT-BASED ARCHITECTURE

The functionality of various components of the InfoSleuth architecture (Figure 6.1) are as follows:

User Agent The user agent is the user's intelligent gateway to the network of InfoSleuth agents. It handles requests from the user via Java applets, routing those requests to appropriate agents and passing responses back to the user. It is capable of storing information (data and queries) for the user, and can maintain a user model. In terms of the agent-based brokering architecture, it is an example of the *consumer agent*.

Broker Agent The broker agent acts as a matchmaker which pairs requests from user agents to resource agents that can fulfill that request. As agents come on line, they can advertise their information, using semantic metadata expressions, to the broker agent. The advertised metadata descriptions are stored in a **metadata repository** which is searched by the broker agent. Any agent can ask the broker for a recommendation on how to fulfill a particular information request, and the broker will respond with addresses of agents that have advertised that information. In terms of the agent-based brokering architecture, this is an example of the *metadata broker agent*. The broker agent handles two kinds of requests.

- Requests from the user agent to locate the ontology appropriate for the information needs of the user.
- Requests from the multi-resource query agent (discussed later) to locate the appropriate resource agents (discussed later) for getting data related to a particular user query. Ontological inferences based on class-subclass relationships are computed by the broker agent. For example, if information corresponding to a particular class is required, resource agents having information corresponding to the subclasses are also considered relevant.

Ontology Agent The ontology agent is responsible for managing the creation, update, and querying of ontology(ies) belonging to multiple information domains. For brokering purposes, it is the querying of an ontology which is of interest, and typically, names of ontologies and descriptions of ontological content in some interchange language are returned. This functionality is a subset of the functionality of the **vocabulary brokering agent** in the agent-based brokering architecture, with a slight difference. Whereas, in the agent-based architecture the vocabulary broker agent manages ontologies corresponding to a particular domain, the ontology agent in the InfoSleuth system manages ontologies across multiple domains.

Multi-Resource Query Agent The multi-resource query agent is responsible for the execution of ontology-based queries. It decomposes the queries into sub-queries based on its knowledge of appropriate resource agents that can satisfy the query, and forwards the decomposed queries to selected agents. The sub-answers returned by the various resource agents are then correlated by the multi-resource query agent to compute the answer for the given query. The results are forwarded to the user agent. In terms of the agent-based brokering architecture, this agent combines the functionality of the **mapping composition** and **correlation** agents.

Resource Agents The resource agent acts as an intelligent front-end interface to the data repositories, accepting high-level ontology-based queries from the network and translating them into the local repository query language. Results are then translated back into the language of the ontology, and returned to the requesting agent. This function is similar to that of the *translator* and *wrapper* modules of the brokering architecture, and is similar to the **provider agent** discussed in the agent-based brokering architecture. This agent also advertises the *ontological fragment* that it can support, along with constraints on the instances (using semantic metadata expressions), to the **broker agent**.

Properties of the InfoSleuth System

The InfoSleuth system in its present version performs brokering primarily at the level of information content. The user can query data repositories by constructing metadata expressions from the vocabulary characterizing the appropriate domain of information. The ontology agent has the ability to handle multiple ontologies across different domains, but lacks the ability to transform metadata expressions constructed from terms in one vocabulary, to those constructed form terms used in another. Hence, the ontology agent may be considered to be a simplified vocabulary brokering agent. Also, the InfoSleuth system lacks the **inter-vocabulary relationships agent** and the corresponding **relationships repository**. Hence, the InfoSleuth system in its present version lacks in adaptability within and across different information domains.

2. METADATA BROKERING IN INFOSLEUTH

We now consider an example information request in the domain of competitive intelligence to demonstrate brokering techniques implemented by the InfoSleuth system. The competitive intelligence ontology on which the information request (expressed in SQL) is based, is illustrated in Figure 6.2.

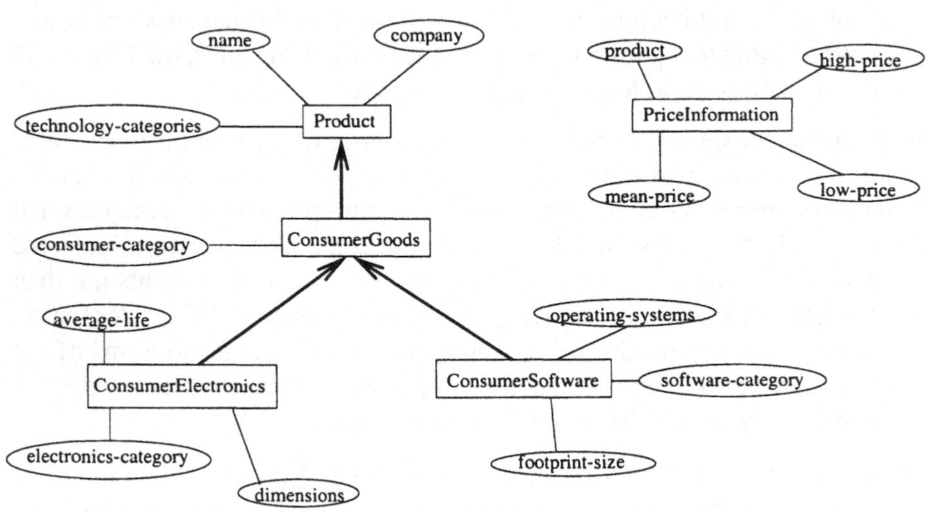

Figure 6.2. The Competitive Intelligence Ontology

The various steps taken by the InfoSleuth system to respond to an information request are as follows.

Content Advertisement Consider five resource agents (R1,...,R5) and their respective advertisements to the broker agent.

R1 ConsumerElectronics(name, company, technology-categories, electronics-categories)

R2 Product(name, company, technology-categories);
constraint: company = "Microsoft"

R3 ConsumerGoods(name, company, consumer-category);
constraint: name is key, non-null

R4 ConsumerSoftware(name, technology-categories, operating-system);
constraint: name is key, non-null

R5 PriceInformation(start-date, end-date, product, low-price, mean-price, high-price)

Ontology Retrieval The user specifies the ontology of interest (in this case the competitive intelligence ontology). The user agent contacts the broker agent and obtains the address of the ontology agent, after which the user agent retrieves the specified ontology from the ontology agent. The user then specifies an information request using the terms of the retrieved ontology. An information request based on the competitive intelligence ontology, expressed in SQL is as follows.

```
SELECT p.name, p.company, i.mean-price, i.low-price, i.high-price
FROM Product p, PriceInformation i
WHERE i.product = p.name AND (p.company = 'Oracle' OR p.company = 'Sun')
AND i.end-date ≥ '1998-08-01' AND i.mean-price < 500.00
AND internet IN p.technology-categories
```

Query Decomposition The multi-resource query agent is responsible for decomposing the query into individual pieces that can be answered by individual resource agents, and then combining the results. It needs to contact the broker agent to determine the resource agents relevant to a query. The sequence of steps performed by the multi-resource query agent is as follows.

Initial Query Decomposition The multi-resource agent initially decomposes the query into a set of queries $\{Q_i\}$, over individual classes in the ontology as follows.

```
Q1 is SELECT p.name, p.company
      FROM Product p
      WHERE (p.company = 'Oracle' OR p.company = 'Sun')
      AND 'internet' IN p.technology-categories
Q2 is SELECT i.product, i.mean-price, i.low-price, i.high-price
      FROM PriceInformation i
      WHERE i.end-date ≥ '1998-08-01' AND mean-price < 500.00
```

```
G is SELECT Q1.name, Q1.company, Q2.mean-price, Q2.low-price,
            Q2.high-price
     FROM Q1, Q2
     WHERE Q2.product = Q1.name
```

Matchmaking The multi-resource query agent asks the broker to find resource agents that can help with Q1 and Q2. R5 is the only resource agent that has information related to PriceInformation that is required by Q2. In the case of Q1, there are four agents that have advertised the relevant class or a subclass thereof. R2 is eliminated from consideration by the broker because its constraint conflicts with that of the query. R1 has all three attributes required by Q1, so it can be assigned a subquery of Q1 by changing Product to ConsumerElectronics. R3 and R4 together have all the attributes necessary for the query, and have common key attributes. Each will receive a sub-query, and their respective results will be joined in an intermediate query.

Final Query Decomposition Based on the results from the matchmaking process and the decomposition analysis, the multi-resource query agent can arrive at the following set of subqueries. This is one possible decomposition, and other runtime heuristics may be employed to further fine-tune the creation of best effort and semantically consistent subqueries.

```
S1 (for R1) SELECT p.name, p.company
            FROM ConsumerElectronics p
            WHERE (p.company = 'Oracle' OR p.company = 'Sun')
            AND 'internet' IN p.technology-categories
S2 (for R3) SELECT p.name, p.company
            FROM ConsumerGoods p
            WHERE (p.company = 'Oracle' OR p.company = 'Sun')
            AND 'internet' IN p.technology-categories
S3 (for R4) SELECT p.name, p.company
            FROM ConsumerSoftware p
            WHERE 'internet' IN p.technology-categories
S4 (for R5) SELECT i.product, i.mean-price, i.low-price, i.high-price
            FROM PriceInformation i
            WHERE i.end-date >= '1998-08-01' AND mean-price < 500.00
```

Correlation The subquery results are passed from the resource agents to the multi-resource query agent, which stores them in its backend database. The intermediate query I1 operates on the results of the subqueries S2 and S3 and appends its result to that of the subquery S1. This result then forms one of the inputs to the final query F. The result of the final query is passed to the agent that sent the original request.

```
I1 INSERT INTO S1(name, company)
   SELECT S2.name, S2.company
   FROM S2, S3
   WHERE S2.name = S3.name
F SELECT S1.name, S1.company, S4.mean-price, S4.low-price, S4.high-price
   FROM S1, S4
   WHERE S1.name = S4.product
```

3. INFOSLEUTH: A SUMMARY

In this chapter, we described an agent-based implementation of some information brokering techniques. The InfoSleuth system uses domain specific ontologies as the basis for brokering across multiple information sources. The contained information can be described by a common domain ontology. There is support for multiple world views on the same data, as resource agents can use multiple ontologies to describe their information. However, information requests constructed from terms in a domain ontology can only be answered by accessing information from resource agents that use the same ontology. There is a critical need for retrieving information from resources that describe information using terms from an ontology, which is different from the one used to specify the information request. This should be done in a manner so as to minimize the change in semantics of the information, and guarantee the soundness of results. This is the focus of the OBSERVER system discussed in the next chapter.

Chapter 7

VOCABULARY BROKERING IN THE OBSERVER SYSTEM

In the previous chapter, we discussed the InfoSleuth system, an agent-based implementation of information brokering based on a common domain ontology. Information sources were described using c-contexts constructed from domain specific ontologies. The c-contexts are associated with underlying data by using mappings that are used to retrieve data. The system determines information sources relevant to a particular information request, provided both, the requests and c-contexts are constructed from terms in a common domain ontology. The agents co-operate with each other and correlate information from different sources to piece together an answer to an information request.

In this chapter, we focus on the *vocabulary problem*. Here, c-contexts in different component systems are constructed using terms in different but related domain ontologies. A representation of c-contexts using a DL, and an implementation of inferences on c-contexts using DL operators was presented in Appendix 5.A. OBSERVER (*O*ntology *B*ased *S*ystem *E*nhanced with (terminological) *R*elationships for *V*ocabulary h*E*terogeneity *R*esolution) is our **vocabulary broker** which enables brokering at the vocabulary level represented by domain specific ontologies. Brokering at the level of information content is discussed to the extent it supports vocabulary brokering. The bibliographic information domain is used as an example domain to illustrate techniques for vocabulary brokering. Information in real-world data repositories is accessed using pre-existing real-world ontologies. OBSERVER enables the user to observe a *semantic conceptual view* of the GII by supporting the ability to browse multiple domain specific ontologies as opposed to individual heterogeneous repositories.

The OBSERVER architecture is expressed as an instantiation of the brokering architecture (Figure 3.1). The ways in which it enhances the MIDAS architecture and the “SEA” properties satisfied by it are also discussed. This is followed by a discussion of the vocabulary brokering performed in OBSERVER. Finally, the properties of OBSERVER as an information brokering system are summarized.

1. ARCHITECTURE OF OBSERVER

The OBSERVER system is an instantiation of the information brokering architecture (Figure 3.1). Brokering is performed at the level of information content, and at the level of vocabulary. In comparison with the MIDAS system, the OBSERVER architecture supports additional functionality at the vocabulary brokering level, and in the metadata systems. The components of the OBSERVER system are discussed next (Figure 7.1).

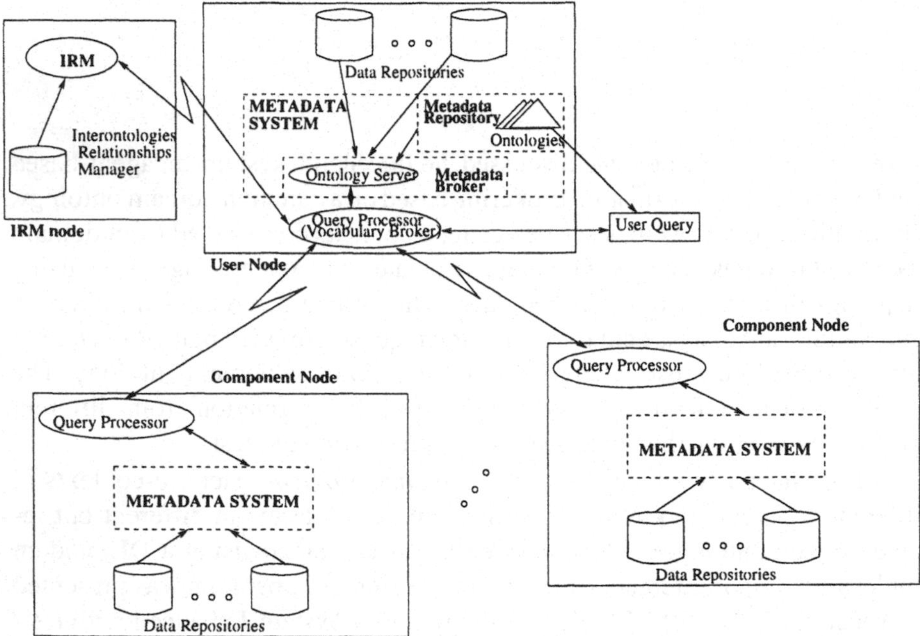

Figure 7.1. Architecture of the OBSERVER System

Query Processor The query processor represents the **vocabulary broker** identified in the brokering architecture. In the MIDAS architecture, it was the metadata broker which (partially) enabled vocabulary brokering within an information domain. The query processor adds extra functionality by enabling vocabulary brokering across information domains. An expression constructed using concepts from a chosen *user ontology* is taken as input. Navigation of other component ontologies on the GII, and translation of terms in the user query into component ontologies are performed by using relationships stored in the **IRM**. A user query may either be partially, or fully translated into component ontologies. The query processor is responsible for combining partial translations from different ontologies to give full translations, while preserving the semantics of the query. It may also convert partial translations into full translations with information loss (lossy translations), and determine the resulting information loss.

Inter-Ontology Relationships Manager (IRM) Terminological relationships between terms in different ontologies are represented in a declarative manner in an independent repository. These relationships (*synonyms* and *hyponyms/hypernyms*) enable different vocabulary brokering functions. Besides relationships between terms, the IRM also stores information about *transformer functions* between domains of synonym roles across ontologies.

Metadata System The metadata system as identified in the brokering architecture (Figure 3.3), is responsible for enabling brokering at the level of information content. The main components of the metadata system are:

Ontology Server This is the main component of the **metadata broker**. Its main functions, performed typically in response to a request by the query processor, are as follows.

- It accesses ontologies stored in the **metadata repository** and provides the term definitions.
- It retrieves data underlying the ontology, corresponding to a given metadata expression. For this purpose, it accesses **mappings** stored in the **metadata repository**, and interacts with other components. These components help compose individual term mappings, decompose composite mappings into mono-repository expressions, and translate them into the local data repository or wrapper query language.

Metadata Repository The metadata repository is responsible for definitions of terms in the metadata, and also for mappings between terms in an ontology and underlying data structures in the local data repositories. Repositories are of two types, *files*, and *knowledge bases*. Here, the emphasis is on retrieval of semantic (e.g., term definitions) and mapping information associated with terms in an ontology.

1.1 ARCHITECTURE OF THE METADATA SYSTEM

We now describe the architecture of the Metadata System in greater detail from two perspectives. The first perspective is that of the Metadata System as an instantiation of the metadata brokering level of the brokering architecture (Figure 3.1). Another perspective is that of enhancements made to the MIDAS architecture. The components of the Metadata System (Figure 7.2) are now described in detail.

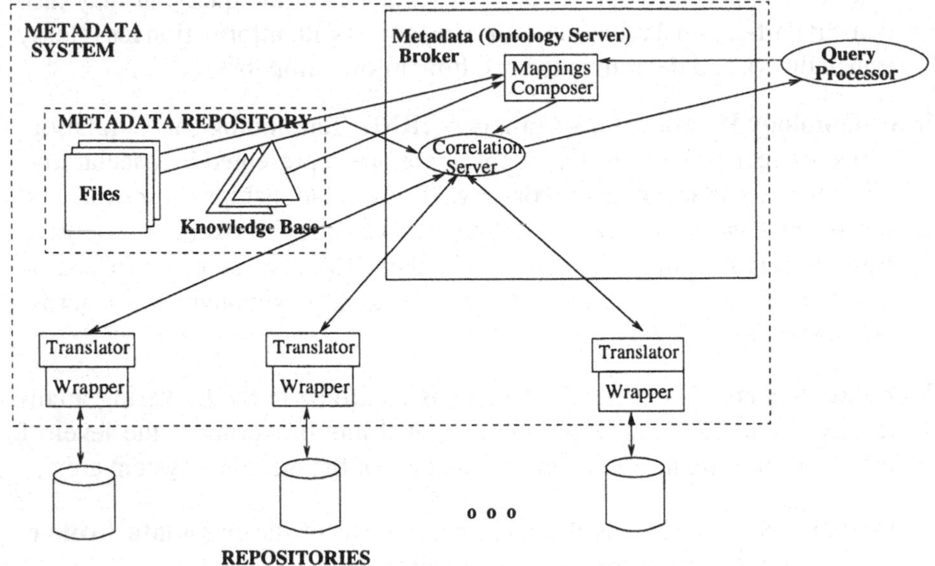

Figure 7.2. Architecture of the OBSERVER Metadata System

1.1.1 THE ONTOLOGY SERVER

The Ontology Server is essentially an instantiation of the **metadata broker** illustrated in the brokering architecture. It shares, with the InfoHarness and MIDAS servers, the basic functionality of handling metadata requests. However, the Ontology Server in the OBSERVER system is designed to handle *c-contexts* which are constructed from concepts in domain specific ontologies. The concepts used therein may have interrelationships in the domain specific ontology. In order to handle this type of metadata, the following components are required:

Mappings Composer In the MIDAS system, individual metadata in *m-contexts* is computed independently by *parameterized routines*, and then combined by the *correlation server*. In the case of *c-contexts*, the individual terms used might have interrelationships in the domain specific ontology. The constructors used in the metadata descriptions require mappings for individual concepts to be combined in special ways. It is the *mappings composer* which is responsible for performing inferences on c-contexts. It then combines the mappings in an appropriate manner into a composite mapping corresponding to the resulting metadata description. The mappings for individual concepts are obtained from the metadata repository. They are a refinement of *parameterized routines*, that contain concept mappings hard-coded within them.

Correlation Server The correlation server is responsible for planning the computation of the composite mapping developed by the mappings composer. This involves decomposition of the composite mapping into mono-repository expressions, results from which are then combined to satisfy various metadata constraints, and compute the final answer.

Translator Another enhancement in the OBSERVER system, is that it enables computation of metadata from data repositories that use different query languages. It is the responsibility of the *translator* to express the mono-repository expression constructed by the *correlation server* in terms of the local repository or query language. The translator uses information describing the repository such as location, query language, etc., obtained from the *metadata repository*. This is also hard-coded in the *parameterized routines* used in the MIDAS system. Another feature of the OBSERVER system is access of **legacy data**, wherein specialized *wrappers* are used to export an *entity-attribute* view of the underlying legacy data.

1.1.2 THE METADATA REPOSITORY

The Metadata repository, as illustrated in Figure 7.2, consists of *files* stored in a UNIX file system, and a DL-based Knowledge Base system used to store component ontologies. The different types of metadata utilized in the OBSERVER system are as follows.

Content Independent Metadata The locations of data repositories used by the Ontology Server are examples of content independent metadata. They are stored on files in a UNIX file system.

Content Descriptive (Domain Independent) Metadata The information about repositories relating to their data organization, and local query languages used by the Ontology Server are examples of domain independent metadata. They are stored on files in a UNIX file system.

Domain Specific Metadata Mappings, that express associations between concepts and underlying data structures are examples of domain specific metadata, and are stored in files. Special kind of domain specific metadata used in OBSERVER are **domain specific ontologies**, which are a collection of interrelated **concepts** and **roles** stored in a DL system. Another kind of domain specific metadata not stored in the metadata repository, are terminological relationships between terms across ontologies stored and managed by the IRM.

1.1.3 THE COMPONENT ONTOLOGIES

We now describe the features of systems based on Description Logics (with examples based on CLASSIC), that are used to define the real world component ontologies used in our prototype. The component ontologies have been designed independently by different researchers in the areas of linguistics and knowledge representation. We **re-use** these ontologies after representing them in a DL. The DL definitions, and the graphical representations of these ontologies can be found in Appendix 7.A. A summary of the ontologies and underlying repositories is given in Table 7.1.

Description Logics Systems

Systems based on Description Logics, also known as terminological systems, are descendants of *KL-ONE* (Brachman and Scmolze, 1985). Some systems based on Description Logics are *CLASSIC* (Borgida et al., 1989), *BACK* (von Luck et al., 1987), *LOOM* (MacGregor, 1987) and *KRIS* (Baader and Hollunder, 1991). The main features of DL systems are as follows.

- The language contains unary relations called *concepts* which represent classes of objects in the domain, and binary relations called *roles* which describe relationships between objects. Concepts and roles are created via *terminological descriptions* built from preexisting concepts, roles and a set of operators (ALL, ATLEAST, ATMOST, etc.). A distinguished role called *self* stores the id of each object belonging to each concept.

- *Primitive and defined terms.* Terms are *primitive* if their descriptions specify only the necessary conditions, and are *defined* if their descriptions specify both the necessary and sufficient conditions.

- *Subsumption of concepts* allows determination of whether a term is more general than another. The *subsumption* relation is exploited by DL system to maintain a classification hierarchy/lattice of terms (which is useful in dealing with large collections of definitions), and to *classify* new terms as well as queries.[1] This classification mechanism allows the system to detect *incoherent* and *disjoint* descriptions.

WN: A subset of WordNet 1.5

WN is an ontology, we have built by re-using a part of the WordNet 1.5 ontology (Miller, 1995a). The concepts in the WN ontology are a subset of terms in the hyponym tree of the noun "print media" (Miller, 1995b). As

[1] A query is considered a definition of properties to be satisfied by the concepts listed in the answer (Borgida, 1992).

no roles are defined in WordNet, we had to define some (name, ISBN, type, number-of-pages, etc.) using criteria like extrinsic and intrinsic properties, and parts ("meronyms") of the concepts identified. This is a case where we represent a *linguistic-based* ontology using a knowledge representation language: the concepts of WN ontology correspond to nouns in WordNet 1.5, and hyponym/hypernym relationships in WordNet 1.5 are modeled as subsumptions in WN. The underlying data are MARC (Piepenburg, 1994) records from the University of Georgia Main Library, stored in plain files. The DL definitions and graphical representations are presented in the Appendix 7.A.

Stanford-I and Stanford-II: DARPA Knowledge Sharing Effort

Two of our other ontologies, Stanford-I and Stanford-II, are subsets of the Bibliographic-Data ontology (Gruber, 1994) developed as a part of the DARPA Knowledge Sharing Effort (http://www-ksl.stanford.edu/knowledge-sharing). The Stanford-II ontology corresponds to the sub-tree under the concept 'reference' of the Bibliographic-Data ontology. Stanford-I corresponds to the rest of the ontology. The data underlying Stanford-I are MARC records from the Library at Monterrey Institute of Technology stored in an Illustra database (object-relational). The data corresponding to Stanford-II is accessed directly through the Z39.50 Web gateway of the Library of Congress (of Congress, 1995). The format and data organization of the Library of Congress repository are unknown and irrelevant for our system. We thus take an *operational view* of this repository. The DL definitions, and graphical representation of these ontologies are presented in Appendix 7.A.

The LSDIS ontology

The LSDIS ontology is a "home-grown" ontology which represents our view of publications related to the LSDIS Lab (http://lsdis.cs.uga.edu/publications). The data consists of several text, HTML, and Postscript documents distributed over various files. The DL definitions and graphical representation are presented in Appendix 7.A.

1.2 THE INTER-ONTOLOGIES RELATIONSHIPS MANAGER (IRM)

The IRM is the critical component which supports ontology-based interoperation. It enhances the **scalability** of query processing by avoiding the need for: (a) designing a common global ontology containing all relevant concepts and roles needed on the GII; and (b) investing time and energy for development of an ontology specific to your needs when "similar" ontologies (containing a large number of relevant concepts and roles) are available on the GII. There will be relationships between terms across ontologies when there exists an

Ontology	Design source	Terms	Data Source	Data Org.
WN	WordNet 1.5	73	subset of UGA Main Library	Files containing MARC records
Stanford-I	Bibliographic-Data (DARPA)	50	subset of Library at Monterrey	Illustra DB storing MARC records
Stanford-II	Bibliographic-Data (DARPA)	51	Library of Congress	Unknown
LSDIS	Locally developed	18	Lab Publications	Text, HTML and Postscript files

Table 7.1. Details of Ontologies and Underlying Repositories

overlapping between domains, e.g., print-media in WN ontology is a synonym of document in Stanford-I ontology. The main assumption behind the IRM is that the number of relationships between terms across ontologies is an order of magnitude smaller than the number of all concepts and roles relevant to the system. Hammer and McLeod (Hammer and McLeod, 1993) have suggested a set of relationship descriptors to capture relationships between terms across different ontologies. A set of terminological relationships have been proposed in (Miller, 1995a). In our approach we focus on the *synonym, hyponym*, and *hypernym* relationships:

Synonym relationships When two terms in different ontologies have the same meaning, they have synonym relationship with each other. However it does not mean that they have the same extension; e.g., document in Stanford-I is a synonym of publication-ref in Stanford-II, but instances corresponding to those terms may be different (yet all of them are publications).

Hyponym relationships When a term in one ontology is semantically more specialized than a term in another ontology, they have a hyponym relationship; e.g., technical-manual in Stanford-I is a hyponym of manual in WN. However, the set of instances corresponding to technical-manual may not be a subset of the set of instances corresponding to manual, as they are from different ontologies, and have different data repositories underlying them.

Hypernym relationships When a term in one ontology is semantically more general than a term in another ontology, they have a hypernym relationship; e.g., book in WN is a hypernym of thesis in Stanford-I. However, the set of instances corresponding to book may not be a superset of the set of instances corresponding to thesis, as they are from different ontologies and have different data repositories underlying them.

When a new component ontology is added to the brokering system, the IRM is responsible for inferring a minimal set of relationships. In general, ontologies may be organized as hierarchies or lattice structures, and capabilities of DL systems may be used to infer redundant relationships.

The relationships discussed above are consulted by the Query Processor to solve the vocabulary problem at the intensional level. In order to solve the vocabulary problem at the extensional level, transformer functions between roles of different ontologies can also be defined. For example, the transformer function capitalize transforms (capitalizes) values of the role keywords in Stanford-II to give values for the role subject in LSDIS.

1.2.1 SERVICES PROVIDED BY THE IRM TO THE QUERY PROCESSOR

The IRM stores information about (a) component ontologies on the GII; (b) relationships defined among terms in different ontologies; and (c) the transformation of values and instances by applying the appropriate transformation function. The following IRM services can be used by the query processor.

- **get-ontologies()** returns the name of component ontologies accessible on the GII. In our present prototype of the OBSERVER system, the result of executing the service is as follows:
  get-ontologies() → {WN, Stanford-I, Stanford-II, LSDIS}.

- **get-synonyms(Term, $\mathbf{Ont_1}$, $\mathbf{Ont_2}$)** returns terms in ontology $\mathbf{Ont_2}$ that are synonyms of **Term** in ontology $\mathbf{Ont_1}$.
  get-synonyms(periodical, WN, Stanford-I) → periodical-publication

- **transform-value(Val, $\mathbf{Role_1}$, $\mathbf{Ont_1}$, $\mathbf{Role_2}$, $\mathbf{Ont_2}$)** returns the equivalent value of **Val** stored in $\mathbf{Role_1}$ (ontology $\mathbf{Ont_1}$) as stored for the role $\mathbf{Role_2}$ (ontology $\mathbf{Ont_2}$) ($\mathbf{Role_1}$ and $\mathbf{Role_2}$ are typically synonyms of each other). If no transformer function is defined between the above two roles, the same value will be returned.
  transform-value('d', content, WN, type-of-work, Stanford-II) → 'dictionary'

1.2.2 STORAGE OF THE RELATIONSHIPS

We store relationships in an independent repository that will be consulted by the IRM when it receives requests from the Query Processor. Storing the inter-ontology term interrelationships in an ontology is avoided due to: (a) introduction of redundancy; and (b) necessity of updating component ontologies when new ontologies are consulted. Storing relationships in an independent repository obviates the need for updating component ontologies, when new ontologies join the system. We only need to update the independent repository without affecting the rest of the system.

The synonym relationships are symmetric in nature (if *a synonym b*, then *b synonym a*). Hence, they will be stored in the following manner: <canonical-

term, term, ontology>. Each new term will be related to a canonical term representing a generic concept or role. If the new term does not *fit* any pre-existing canonical term, a new one will be added to represent that concept/role. In this way, for each new term we only need to choose its canonical term, which helps avoid redundancy of these relationships. The IRM deduces that terms with the same canonical term are synonyms. If these relationships were represented as Term_1 in ontology Ont_1 is a synonym of Term_2 in ontology Ont_2, we would need to define *n* synonym relationships (to relate the new term to all its synonyms) for each new term in a new ontology, where *n* is the number of component ontologies with synonym terms.

The hyponym and hypernym relationships are, however, not symmetrical, i.e., we have to store the relationships in the following manner: <Term_1, Ont_1, Rel, Term_2, Ont_2 >. However, there is an inverse relationship between hyponym and hypernym, i.e. if *a hyponym b*, then *b hypernym a*. Thus, we store only hyponym relationships (*relationship* will be always 'hyponym') and the IRM will deduce hypernym relationships appropriately.

The transformer functions are stored in the format <function-name, domain, range> where *domain* and *range* are sets of pairs of the format <role, ont> (role is defined in ontology ont), and function-name is the name of the function that translates values of the roles in *domain* into semantically equivalent values of the roles of *range*. The implementations of such functions must be accessible by the IRM. A transformer function is stored as follows.

<capitalize, {<keywords,Stanford-II>, <creator,WN>, <authors,LSDIS>},
{<subject,LSDIS>, <author-doc-name,Stanford-I>,
<author-name,Stanford-I>}>

An interesting case of a transformer function is when the domain of the function are complex objects. For example, the role pages in the Stanford-I ontology has values of the type <minPage, maxPage>. The values of the corresponding synonym role in the Stanford-II ontology number-of-pages are related to pages as follows:

<compute_pages, {<pages, Stanford-I>}, {number-of-pages, Stanford-II}>
where, compute_pages(<minPage, maxPage>) = maxPage - minPage + 1

If the IRM repository becomes so huge that efficiency of the information system is affected, it could be mirrored or partitioned without affecting the rest of the system. This is possible due to the independence of the IRM. Issues related to distributed repositories are well understood, and can be handled using distributed database technology.

1.3 PROPERTIES OF THE OBSERVER ARCHITECTURE

The OBSERVER architecture performs brokering at the metadata and vocabulary levels of the brokering architecture (Figure 3.1). Hence, issues relating to adaptability arise in a very significant manner, primarily at the vocabulary, and to some extent, the metadata level. We now discuss the extent to which "SEA" properties are possessed by the OBSERVER architecture.

1.3.1 SCALABILITY OF THE OBSERVER ARCHITECTURE

In the OBSERVER system, metadata computation is performed in a top-down manner. The scalability of the architecture, thus, is a consequence of (possibly partial) pre-computation of metadata. However, the following factors also enhance scalability of the OBSERVER architecture.

- The use of component ontologies in OBSERVER, and storage and utilization of inter-ontology relationships by the IRM and Query Processor, enhance scalability vis-a-vis the global ontology approach. The extensions of semantically similar terms can be appropriately combined using terminological relationships stored and managed by the IRM. Besides, the key assumption, which makes this approach scalable, is that the number of terminological relationships between terms across ontologies, which need to be explicitly represented, are an order of magnitude less than all the terms in all the ontologies on the GII.

- An alternative approach of enhancing scalability proposed in the case of the MIDAS system, was to support brokering at different levels of abstraction. This is more cleanly implemented in the OBSERVER architecture because: (a) the component ontologies contain terms and their interrelationships, which can be used to rewrite queries; and (b) the Ontology Server constructs a suitable plan for translating the composite mapping expression into mono-repository queries, and combining them for the final results. This may be viewed as a refinement of the control strategy used in MIDAS to compute metadata.

1.3.2 EXTENSIBILITY OF THE OBSERVER ARCHITECTURE

Use of *parameterized routines* was responsible for enhancing extensibility of the MIDAS system. However, as discussed earlier, critical information like mappings between domain specific metadata, and underlying data structures in the repositories is hard-coded in the parameterized routines. The OBSERVER system is more extensible than the MIDAS system because:

- The mappings between terms in ontologies and underlying data structures in the repositories are explicitly represented in the metadata repository. Hence, every time a new repository is added to the system, appropriate mappings can be defined and stored in the metadata repository, as opposed to defining new parameterized routines to compute metadata.

- As far as extensibility at the level of ontology is concerned, new synonym concepts can be easily added to the ontology as they are automatically classified at the right position by the DL system.

- Extensibility, at the level of multiple ontologies, is enabled by utilizing the IRM component of the architecture. In the case of synonyms, all we need to do is to add relationships between terms in that ontology with terms in pre-existing ontologies, to the IRM repository. As far as hyponyms/hypernyms are concerned, pairwise integration of the new ontology to pre-existing ontologies is required to determine the minimal set of relationships. This is more extensible than complex integration of the new ontology with a pre-integrated set of existing ontologies in the system, as would be the case with the common/global ontology approach.

1.3.3 ADAPTABILITY OF THE OBSERVER ARCHITECTURE

The presence of the vocabulary brokering level makes OBSERVER a more adaptable system than either the InfoHarness or MIDAS systems. Whereas the MIDAS system enables *intra-domain adaptability*, the vocabulary brokering layer in the OBSERVER system, enables both *intra* and *inter-domain adaptability*. The reasons for adaptability of OBSERVER are as follows.

- As far as intra-domain adaptability is concerned, a defined term can be expressed using other terms occurring in its description. Thus, if a term is not directly supported by an underlying repository, it can be substituted by an equivalent expression, using terms that can be mapped to the underlying repository by the ontology server.

- A query expression constructed by using terms from one ontology can be "adapted" by using related terms from other ontologies. This is achieved by utilizing terminological relationships, and translating an expression in one ontology, into expressions in other ontologies. The Query Processor also supports combination of translations, and further translation to enable a complete translation of the user query. This shall be the focus of our discussion in the next section of this chapter.

2. VOCABULARY BROKERING BY THE QUERY PROCESSOR

With the help of examples, we now illustrate vocabulary brokering functions performed by the Query Processor. We assume that the user aligns himself to an ontology which is referred to as the *user ontology*. Vocabulary brokering then consists of translating a DL expression constructed from terms in a user ontology, into one constructed by terms in the component ontologies. The two cases that arise are: (a) utilizing *synonym* relationships for translation, preserving the semantics of the query; and (b) utilizing *hyponym/hypernym* relationships for translation resulting in transformation of the query semantics, and loss of information. We now discuss these cases in greater detail. A small example of brokering at the level of information content, performed by the Ontology Server to support vocabulary brokering performed by the Query Processor, is also described.

2.1 SEMANTICS PRESERVING VOCABULARY BROKERING

We now discuss the case where the Query Processor uses synonyms to perform semantics-preserving translations into component ontologies of the system. The query processor performs the following important steps:

- Translation of terms in the query into terms in each component ontology. For this the Query Processor needs to access:
  - The IRM which stores terminological relationships between terms across ontologies.
  - The Ontology Server of the component ontology in order to obtain the term definitions.
- Combining partial translations, in such a way that semantics of the user query is preserved.
- Accessing the Ontology Server to obtain data under the component ontology that satisfies the translated query.
- Correlation of objects retrieved from various data repositories/ontologies.

2.1.1 CONSTRUCTING QUERY METADATA USING ONTOLOGICAL TERMS

The user query will be expressed in the format:

[<list-of-roles>] for <DL-expression>

where list-of-roles is a list of roles to be projected (the roles for which the user asks about) and DL-expression is a list of constraints expressed in a DL (the conditions that the answer must satisfy). If list-of-roles is empty, the distinguished role *self*, will be included as the only projection. Consider an example query and metadata corresponding to the query using terms in the user ontology Stanford-II (Appendix 7.A). The query metadata and the english paraphrase are as follows.

Query Metadata: [title author document number-of-pages] for
(**AND** doctoral-thesis-ref (**FILLS** keywords "metadata")
(**ATLEAST** 1 publisher))

English Paraphrase: Get the titles, authors, documents, and number of pages of doctoral theses dealing with "metadata" and that have been published at least once.

2.1.2 SEMANTICS-PRESERVING TRANSLATIONS INTO COMPONENT ONTOLOGIES

The translation algorithm substitutes each concept or role in the user query, by its corresponding translations in the component ontology. If a translation is not found for a concept, its definition in the user ontology is obtained and translated into the component ontology. If a definition is not found, then the concept is marked as untranslated with respect to the component ontology. We illustrate the algorithm by using the example query above. The detailed algorithm is presented in Appendix 7.B. To obtain synonyms and transformed values, the IRM will be invoked. To obtain the definition of a term, the Ontology Server of the user ontology is consulted. The previous process will be applied to each component ontology in the system, where translation is performed between the user ontology and a component ontology. We now present some definitions used in the translation process.

User Query: The user query can be represented as a collection of constraints:

$$\mathcal{Q} = \{Q_1 \ldots Q_n\} \qquad Q_i \ \mathit{constraints}$$

Partial Translation: The result of translating a query using terms from a different ontology will be a tuple of four elements:

- The name of the target ontology.
- The translated roles to be projected.
- The translation of those constraints in the user query which were translated completely using terms of the target ontology.
- Those constraints that do not have a translation.

$$\mathcal{P} = < \mathit{ontology}, \mathit{roles}, P_T, P_{NT} > \begin{cases} P_T = \{P_{T_1} \ldots P_{T_i}\} \qquad P_{T_k} \equiv Q_m \\ P_{NT} \subseteq \mathcal{Q} \\ s.t. \ \ \forall Q_i \in P_{NT} \rightarrow \nexists P_{T_j} \in P_T / P_{T_j} \equiv Q_i \end{cases}$$

$$P_T \bigcup P_{NT} \equiv \mathcal{Q}$$

Full Translation: This represents the case where all constraints in a particular query are translated using terms from another ontology. In this case, the fourth component is **empty**.

$$\mathcal{P} = < ontology, roles, P_T, \phi > \qquad P_T \equiv \mathcal{Q}$$

Extension: This enumerates the objects satisfying a set of constraints C in the query. These objects are obtained from data repositories underlying the ontology *Ont*.

$$Objects(\mathcal{C}, Ont) = \{o \mid C_i(o)\ \forall i\ C_i \in \mathcal{C}\} \qquad C_i\ constraint$$

Examples: Consider the example query discussed above, and the synonyms enumerated in the Appendix 7.C. The translation of the query into the component ontologies is as follows:

- Note that the user query always represents a full translation into the user ontology.
  <Stanford-II, [title author document number-of-pages],
  {doctoral-thesis-ref, (**FILLS** keywords "metadata"), (**ATLEAST** 1 publisher)}, ϕ >

- This is an example of a **partial translation**.
  <Stanford-I, [title author NULL pages],
  {doctoral-thesis, (**ATLEAST** 1 publisher)}, {(**FILLS** keywords "metadata")}>

- This is an example where a term is substituted by its definition.
  doctoral-thesis-ref ≡ (**AND** thesis-ref (**FILLS** type-of-work "doctoral"))
  thesis-ref ≡ (**AND** publication-ref (**FILLS** type-of-work "thesis"))
  <WN, [name creator NULL number-of-pages],
  {print-media, (**FILLS** content "thesis" "doctoral"), (**ATLEAST** 1 publisher),
  (**FILLS** general-topics "metadata")}, ϕ >

- This is an example of a **partial translation** where the value of the role-filler of keywords is transformed by the transformer function relating keywords (Stanford-II) and subject (LSDIS).
  <LSDIS, [title authors location-document NULL],
  {publications, (**FILLS** type "doctoral" "thesis"), (**FILLS** subject "METADATA")},
  {(**ATLEAST** 1 publisher)}>

Consider the list of roles in a user query to be projected, and the translation of the example query into the WN ontology (discussed in the previous section). It is still a full translation (all instances of print-media retrieved would satisfy constraints in the user query), but only information about the name and creator can be provided from the underlying repositories. In this case, roles without a translation will be represented as NULL values. After accessing the data corresponding to that translation, the answer from WN can be correlated with answers from other ontologies (e.g., LSDIS, Stanford-II), and the NULL columns will be overwritten with other values.

2.1.3 COMBINING PARTIAL TRANSLATIONS

As illustrated in the previous section, there are cases when the user query is only partially translated into some ontologies. We illustrate with the help of an example, how partial translations in different ontologies may be combined to give an expression equivalent to the original query.

Example: Consider partial translations of the user query at the ontologies Stanford-I and LSDIS illustrated above. If the intersection of non-translated parts of the partial translations into Stanford-I and LSDIS is empty, then the intersection of both partial answers must satisfy all the constraints in the query. Intuitively,

- From Stanford-I, doctoral theses (about any subject), that have been published at least once will be retrieved;
- From LSDIS, documents about metadata that may have not been published will be retrieved.
- The intersection of the above, returns documents classified as doctoral theses about metadata, and have been published at least once, which is exactly the user query.

In Appendix 7.B, we present an algorithm which, given a new partial translation, tries to determine whether it can be combined with any of the partial translations into previously visited ontologies. It also tries to combine the new partial translation with any combination of the previously obtained partial translations. If the maximum[2] number of constraints of a given user query is K, the previous algorithm will never construct combinations of more than K-1 elements/partial translations. This reduces the explosion of the search space. We also maintain different combinations of ontologies that can form new full translations, and only minimal full translations[3] are returned by the algorithm.

2.1.4 ONTOLOGY SERVER: ACCESSING THE DATA REPOSITORIES

We now discuss how the Ontology Server helps enable brokering at the level of information content by mapping c-contexts expressed as DL expressions

---

[2]Since the original constraints can be substituted by others constraints when using definitions of defined terms.

[3]If translations at ontologies A and B and translations at ontologies A, B and C can be combined to obtain a full translation, then the combination A and B is minimal, whereas the combination A, B and C is not.

to the local repository query language. The services provided to the Query Processor are:

- To provide the term definitions in the query by consulting the user ontology, and invoking appropriate functions of the DL system.
  Get-definition(dictionary, WordNet) → (**AND** print-media (**FILLS** content "d"))

- To retrieve data corresponding to a query over a component ontology. Given a query and an ontology name, it returns corresponding data stored in repositories underlying the ontology, as a relation.
  Get-extension('[pages] for dictionary', WN) → <relation>
  The Ontology Server utilizes **mappings** between terms in the ontology and data structures in the underlying repositories.

In the following, we illustrate the (combined) mappings corresponding to each of the translations above and their transformation into the local repository query language. To retrieve objects satisfying a query formulated over an ontology we need mapping information that links each term in the ontology with structures in data repositories. The mappings between DL terms and the underlying data are expressed using *extended relational algebra (ERA)* expressions. The techniques used to combine mappings for individual terms into a composite mapping for the DL expression have been discussed in (Goñi et al., 1995). The mappings from terms in component ontologies to the underlying data structures in the repositories are presented in Appendix 7.D.

- **Stanford-II**: [self title author document number-of-pages] for
  (**AND** doctoral-thesis-ref (**FILLS** keywords "metadata")
  (**ATLEAST** 1 publisher))

  Mappings:
  <(SELECTION,stanford-II.doc,(AND,(=,stanford-II.doc.Series,"doctoral"),
  (=,stanford-II.doc.Series,"thesis"),
  (=,stanford-II.doc.Subjects, "metadata"),
  (NOT-NULL,stanford-II.doc.Publisher))),
  (stanford-II.doc.LC_Call_No,stanford-II.doc.Title,stanford-II.doc.Author,
  stanford-II.doc.document,stanford-II.doc.Description),
  (string,string,string,postscript,string)>

Local Repository Language (Z39.50 Gateway to Library of Congress):
firstrecord = 1 & maxrecords = 1000 & dbname = BOOKS & term_term_1 = doctoral & term_use_1 = Series Title & term_struct_1 = Word & operator_2 = and & term_term_2 = thesis & term_use_2 = Series Title & term_struct_2 = Word & operator_3 = and & term_term_3 = metadata & term_use_3 = Subjects & term_struct_3 = Word & operator_3 = and not & term_term_4 = NULL & term_use_4 = publisher & term_structure_4 = Word & port = 2210 & esn = F
host = ibm2.loc.gov & attrset = BIB1 & rtype = USMARC
& DisplayRecordSyntax = HTML

- **Stanford-I**: [self title author NULL pages] for
  (**AND** doctoral-thesis (**ATLEAST** 1 publisher))

  Mappings:
  <(SELECTION,stanford-I.document,
  (AND,(=,stanford-I.document.series_title,"doctoral thesis"),
  (NOT-NULL,stanford-I.doc.publisher)))
  (stanford-I.document.loc, stanford-I.document.title,
  stanford-I.document.name, NULL, stanford-I.document.pages),
  (string,string,string,NULL,<string,string>)>

  Local Repository Query Language (SQL):
  SELECT loc, title, name, "NULL", pages
  FROM document
  WHERE doc_type like "%doctoral thesis%" AND publisher NOT NULL;

- **WN**: [self name creator NULL number-of-pages] for
  (**AND** print-media (**FILLS** content "thesis") (**ATLEAST** 1 publisher)
  (**FILLS** content "doctoral") (**FILLS** general-topics "metadata"))

  Mappings:
  <(SELECTION,wn.record,(AND,(=,wn.record.008$[24-27],"doctoral"),
  (=,wn.record.008$[24-27],"thesis"),
  (NOT-NULL,wn.record.260$b),
  (=,wn.record.650$a,"metadata"))),
  (wn.record.010$a,wn.record.245$a,wn.record.100$a,wn.record.300$a),
  (string,string,string,NULL,string)>

  Local Repository Query Language:
  FILES: /home/grad/mena/MARC/UGA/oclcwkly.unicat
  PROJECTIONS: 010$a | 245$a | 100$a | NULL | 300$a
  CONDITIONS: 008$[24-27] = doctoral | 008$[24-27] = thesis | 650$a = metadata | 260b$ <> NULL

- **LSDIS**: [self title authors location-document NULL] for
  (**AND** publications (**FILLS** type "doctoral" "thesis")
  (**FILLS** subject "METADATA"))

Mappings:

```
<(JOIN,(SELECTION,lsdis.pub,(AND,(=,lsdis.pub.type,"doctoral"),
                                 (=,lsdis.pub.type,"thesis"),
                                 (=,lsdis.pub.subjects,"METADATA"))),
        lsdis_html.pub,
        (=, lsdis.pub.id,lsdis_html.pub.id)),
(lsdis.pub.id,lsdis.pub.title,lsdis.pub.authors, lsdis_html.pub.document, NULL),
(string, string, string, postscript, NULL)>
```

Local Repository Query Language:

```
FILES: /home/grad/mena/PROGS/publication-list.txt |
/research2/www/htdocs/publications/pub_ALL.html
PROJECTIONS: id | title | authors | location-document | NULL
CONDITIONS: subjects = METADATA | publisher <> NULL
```

2.1.5 CORRELATION OF THE EXTENSIONS

After obtaining corresponding data from each ontology involved in the user query, that data must be combined to give an answer to the user. First, the data retrieved is checked for format and value heterogeneity. For each answer, the Query Processor invokes the IRM for appropriate transformer functions to be applied. The transformer functions transform values in the format of the user ontology. After this initial step, the different partial answers can be correlated since all of them are expressed in the *language* of the user ontology. In the following discussion, we describe how different partial answers can be combined.

- Let C be the set of constraints in a query Q constructed from a user ontology Ont. Let C' and C" be **full translations** of the query Q at ontologies Ont' and Ont" respectively. Let Objects (C, Ont) be the set of objects retrieved from ontology Ont that satisfy constraints in C. Then the final answer is given as:
  Objects(C, Ont) = Objects(C', Ont') ∪ Objects(C", Ont")

- Let C' be a partial translation of C at ontology Ont' and C" be a partial translation of C at ontology Ont" respectively, where the combination of C' and C" is a **full translation**.
  The final answer is then given as:
  Objects(C, Ont) = Objects(C', Ont') ∩ Objects(C", Ont").

We now present the correlation plan which is applied to translations of the user query into component ontologies.

User_Query_Objects
= Objects('[self title author document number-of-pages] for
(**AND** doctoral-thesis-ref (**FILLS** keywords "metadata")
(**ATLEAST** 1 publisher))')

Stanford-II_Objects
= Objects('[self title author document number-of-pages] for
(**AND** doctoral-thesis-ref (**FILLS** keywords "metadata")
(**ATLEAST** 1 publisher))', Stanford-II)

Stanford-I_Objects
= Objects('[self title author NULL pages] for
(**AND** doctoral-thesis (**ATLEAST** 1 publisher))', Stanford-I)

WN_Objects
= Objects('[self name creator NULL number-of-pages] for
(**AND** print-media (**FILLS** content "thesis" content "doctoral")
(**FILLS** general-topics "metadata"))', WN)

LSDIS_Objects
= Objects('[self title authors location-document NULL] for
(**AND** publications (**FILLS** type "doctoral" "thesis")
(**FILLS** subject "METADATA")', LSDIS))

User_Query_Objects $\supseteq$ **Stanford-II_Objects** $\cup$ **WN_Objects**
$\cup$ [**Stanford-I_Objects** $\cap$ **LSDIS_Objects**]

We can see that the final answer is composed of two full translations (Stanford-II, which plays the role of the user ontology, and WN) and two partial translations (Stanford-I and LSDIS) combined to give a third full translation. Once the set of objects corresponding to the answer have been identified, the following steps need to be taken:

- The values for the NULL roles must be filled out, if they are available at some ontology.

- A transformer function may need to be applied to the results to convert the role values. For example, the Stanford-I ontology returns the pages (<minPage, maxPage>) of a document, whereas the final answer required in the language of the Stanford-I ontology is in terms of number-of-pages. Hence, the transformation function is applied as follows:
  Stanford-II.number-of-pages = compute_pages(Stanford-I.pages)

- To perform correlation between data from different ontologies, we must be able to identify common objects retrieved from different ontologies. For intersection, we show only the common objects; and for union, we eliminate the duplicate objects. The queries sent to the Ontology Servers always include the distinguished role *self* (see examples in the previous section), so that correlation can be performed based on that column to identify different instances.

2.2 VOCABULARY BROKERING WITH LOSS OF INFORMATION

We now discuss how *hyponym/hypernym* relationships across terms in different ontologies may be utilized to obtain translations into component ontologies. This results in a change in the query semantics, and techniques to measure the consequent loss of information in the answer are proposed. The following important steps are performed:

- Temporary Merging of the user and component ontology into which the translation is to be made.
- Translation of the query into this combined ontology in a manner that only terms from the target component ontology are used.
- Estimating the loss of information incurred due to the various candidate translations, and updating the loss of information of the final answer presented to the user.

Example: Consider the following query metadata, and the corresponding english paraphrase constructed using terms from the WN ontology (Appendix 7.A):

English Paraphrase: Get the titles of all books written by "Carl Sagan"
Query Metadata: [name] for (**AND** book (**FILLS** creator "Carl Sagan"))

We now present the translation of this query into various component ontologies using synonym relationships.

- The query always represents a **full translation** into the user ontology.
  < WN, [name], {book, (**FILLS** creator "Carl Sagan")}, ϕ >
- <Stanford-I, [title], {(**FILLS** doc-author-name "Carl Sagan")}, {book}>
- <Stanford-II, [title], {(**FILLS** author "Carl Sagan")}, {book-ref}>
- < LSDIS,[title], {(**FILLS** authors "Carl Sagan")}, {book}>

We see that, other than the translation at the user ontology, no full translation is obtained. Notice, that although there are terms named 'book' and 'book-ref' in Stanford-I and Stanford-II, respectively, and have been classified as synonyms (Appendix 7.C), they are homonyms of the term 'book' in the WN ontology. Data underlying the WN ontology is accessed and presented to the user, but the system is not able to use other ontologies to upgrade such an answer, at least not without loss of information. In the process of refining the answer presented to the user, she/he can choose between translating the query into new ontologies using synonyms, or trying to fully translate the unused partial translations already found, by substituting the non-translated terms with their hyponym/hypernyms.

2.2.1 TEMPORARY MERGING OF ONTOLOGIES

A non-translated term can be substituted by the intersection (*and*) of its immediate parents or by the union (*or*) of its immediate children. This method is applied recursively until a full translation of the conflicting term is obtained. To obtain the immediate parents and children of a term in the user ontology, two different kinds of relationships are involved:

1. Synonyms, hyponyms, and hypernyms between terms in the user and target ontologies obtained from the IRM.

2. Synonyms, hyponyms, and hypernyms in the user ontology, and synonyms, hyponyms and hypernyms in the target ontology.

The task of getting the immediate parents/children is not easy to perform. To obtain the parents/children within the user ontology, the corresponding functions (e.g., subsumption) of the DL systems can be used. But we must combine that answer with the immediate parents/children in the target ontology. Taking into account that some relationships stored in the IRM can be redundant (they were independently defined by different ontology administrators), such a task can be quite difficult. We would need a DL system dealing with "distributed" ontologies.

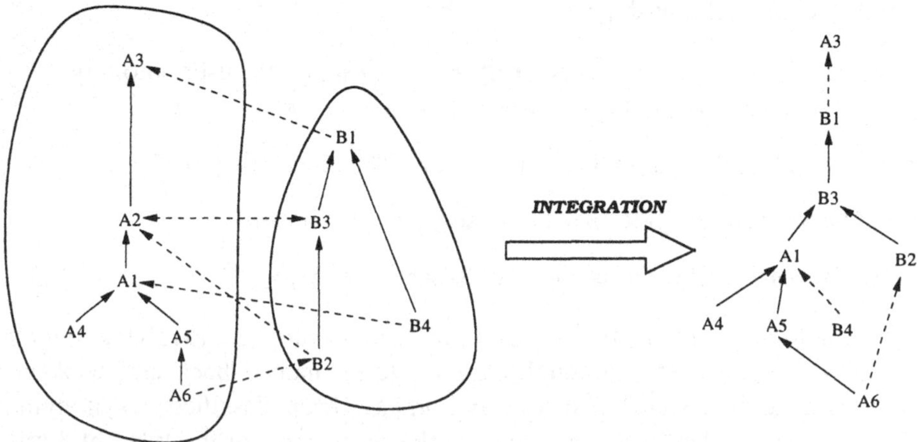

Figure 7.3. Integration of Two Component Ontologies

In Figure 7.3, we show two ontologies with some relationships between them (arrows are hyponym relationships, dashed double arrows are synonyms, and dashed lines are inter-ontology relationships), and the integrated ontology (synonyms are grouped into one term). We can see that obtaining the immediate parents is not evident; for instance, to get the immediate parents of B4 we must deduce that A1 is a child of B1. There are also redundant relationships like the one between A2 and B2. In order to work with these relationships in a homogeneous way, the solution seems to be the integration of the user and target ontologies. The deductive power of the DL system is used to obtain the immediate parents/children (Blanco et al., 1994b). The process of ontology integration is accomplished as follows:

1. Rename and load the user and target ontologies in the DL system.
2. For each term A of the user ontology, get its inter-ontology relationships with terms (referred to as B) in the target ontology, if:
   - *A synonym B*: rename A as B[4]. E.g., A2 and B3 in Figure 7.3.
   - *A hypernym B*: rewrite B including A in the definition
   - *A hyponym B*: rewrite A including B in the definition.

Although some of the previous relationships can be redundant, the DL system will classify the terms at the right place in the ontology. To determine if the resulting terms of the integrated ontology are *primitive* or *defined* (depending on whether A and B are primitive or defined), the rules described in (Blanco et al., 1994a) are applied. The advantages of applying this method are as follows.

- *Costly deductive algorithms* to determine immediate hyponyms and hypernyms of a term can be avoided as that task is now done automatically by the DL system.
- The same method can be used by the IRM to detect inconsistencies and redundancies, and obtain a minimal set of relationships when new inter-ontology relationships are defined in the system.

Besides the above advantages in using DL systems to accomplish the merging of ontologies, there are issues related to the limitations and performance of DL systems that need to be considered.

- DL systems are not able to handle terminological cycles. Hence, if there occurs a terminological cycle in one of the ontologies, or one is generated

[4]We are only interested in terms in the target ontology as we are looking for substituting conflicting terms of the user ontology by terms in the target ontology.

during the merging of ontologies, the system will flag an error. An interesting case related to the above, is illustrated with the help of the following example. Let A_1 and A_2 be two unrelated concepts in one ontology, and B be a concept in another ontology. If the inter-ontology relationships: A_1 hypernym B; and B hypernym A_2 are specified, then a new relationship A_1 hypernym A_2 which did not exist before can be inferred. This may be looked upon in two ways:

- One may consider ontologies as having complete knowledge of the domain they describe and hence consider the new relationship to be an error. This may then lead to a re-examination of the inter-ontology relationships that lead to this inference and determining which of them was erroneous in the first place. The relationship(s) thus chosen may then be retracted by the IRM.
- One may consider that the new ontology and the inter-ontology relationships specified constitute new evidence, based on which the knowledge in the original ontology can be enhanced. This would lead to modification of the ontology, and users of the system should be suitably warned about this.

■ Studies on the performance of the DL systems (Speel, 1995) show that it is possible to integrate two ontologies of around 1000 terms[5] in times of less than a minute. Hence, this process can be used for run-time integration of ontologies.

Figure 7.4 shows the result of integrating the WN and Stanford-I ontologies by applying the relationships in Appendix 7.C. Terms from the ontology WN are in uppercase and terms from Stanford-I are shown in lowercase. Notice that only synonym terms from Stanford-I (document, journal, newspaper and magazine) appear, as it will be the target ontology in the coming examples.

Generating translations with loss of information

Before integrating the user and target ontologies, a **defined term** Q describing the non-translated part of the query is created. Once the merged ontology is built, the system fully translates Q into terms from the target ontology. Notice that it is always possible to get at least one full translation of a conflicting term in both directions since, **Anything** and **Nothing** always exist in the target ontology. Using hyponym and hypernym relationships as described above can result in several possible translations of a non-translated term into a target

[5]Ontologies describing concrete domains, as opposed to systems using only one global ontology, are presumed to be "small" since knowledge is distributed among several ontologies and combined when needed by our system.

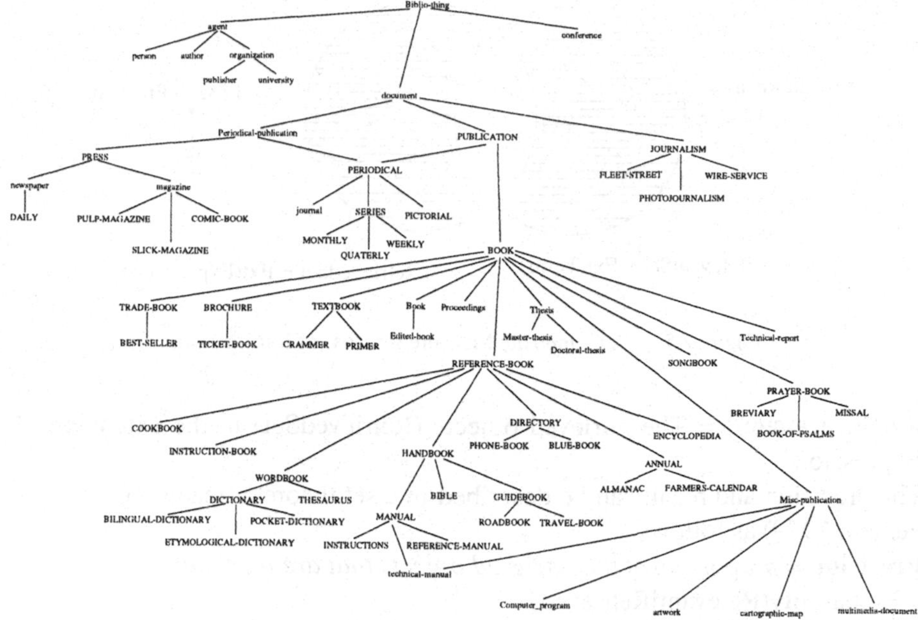

Figure 7.4. Integration of the WN and Stanford-I Ontologies

ontology. The loss of information is measured for all possible cases and the translation with least loss of information is chosen. The complete algorithm to obtain translations with loss of information is presented in Appendix 7.E.

2.2.2 MEASURING THE LOSS OF INFORMATION

A key component of the algorithm is evaluation of the resulting loss of information for each plan/translation, and the choice of that translation which results in the least loss of information. In this section, we evaluate loss of information based on *precision* and *recall* metrics (Salton, 1989), that have been widely used in Information Retrieval literature. They measure the loss of information based on the proportion of irrelevant documents retrieved in response to a user query.

We present measures based on underlying extensions of terms in the ontologies, and propose an adaptation of well established measures like *precision* and *recall*, to measure the information loss when a term is translated by its hyponyms or hypernyms. A composite measure combining precision and recall (van Rijsbergen, 1979), (also known as the E measure in Information Retrieval), is used to choose a translation with least loss of information.

Let **Term** = term to be translated into the target ontology

Ext(Term) = The relevant objects (RelevantSet) in the extension of the term.

Expression = "lossy" translation of the term

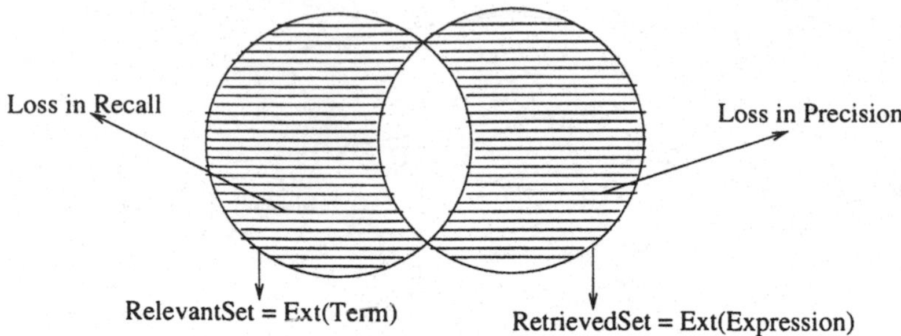

Figure 7.5. A Composite Measure for Loss of Information

Ext(Expression) = The retrieved objects (RetrievedSet) in the extension of Expression

The precision and recall can be described in a set theoretic manner (van Rijsbergen, 1979) as follows:

Precision = *proportion of the retrieved objects that are relevant*

= Probability(Relevant|Retrieved)

$= \frac{|RetrievedSet \cap RelevantSet|}{|RetrievedSet|}$

$= \frac{|Ext(Term) \cap Ext(Expression)|}{|Ext(Expression)|}$

Recall = *proportion of relevant objects that are retrieved*

= Probability(Retrieved|Relevant)

$= \frac{|RetrievedSet \cap RelevantSet|}{|RelevantSet|}$

$= \frac{|Ext(Term) \cap Ext(Expression)|}{|Ext(Term)|}$

In the process of answering a user query, we substitute Term (whose extension constitutes the RelevantSet) with Expression (whose extension constitutes the RetrievedSet). In trying to devise a composite measure for loss of information we seek to measure the extent to which the two sets do not match. This is denoted by the shaded area in Figure 7.5. The area is in fact the symmetric difference:

RelevantSet Δ RetrievedSet

= (RelevantSet $\cup$ RetrievedSet) - (RelevantSet $\cap$ RetrievedSet)

We are interested in the proportion (rather than the absolute number) of relevant and non-relevant objects retrieved, so we need to normalize the measure. A simple normalization gives:

Loss = $\frac{|RelevantSet \Delta RetrievedSet|}{|RelevantSet| + |RetrievedSet|}$

In terms of precision and recall we have:

Loss = 1 - $\frac{1}{\frac{1}{2}(\frac{1}{Precision}) + \frac{1}{2}(\frac{1}{Recall})}$

The OBSERVER system has to satisfy information needs of a widely varying cross-section of users. They may have widely varying preferences when it comes to choosing between precision and recall. We introduce a parameter α ($0 \leq \alpha \leq 1$) to capture the preference of the user where α denotes the importance attached by a user to precision. The modified composite measure may now be given as:

Loss = 1 - $\frac{1}{\alpha(\frac{1}{Precision})+(1-\alpha)(\frac{1}{Recall})}$

Depending on the importance attached by the user to precision and recall (captured by various values of α) we now enumerate various possibilities of computing the composite measure.

- $\alpha = 1/2$ corresponds to a user who attaches equal importance to precision and recall. In this case the information loss reduces to the symmetric difference between RelevantSet and RetrievedSet as discussed before.

- $\alpha \rightarrow 0$ corresponds to a user who attaches no importance to precision. In this case, Loss $\rightarrow$ 1 - Recall, which is true as precision no longer remains a consideration.

- $\alpha \rightarrow 1$ corresponds to a user who attaches no importance to recall. In this case, Loss $\rightarrow$ 1 - Precision, which is true as recall no longer remains a consideration.

Given the translation of a term (expression), we must be able to approximate its extension in order to calculate the loss of information between a conflicting term and its translation. The expression is a combination of unions and intersections of terms in the target ontology; since to get a translation, the system substitutes conflicting terms by intersection of parents and union of children, taking into account all possible combinations. The extension may then be evaluated by updating lower and upper bounds as follows:

- $|Ext(Expr_1) \cap Ext(Expr_2)|$.low = 0
  $|Ext(Expr_1) \cap Ext(Expr_2)|$.high = min[$|Ext(Expr_1)|$.high,
  $|Ext(Expr_2)|$.high]

- $|Ext(Expr_1) \cup Ext(Expr_2)|$.low = max[$|Ext(Expr_1)|$.high,
  $|Ext(Expr_2)|$.high]
  $|Ext(Expr_1) \cup Ext(Expr_2)|$.high = $|Ext(Expr_1)|$.high
  + $|Ext(Expr_2)|$.high

- When $Expr_1$ or $Expr_2$ is a term, both bounds are the number of objects under that term.

Semantic Adaptation of Precision and Recall

We seek to give higher priority to semantic relationships over those suggested by underlying extensions (we want semantically equivalent expressions). Only when no semantics are available, does the system resort to the use of extensional information. Depending on the relationship between the conflicting term and a translation, precision and recall are adapted as follows:

- Term subsumes Expression $\Rightarrow$
  Ext(Term) $\cap$ Ext(Expression) = Ext(Expression).
  Precision = $\frac{|Ext(Term) \cap Ext(Expression)|}{|Ext(Expression)|} = \frac{|Ext(Expression)|}{|Ext(Expression)|} = 1$
  since semantically we are providing no wrong data from expression from the point of view of Term.
  Recall = $\frac{|Ext(Term) \cap Ext(Expression)|}{|Ext(Term)|} = \frac{|Ext(Expression)|}{|Ext(Term)|}$
  Since terms in *Expression* are from a different ontology than *Term*, the extension of *Expression* can be bigger than the extension of *Term*, 0 *Term* subsumes *Expression* semantically. In this case we consider the extension of *Term* to be the union of it's own extension and that of *Expression*. Thus:
  Recall = $\frac{|Ext(Expression)|}{|Ext(Expression) \cup Ext(Term)|} \Rightarrow$
  Recall.low = $\frac{|Ext(Expression)|.low}{|Ext(Expression)|.low + |Ext(Term)|}$
  Recall.high = $\frac{|Ext(Expression)|.high}{max[|Ext(Expression)|.high, |Ext(Term)|]}$

- Expression subsumes Term $\Rightarrow$ Ext(Term) $\cap$ Ext(Expression) = Ext(Term).
  This case is the dual case of the previous one and applying similar reasoning, the Precision and Recall measures may be given as:
  Precision.low = $\frac{|Ext(Term)|}{|Ext(Expression)|.high + |Ext(Term)|}$
  Precision.high = $\frac{|Ext(Term)|}{max[|Ext(Expression)|.low, |Ext(Term)|]}$
  Recall = 1

- *Term* and *Expression* are not related by any subsumption relationship. The general case is applied directly since intersection cannot be simplified.
  Precision.low = 0
  Precision.high[6]
  $= max[\frac{min[|Ext(Term)|, |Ext(Expression)|.high]}{|Ext(Expression)|.high}, \frac{min[|Ext(Term)|, |Ext(Expression)|.low]}{|Ext(Expression)|.low}]$
  Recall.low = 0
  Recall.high = $\frac{min[|Ext(Term)|, |Ext(Expression)|.high]}{|Ext(Term)|}$

- When *Term* is a *defined* term and *Expression* is the intersection of its immediate parents, *Term* subsumes *Expression* and *Expression* subsumes *Term*, i.e., Precision = 1 and Recall = 1.

[6] As we change in numerator and denominator, we do not know which option is greater.

2.2.3 TRANSLATION OF THE EXAMPLE QUERY

We now present steps in transforming the partial translation of the example query discussed earlier into a full translation in the Stanford-I ontology. The resulting loss of information is also evaluated.

< Stanford-I, [title number-of-pages],
{(**FILLS** doc-author-name "Carl Sagan")}, {book}>

As illustrated above, there is no translation for the term 'book' in the Stanford-I ontology. We use inter-ontological relationships between Stanford-I and WN (including hyponyms) to create the integrated ontology illustrated in Figure 7.4. We also illustrate how extra constraints represented in the user ontology can be used to reduce the number of translations under consideration. In particular, we consider the constraint that the concepts PERIODICAL and BOOK are disjoint, and illustrate the translation process for cases where the above constraint may or may not be represented. The term BOOK can be substituted by:

1. Intersection of Parents ⇒ 'PUBLICATION'.
   Since 'PUBLICATION' is not a term of the target ontology, it can be substituted by:
   (a) Intersection of Parents ⇒ 'document'.
   Since 'document' is a term in the target ontology, it is a candidate translation plan for the term 'PERIODICAL'.
   (b) Union of Children ⇒ 'PERIODICAL'.
   It may be noted that 'PUBLICATION' is not considered as it is the lower boundary for itself. Since 'PERIODICAL' is not a term of the target ontology, it can be substituted by:
      i. Intersection of Parents ⇒ 'periodical-publication'.
      Since 'periodical-publication' is a term in the target ontology, it is a candidate translation plan for the term 'PERIODICAL'.
      ii. Union of Children ⇒ 'journal' ∪ 'SERIES' ∪ 'PICTORIAL'.
      Since 'SERIES' and 'PICTORIAL' lead to NOTHING, they are ignored. Hence 'journal' is a candidate translation plan for 'PERIODICAL'. It may be noted that in case the disjointness constraint between 'BOOKS' and 'PERIODICAL' is represented, this option is not explored.
      iii. Candidate Plans for 'PERIODICAL' without the disjointness constraint:
      = {'periodical-publication', 'journal'}
      iv. Candidate Plans for 'PERIODICAL' with the disjointness constraint:
      = {'periodical-publication'}
   (c) Candidate Plans for 'PUBLICATION' without the disjointness constraint:
   = {'document', 'periodical-publication', 'journal'}
   Even though 'document' subsumes 'periodical-publication', either of them may be preferred depending on the bias of the user for precision or recall.
   (d) Candidate Plans for 'PUBLICATION' with the disjointness constraint:
   = {'document', 'periodical-publication'}
2. Union of Children ⇒ 'TRADE-BOOK' ∪ 'BROCHURE' ∪ 'TEXTBOOK' ∪ 'Book' ∪ 'Proceedings' ∪ 'REFERENCE-BOOK' ∪ 'Thesis' ∪ 'Misc-publication' ∪ 'SOUND-BOOK' ∪ 'PRAYER-BOOK' ∪ 'Technical-report'.

'TRADE-BOOK', 'BROCHURE', 'TEXTBOOK', 'SONGBOOK' and 'PRAYER-BOOK' lead to NOTHING and are ignored. The only term that needs to be translated is 'REFERENCE-BOOK'. As the only parent of 'REFERENCE-BOOK' is 'BOOK', it is ignored.

(a) Union of Children ⇒ 'COOKBOOK' ∪ 'INSTRUCTION-BOOK' ∪ 'WORDBOOK' ∪ 'HANDBOOK' ∪ 'DIRECTORY' ∪ 'ANNUAL' ∪ 'ENCYCLOPEDIA'.
All the terms in the above translation except 'HANDBOOK' lead to NOTHING. 'HANDBOOK' is ultimately substituted by 'technical-manual'.

(b) Candidate Plans for 'REFERENCE-BOOK' = {'technical-manual'}

(c) Candidate Plans for Union of Children of 'BOOK'
= { 'Book' ∪ 'Proceedings' ∪ 'technical-manual' ∪ 'Thesis' ∪ 'Misc-publication'∪ 'Technical-report'}
Since 'Misc-publication' subsumes 'technical-manual ⇒
= { 'Book' ∪ 'Proceedings' ∪ 'Thesis' ∪ 'Misc-publication'∪ 'Technical-report'}

3. Candidate Plans for 'BOOK' without the disjointness constraint:
= { 'document', 'periodical-publication', 'journal',
'Book' ∪ 'Proceedings' ∪ 'Thesis' ∪ 'Misc-publication'∪ 'Technical-report'}

4. Candidate Plans for 'BOOK' with the disjointness constraint:
= { 'document', 'periodical-publication',
'Book' ∪ 'Proceedings' ∪ 'Thesis' ∪ 'Misc-publication'∪ 'Technical-report'}

Now let us compute the precision, recall, and loss of information for each candidate translation plan of 'BOOK'. We assume the value of α to be 0.5:

document $|Ext(\text{'}BOOK')| = 1105$; $|Ext(\text{'}document')| = 24570$

Precision.low = $\frac{|Ext(\text{'}BOOK')|}{|Ext(\text{'}BOOK')|+|Ext(\text{'}document')|} = 0.043$

Precision.high = $\frac{|Ext(\text{'}BOOK')|}{max[|Ext(\text{'}BOOK')|,|Ext(\text{'}document')|]} = 0.044$

Recall = 1

Loss.low = 1- $\frac{1}{\frac{\alpha}{Precision.high}+\frac{\alpha}{Recall.high}} = 0.91571$

Loss.high = 1- $\frac{1}{\frac{\alpha}{Precision.low}+\frac{\alpha}{Recall.low}} = 0.91755$

periodical-publication $|Ext(\text{'}BOOK')| = 1105$;
$|Ext(\text{'}periodical-publication')| = 0$
Precision = 0; Recall = 0, Loss = 1

journal $|Ext(\text{'}BOOK')| = 1105$; $|Ext(\text{'}journal')| = 0$
Precision = 0; Recall = 0, Loss = 1

Union of Children of BOOK $|Ext(\text{'}BOOK')| = 1105$; $|Ext(\text{'}book')| = 14199$;
$|Ext(\text{'}proceedings')| = 6$; $|Ext(\text{'}thesis')| = 0$; $|Ext(\text{'}misc-publication')| = 31$;
$|Ext(\text{'}technical-report')| = 1$

SizeUnion.low = max[$|Ext(\text{'}book')|$, $|Ext(\text{'}proceedings')|$, $|Ext(\text{'}thesis')|$, $|Ext(\text{'}misc-publication')|$, $|Ext(\text{'}technical-report')|$] = 14199

SizeUnion.high = $|Ext(\text{'}book')| + |Ext(\text{'}proceedings')| + |Ext(\text{'}thesis')| + |Ext(\text{'}misc-publication')| + |Ext(\text{'}technical-report')| = 14237$

Precision = 1 (Since 'BOOK' subsumes each of them, it subsumes the Union)

Recall.low = $\frac{SizeUnion.low}{|Ext(\text{'}BOOK')|+SizeUnion.low} = 0.92780$

Recall.high = $\frac{SizeUnion.high}{max[|Ext(\text{'}BOOK')|,SizeUnion.high]} = 1$

$$\text{Loss.low} = 1 - \frac{1}{\frac{\alpha}{Precision.high} + \frac{\alpha}{Recall.high}} = 0$$

$$\text{Loss.high} = 1 - \frac{1}{\frac{\alpha}{Precision.low} + \frac{\alpha}{Recall.low}} = 0.0722$$

The fourth candidate translation is chosen as it minimizes loss of information.

3. OBSERVER: A SUMMARY

The OBSERVER system is one alternative to extend the InfoSleuth system that enables information brokering, by addressing the critical issue of vocabulary differences across different systems on the GII. We have used *pre-existing domain specific ontologies* to characterize the vocabulary used for construction of domain specific metadata. Though the system performs brokering also at the metadata level, the focus of the system is on vocabulary brokering that utilizes relationships across terms in different ontologies. The OBSERVER architecture is an enhancement of the InfoSleuth and MIDAS architectures. it is more *adaptable* because of its ability to transform information requests across different domain ontologies, and the ability to minimize loss of information.

In the InfoHarness and MIDAS systems, we investigated trade-offs related to the performance of the information brokering system. We characterize them as *infrastructure based* trade-offs, where the emphasis is on techniques related to optimizing access and manipulation of structures underlying the information. In the OBSERVER system, we make a transition to *information based* trade-offs, where we evaluate loss of information incurred in the process of translation to different ontologies. The use of component ontologies (as opposed to a global ontology) enhances both the adaptability and scalability of information access. As the information overload on the user increases, it is our belief that information based trade-offs would become more important and in most (if not all) cases precede infrastructure based trade-offs for feasible access to relevant information on the GII.

APPENDIX 7.A: Ontologies used in the OBSERVER Prototype

WN: A Subset of WordNet 1.5

The DL Definitions

```
; WN Ontology
(cl-define-primitive-concept 'print-media 'CLASSIC-THING)
(cl-define-primitive-role 'name)
(cl-define-primitive-role 'creator)
(cl-define-primitive-role 'type)
(cl-define-primitive-role 'target-audience)
(cl-define-primitive-role 'content)
(cl-define-primitive-role 'general-topics)
; PRESS
(cl-define-primitive-concept 'press 'print-media)
(cl-define-primitive-role 'frequency)
(cl-define-primitive-concept 'newspaper 'press)
(cl-define-concept 'daily '(and newspaper (fills frequency "daily")))
(cl-define-primitive-role 'ISSN)
```

```
(cl-define-concept 'magazine '(and press (atleast 1 ISSN)))
(cl-define-primitive-concept 'pulp-magazine 'magazine)
(cl-define-primitive-concept 'slick-magazine 'magazine)
(cl-define-primitive-concept 'comic-book 'magazine)
; JOURNALISM
(cl-define-primitive-concept 'journalism 'print-media)
(cl-define-primitive-concept 'fleet-street 'journalism)
(cl-define-primitive-concept 'wire-service 'journalism)
(cl-define-primitive-concept 'photojournalism 'journalism)
; PUBLICATION
(cl-define-primitive-role 'pages)
(cl-define-primitive-role 'language)
(cl-define-primitive-role 'dimensions)
(cl-define-primitive-role 'awards)
(cl-define-primitive-role 'place-publication)
(cl-define-concept 'publication '(and print-media (atleast 1 place-publication)))
; Book
(cl-define-primitive-role 'ISBN)
(cl-define-concept 'book '(and publication (atleast 1 ISBN)))
(cl-define-primitive-role 'publisher)
(cl-define-primitive-role 'date)
(cl-define-primitive-concept 'trade-book 'book)
(cl-define-primitive-concept 'best-seller 'trade-book)
(cl-define-primitive-concept 'brochure 'book)
(cl-define-primitive-concept 'ticket-book 'brochure)
(cl-define-primitive-concept 'textbook 'book)
(cl-define-primitive-concept 'crammer 'textbook)
(cl-define-primitive-concept 'primmer 'textbook)
(cl-define-primitive-concept 'songbook 'book)
(cl-define-primitive-concept 'prayer-book 'book)
(cl-define-primitive-concept 'breviary 'prayer-book)
(cl-define-primitive-concept 'missal 'prayer-book)
(cl-define-primitive-concept 'book-of-Psalms 'prayer-book)
; reference-book
(cl-define-primitive-concept 'reference-book 'book)
(cl-define-primitive-concept 'cookbook 'reference-book)
(cl-define-primitive-concept 'instruction-book 'reference-book)
(cl-define-primitive-concept 'wordbook 'reference-book)
(cl-define-concept 'dictionary '(and book (fills content "d")))
(cl-define-primitive-concept 'bilingual-dictionary 'dictionary)
(cl-define-primitive-concept 'etymological-dictionary 'dictionary)
(cl-define-primitive-concept 'pocket-dictionary 'dictionary)
(cl-define-primitive-concept 'thesaurus 'wordbook)
(cl-define-concept 'handbook '(and book (fills content "f")))
(cl-define-primitive-concept 'manual 'handbook)
(cl-define-primitive-concept 'instructions 'manual)
(cl-define-primitive-concept 'reference-manual 'manual)
(cl-define-primitive-concept 'bible 'handbook)
(cl-define-primitive-concept 'guidebook 'handbook)
(cl-define-primitive-concept 'roadbook 'guidebook)
(cl-define-primitive-concept 'travel-guidebook 'guidebook)
(cl-define-concept 'directory '(and book (fills content "r")))
(cl-define-primitive-concept 'phone-book 'directory)
(cl-define-primitive-concept 'blue-book 'directory)
(cl-define-primitive-concept 'annual 'reference-book)
(cl-define-primitive-concept 'almanac 'annual)
(cl-define-primitive-concept 'farmers-calendar 'annual)
(cl-define-concept 'encyclopedia '(and book (fills content "e")))
; Periodical
(cl-define-primitive-concept 'periodical 'publication)
(cl-define-primitive-concept 'pictorial 'periodical)
(cl-define-primitive-concept 'series 'periodical)
(cl-define-primitive-concept 'monthly 'series)
(cl-define-primitive-concept 'quarterly 'series)
(cl-define-primitive-concept 'weekly 'series)
(cl-define-primitive-concept 'journals 'periodical)
```

The Graphical Representation

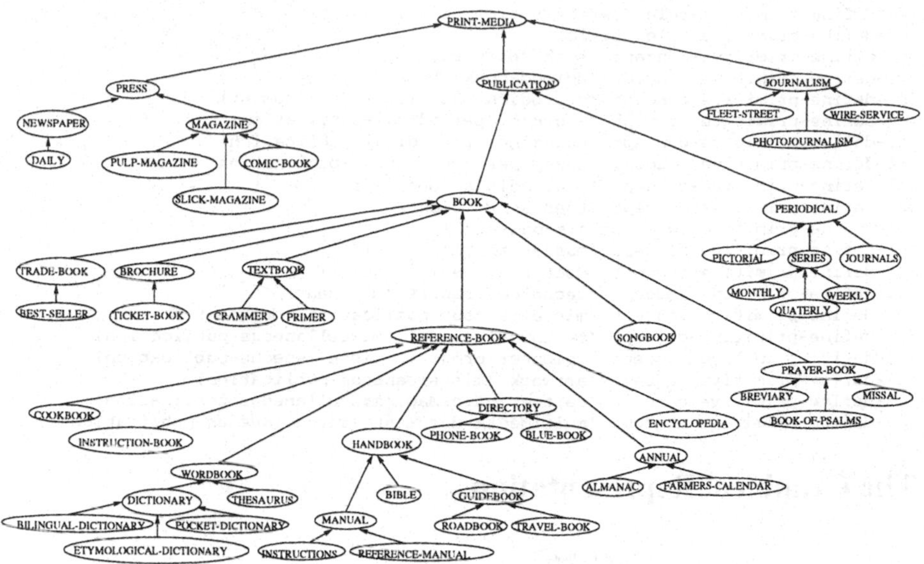

Figure 7.A.1. WN: A Subset of the WordNet 1.5 Ontology

Stanford-I: A Subset of Bibliography Data Ontology

The DL Definitions

```
; STANFORD-I Ontology
(cl-define-primitive-concept 'biblio-thing 'CLASSIC-THING)
; AGENT
(cl-define-primitive-concept 'agent 'biblio-thing)
(cl-define-primitive-role 'agent-name)
(cl-define-primitive-concept 'person 'agent)
(cl-define-primitive-concept 'author 'agent)
(cl-define-primitive-role 'author-name)
(cl-define-primitive-role 'penname)
(cl-define-primitive-concept 'organization 'agent)
(cl-define-primitive-role 'organization-name)
(cl-define-primitive-concept 'publisher 'organization)
(cl-define-primitive-role 'publisher-name)
(cl-define-primitive-role 'publisher-address)
(cl-define-primitive-concept 'university 'organization)
; CONFERENCE
(cl-define-primitive-concept 'conference 'biblio-thing)
(cl-define-primitive-role 'conf-name)
(cl-define-primitive-role 'conf-date)
(cl-define-primitive-role 'conf-address)
(cl-define-primitive-role 'conf-organization)
; DOCUMENT
(cl-define-primitive-concept 'document 'biblio-thing)
(cl-define-primitive-role 'author)
(cl-define-primitive-role 'doc-author-name)
(cl-define-primitive-role 'editor)
(cl-define-primitive-role 'series-editor)
(cl-define-primitive-role 'translator)
(cl-define-primitive-role 'conference)
(cl-define-primitive-role 'edition)
(cl-define-primitive-role 'institution)
```

```
(cl-define-primitive-role 'pages)
(cl-define-primitive-role 'publication-date)
(cl-define-primitive-role 'publisher)
(cl-define-primitive-role 'series-title)
(cl-define-primitive-role 'title)
(cl-define-primitive-concept 'book 'document)
(cl-define-primitive-concept 'edited-book 'book)
(cl-define-primitive-concept 'periodical-publication 'document)
(cl-define-primitive-concept 'journal 'periodical-publication)
(cl-define-primitive-concept 'magazine 'periodical-publication)
(cl-define-primitive-concept 'newspaper 'periodical-publication)
(cl-define-primitive-concept 'proceedings 'document)
(cl-define-primitive-concept 'thesis 'document)
(cl-define-primitive-role 'thesis-university)
(cl-define-primitive-concept 'master-thesis 'thesis)
(cl-define-primitive-concept 'doctoral-thesis 'thesis)
(cl-define-primitive-concept 'technical-report 'document)
(cl-define-primitive-concept 'miscellaneous-publication 'document)
(cl-define-primitive-concept 'technical-manual 'miscellaneous-publication)
(cl-define-primitive-concept 'computer-program 'miscellaneous-publication)
(cl-define-primitive-concept 'artwork 'miscellaneous-publication)
(cl-define-primitive-concept 'cartographic-map 'miscellaneous-publication)
(cl-define-primitive-concept 'multimedia-document 'miscellaneous-publication)
```

The Graphical Representation

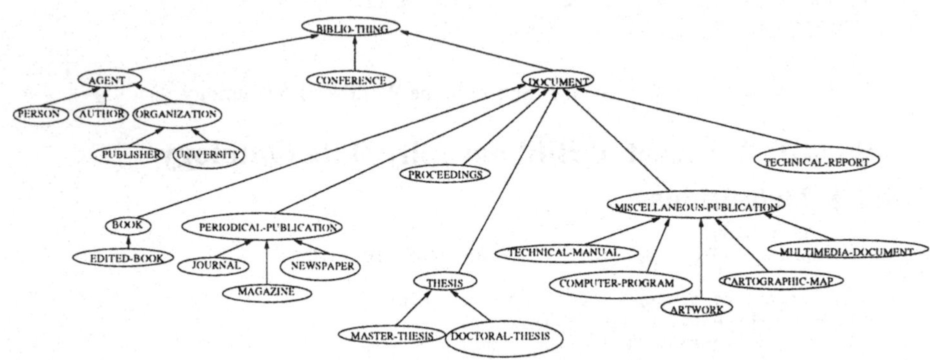

Figure 7.A.2. Stanford-I: A Subset of the Bibliographic Data Ontology

Stanford-II: A Subset of Bibliography Data Ontology

The DL Definitions

```
; STANFORD-II Ontology
; REFERENCE
(cl-define-primitive-concept 'reference 'CLASSIC-THING)
(cl-define-primitive-role 'author)
(cl-define-primitive-role 'editor)
(cl-define-primitive-role 'keywords)
(cl-define-primitive-role 'notes)
(cl-define-primitive-role 'secondary-author)
(cl-define-primitive-role 'secondary-title)
(cl-define-primitive-role 'series-editor)
(cl-define-primitive-role 'tertiary-author)
(cl-define-primitive-role 'translator)
(cl-define-primitive-role 'abstract)
(cl-define-primitive-role 'booktitle)
(cl-define-primitive-role 'day)
(cl-define-primitive-role 'document)
```

```
(cl-define-primitive-role 'edition)
(cl-define-primitive-role 'issue)
(cl-define-primitive-role 'month)
(cl-define-primitive-role 'number-of-volumes)
(cl-define-primitive-role 'organization)
(cl-define-primitive-role 'number-of-pages)
(cl-define-primitive-role 'periodical)
(cl-define-primitive-role 'publisher)
(cl-define-primitive-role 'report-number)
(cl-define-primitive-role 'title)
(cl-define-primitive-role 'type-of-work)
(cl-define-primitive-role 'volume)
(cl-define-primitive-role 'year)
; PUBLICATION-REFERENCE
(cl-define-primitive-concept 'publication-ref 'reference)
(cl-define-primitive-concept 'book-ref 'publication-ref)
(cl-define-primitive-concept 'edited-book-ref 'book-ref)
(cl-define-primitive-concept 'book-section-ref 'publication-ref)
(cl-define-primitive-concept 'article-ref 'publication-ref)
(cl-define-concept 'journal-article-ref
                   '(and article-ref (fills type-of-work "journal")))
(cl-define-concept 'magazine-article-ref
                   '(and article-ref (fills type-of-work "magazine")))
(cl-define-primitive-role 'magazine-name)
(cl-define-concept 'newspaper-article-ref
                   '(and article-ref (fills type-of-work "newspaper")))
(cl-define-primitive-role 'newspaper-name)
(cl-define-concept 'proceedings-paper-ref
                   '(and publication-ref (fills type-of-work "proceeding")))
(cl-define-concept 'thesis-ref
                   '(and publication-ref (fills type-of-work "thesis")))
(cl-define-concept 'master-thesis-ref
                   '(and thesis-ref (fills type-of-work "master")))
(cl-define-concept 'doctoral-thesis-ref
                   '(and thesis-ref (fills type-of-work "doctoral")))
(cl-define-concept 'technical-report-ref
                 '(and publication-ref (fills type-of-work "technical report")))
(cl-define-primitive-concept 'misc-publication-ref 'publication-ref)
(cl-define-concept 'technical-manual-ref
           '(and misc-publication-ref (fills type-of-work "technical manual")))
(cl-define-concept 'computer-program-ref
           '(and misc-publication-ref (fills type-of-work "computer program")))
(cl-define-primitive-concept 'artwork-ref 'misc-publication-ref)
(cl-define-concept 'cartographic-map-ref
                   '(and misc-publication-ref (fills type-of-work "map")))
(cl-define-primitive-concept 'multimedia-document-ref 'misc-publication-ref)
; NON-PUBLICATION REFERENCE
(cl-define-primitive-concept 'non-publication-ref 'reference)
(cl-define-primitive-concept 'personal-communication-ref 'non-publication-ref)
(cl-define-primitive-concept 'generic-unpublished-ref 'non-publication-ref)
```

The Graphical Representation

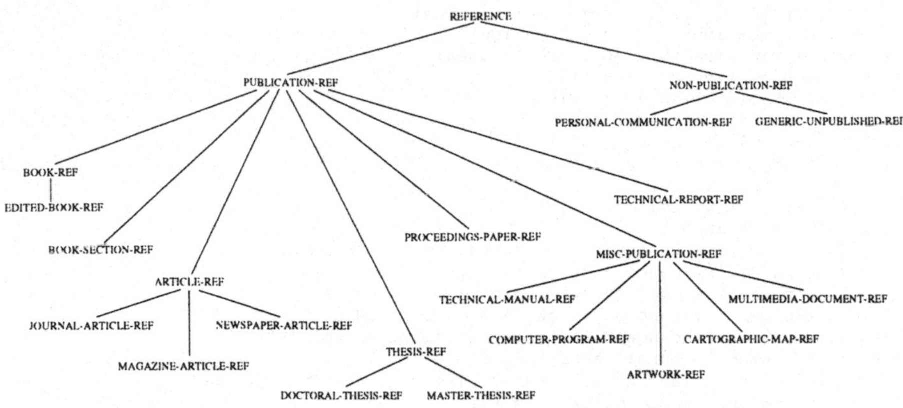

Figure 7.A.3. Stanford-II: A Subset of the Bibliographic Data Ontology

The LSDIS Ontology

The DL Definitions

```
; LSDIS Ontology
(cl-define-primitive-concept 'publications 'CLASSIC-THING)
(cl-define-primitive-role 'title)
(cl-define-primitive-role 'authors)
(cl-define-primitive-role 'published-in)
(cl-define-primitive-role 'type)
(cl-define-primitive-role 'subject)
(cl-define-primitive-role 'location-document)
; SUBJECT-BASED
(cl-define-primitive-concept 'subject-based 'publications)
(cl-define-concept 'workflow-pub '(AND publications (FILLS subject "WORKFLOW")))
(cl-define-concept 'information-modeling-pub
                   '(AND publications (FILLS subject "MODELING")))
(cl-define-concept 'metadata-pub '(AND publications (FILLS subject "METADATA")))
(cl-define-concept 'integration-pub
                   '(AND publications (FILLS subject "INTEGRATION")))
(cl-define-concept 'consistency-pub
                   '(AND publications (FILLS subject "CONSISTENCY")))
; TYPE-BASED
(cl-define-primitive-concept 'type-based 'publications)
(cl-define-concept 'technical-reports
                   '(AND publications (FILLS type "technical-report")))
(cl-define-concept 'journal-article '(AND publications (FILLS type "article")))
(cl-define-concept 'paper '(AND publications (FILLS type "proceeding")))
(cl-define-concept 'thesis '(AND publications (FILLS type "thesis")))
```

The Graphical Representation

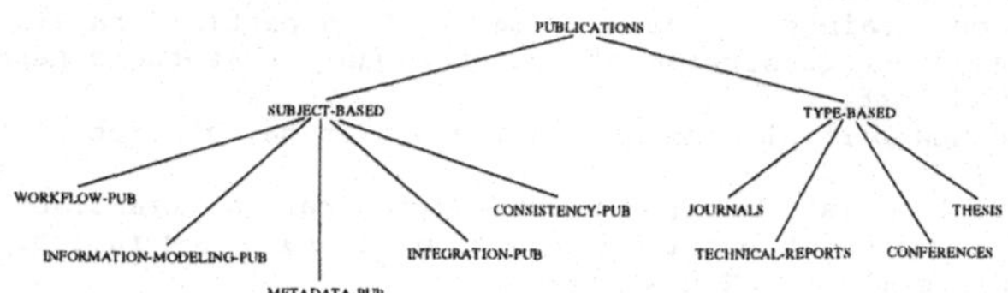

Figure 7.A.4. The LSDIS Ontology

APPENDIX 7.B: Algorithms for Semantics-preserving Translations

Translation Algorithm

```
/* Given a user query and a target ontology it transforms the user query to an
equivalent one expressed in terms of the target ontology */
TRANSLATE-PRESERVING-SEMANTICS (user-query, target-ontology) {
  fills = 0
  untranslated = 0
  FOR each constraint in the user query DO
    FOR each component of the constraint DO
      CASE component is:
        term: /* concept or role */
          IF exists synonym from user to target ontology THEN {
            substitute(term, synonym-of-term)
              IF fills THEN {
                                role = term
                                new-role = synonym-of-term
                              }
                      }
              ELSE IF term is defined THEN {
                                substitute(term, definition-of-term)
IF translate-preserving-semantics(definition-of-term, target-ontology)
              == FAILURE THEN
                 untranslated = 1
              }
              ELSE
                 untranslated = 1
        value:
IF fills AND exists transformer function between role and new-role THEN {
            equivalent-value = transformer_function(value)
            substitute(value, equivalent-value)
            fills = 0
           }
           ELSE
             untranslated = 1
        operator: /* ALL, AT-LEAST, FILLS, ... */
          IF it is 'fills' THEN
            fills = 1
          ELSE
            fills = 0
         ENDCASE
    ENDFOR
  ENDFOR
  IF untranslated == 1 THEN
         return(FAILURE)
  ELSE
         return(SUCCESS)
```

Translation Combination Algorithm

```
COMBINE_PARTIAL_TRANSLATIONS ( non_full_combs, new_partial)
/* Non_full_combs: previous combinations of partial translations which do not
satisfy all the constraints in the user query. Each partial translation
translates at least one constraint of the user query that the others in the
same combination do not.
New_partial: the new partial translation the system has just obtained */
{
  full={} /* full translations from combining new partial translation */
  new_fulls={} /* component ontologies involved in each new full translation */
  n_f_c = non_full_combs UNION new_partial
  /* New partial is a non full combination */
  WHILE not_empty(non_full_combs) DO {
    comb = first(non_full_combs)
    new_comb = comb UNION new_partial
    IF  (#_non_translated(new_comb) < #_non_translated(comb)) AND
      (ontologies(new_comb) is not a superset of any element in new_fulls) THEN
{
            /* some nontranslated constraints in the combination are translated
             in the new partial translation */
                IF full(new_comb) THEN {
                /* equiv. #_non_translated(new_comb)=0 */
                          full = full UNION new_comb
                          new_fulls = new_fulls UNION ontologies(new_comb)
                         }
                    ELSE n_f_c = n_f_c UNION new_comb
              }
           /* ELSE The new partial is not interesting for that combination
              or it is not minimal) */
         non_translated_combs = remove_first(non_translated_combs)
       }
  return < full, n_f_c >
}
/* Returns new full translations when using the new partial and the new
interesting non full combinations */
```

APPENDIX 7.C: Inter-Ontology Relationships in the OBSERVER System

Synonym Relationships

CANONICAL	TERM	ONTOLOGY
---------	----	--------
ISBN	ISBN	wn
ISSN	ISSN	wn
article	article-ref	stanford-II
artwork	artwork	stanford-I
artwork	artwork-ref	stanford-II
author	authors	lsdis
author	creator	wn
author	author	stanford-II
author	doc-author-name	stanford-I
awards	awards	wn
book	book	stanford-I
book	book-ref	stanford-II
computer-program	computer-program	stanford-I
computer-program	computer-program-ref	stanford-II
dimensions	dimensions	wn
doctoral-thesis	doctoral-thesis	stanford-I
doctoral-thesis	doctoral-thesis-ref	stanford-II
document	location-document	lsdis
document	document	stanford-II
edited-book	edited-book	stanford-I
edited-book	edited-book-ref	stanford-II
editor	editor	stanford-I
editor	ref-editor	stanford-II

newspaper	newspaper	stanford-I
notes	notes	stanford-II
publication-date	publication-date	stanford-I
publications	print-media	wn
publications	publication-ref	stanford-II
publications	document	stanford-I
publications	publications	lsdis
published-in	published-in	lsdis
published-in	place-publication	wn
publisher	publisher	wn
publisher	publisher	stanford-I
publisher	publisher	stanford-II
secondary-author	secondary-author	stanford-II
secondary-title	secondary-title	stanford-II
series-editor	series-editor	stanford-I
series-editor	series-editor	stanford-II
subject	subject	lsdis
subject	general-topics	wn
subject	keywords	stanford-II
target-audience	target-audience	wn
technical-reports	technical-reports	lsdis
technical-reports	technical-report	stanford-I
technical-reports	technical-report-ref	stanford-II
thesis	thesis	lsdis
thesis	thesis	stanford-I
thesis	thesis-ref	stanford-II
title	title	lsdis
title	title	stanford-I
title	title	stanford-II
title	name	wn
translator	translator	stanford-I
translator	translator	stanford-II
type	type	lsdis
type	type-of-work	stanford-II
type	content	wn
periodical-pub	periodical-publication	stanford-I
periodical	periodical	stanford-II
paper	proceedings-paper-ref	stanford-II
paper	paper	lsdis
pages	pages	stanford-II
pages	number-of-pages	stanford-I
pages	number-of-pages	wn
organization	organization	stanford-II
organization	institution	stanford-I

Hyponyms used in the OBSERVER System

TERM 1	ONT 1	IS A HYPONYM OF	TERM 2	ONT 2
technical-manual	Stanford-I		manual	WN
book	Stanford-I		book	WN
proceedings	Stanford-I		book	WN
thesis	Stanford-I		book	WN
misc-publication	Stanford-I		book	WN
technical-reports	Stanford-I		book	WN
press	WN		periodical-publ.	Stanford-I
periodical	WN		periodical-publ.	Stanford-I

APPENDIX 7.D: Mappings from Ontological Terms to underlying Data Structures

Mappings for the WN Ontology

CONCEPT print-media wn.record wn.record.010$a string

ROLE name wn.record wn.record.010$a string wn.record.245$a string none

ROLE creator wn.record wn.record.010$a string wn.record.100$a string none

ROLE type wn.record wn.record.010$a string wn.record.000$[6] string none

ROLE target-audience wn.record wn.record.010$a string wn.record.000$[22] string none

ROLE content wn.record wn.record.010$a string wn.record.008$[24-27] string none

ROLE general-topics wn.record wn.record.010$a string wn.record.650$a string none

CONCEPT publication wn.record wn.record.010$a string

ROLE pages wn.record wn.record.010$a string wn.record.300$a string none

ROLE language wn.record wn.record.010$a string wn.record.008$[35-37] string none

ROLE place-publication wn.record wn.record.010$a string wn.record.260$a string none

ROLE ISSN wn.record wn.record.010$a string wn.record.022$a string none

CONCEPT magazine [SELECTION, wn.record, [NOT NULL wn.record.022$a]] wn.record.010$a string

ROLE pages wn.record wn.record.010$a string wn.record.300$a string none

ROLE dimensions wn.record wn.record.010$a string wn.record.300$c string none

ROLE awards wn.record wn.record.010$a string wn.record.586$a string none

CONCEPT book [SELECTION, wn.record, [NOT NULL wn.record.020$a]] wn.record.010$a string

ROLE publisher wn.record wn.record.010$a string wn.record.260$b string none

ROLE isbn wn.record wn.record.010$a string wn.record.020$a string none

CONCEPT handbook [SELECTION, wn.record, [=, wn.record.008$[24-27],"f"]] wn.record.010$a string

CONCEPT directory [SELECTION, wn.record, [=, wn.record.008$[24-27],"r"]] wn.record.010$a string

CONCEPT dictionary [SELECTION, wn.record, [=, wn.record.008$[24-27],"d"]] wn.record.010$a string

CONCEPT encyclopedia [SELECTION, wn.record, [=, wn.record.008$[24-27],"e"]] wn.record.010$a string

Mappings for the Stanford-I Ontology

CONCEPT print-media wn.record wn.record.010$a string

ROLE name wn.record wn.record.010$a string wn.record.245$a string none

ROLE creator wn.record wn.record.010$a string wn.record.100$a string none

ROLE type wn.record wn.record.010$a string wn.record.000$[6] string none

ROLE target-audience wn.record wn.record.010$a string wn.record.000$[22] string none

ROLE content wn.record wn.record.010$a string wn.record.008$[24-27] string none

ROLE general-topics wn.record wn.record.010$a string wn.record.650$a string none

CONCEPT publication wn.record wn.record.010$a string

ROLE pages wn.record wn.record.010$a string wn.record.300$a string none

ROLE language wn.record wn.record.010$a string wn.record.008$[35-37] string none

ROLE place-publication wn.record wn.record.010$a string wn.record.260$a string none

ROLE ISSN wn.record wn.record.010$a string wn.record.022$a string none

CONCEPT magazine [SELECTION, wn.record, [NOT NULL wn.record.022$a]] wn.record.010$a string

ROLE pages wn.record wn.record.010$a string wn.record.300$a string none

ROLE dimensions wn.record wn.record.010$a string wn.record.300$c string none

ROLE awards wn.record wn.record.010$a string wn.record.586$a string none

CONCEPT book [SELECTION, wn.record, [NOT NULL wn.record.020$a]] wn.record.010$a string

ROLE publisher wn.record wn.record.010$a string wn.record.260$b string none

ROLE isbn wn.record wn.record.010$a string wn.record.020$a string none

CONCEPT handbook [SELECTION, wn.record, [=, wn.record.008$[24-27],"f"]] wn.record.010$a string

CONCEPT directory [SELECTION, wn.record, [=, wn.record.008$[24-27],"r"]] wn.record.010$a string

CONCEPT dictionary [SELECTION, wn.record, [=, wn.record.008$[24-27],"d"]] wn.record.010$a string

CONCEPT encyclopedia [SELECTION, wn.record, [=, wn.record.008$[24-27],"e"]] wn.record.010$a string

Mappings for the Stanford-II Ontology

CONCEPT reference stanford-II.doc stanford-II.doc.LC_Call_No string

ROLE author stanford-II.doc stanford-II.doc.LC_Call_No string stanford-II.doc.Author string none

ROLE keywords stanford-II.doc stanford-II.doc.LC_Call_No string stanford-II.doc.Subjects string none

ROLE notes stanford-II.doc stanford-II.doc.LC_Call_No string stanford-II.doc.Notes string none

ROLE secondary-author stanford-II.doc stanford-II.doc.LC_Call_No string

stanford-II.doc.Other_authors string none

ROLE secondary-title stanford-II.doc stanford-II.doc.LC_Call_No string

stanford-II.doc.Other_titles string none

ROLE booktitle stanford-II.doc stanford-II.doc.LC_Call_No string stanford-II.doc.Series string none

ROLE organization stanford-II.doc stanford-II.doc.LC_Call_No string

stanford-II.doc.Corporate_Name string none

ROLE pages stanford-II.doc stanford-II.doc.LC_Call_No string stanford-II.doc.Description string none

ROLE periodical stanford-II.doc stanford-II.doc.LC_Call_No string stanford-II.doc.Series string none

ROLE title stanford-II.doc stanford-II.doc.LC_Call_No string stanford-II.doc.Title string none

ROLE type-of-work stanford-II.doc stanford-II.doc.LC_Call_No string stanford-II.doc.Series string none

CONCEPT publication-ref stanford-II.doc stanford-II.doc.LC_Call_No string

CONCEPT journal-article-ref [SELECTION,stanford-II.doc,[=,stanford-II.doc.Series,"journal"]]

stanford-II.doc.LC_Call_No string

CONCEPT magazine-article-ref [SELECTION,stanford-II.doc,[=,stanford-II.doc.Series,"magazine"]]

stanford-II.doc.LC_Call_No string

ROLE magazine_name [SELECTION,stanford-II.doc,[=,stanford-II.doc.Series,"magazine"]]

stanford-II.doc.LC_Call_No string stanford-II.doc.Series string none

CONCEPT newspaper-article-ref [SELECTION,stanford-II.doc,[=,stanford-II.doc.Series,"newspaper"]]

stanford-II.doc.LC_Call_No string

ROLE newspaper_name [SELECTION,stanford-II.doc,[=,stanford-II.doc.Series,"newspaper"]]

stanford-II.doc.LC_Call_No string stanford-II.doc.Series string none

CONCEPT proceedings-paper-ref [SELECTION,stanford-II.doc,[=,stanford-II.doc.Series,"proceeding"]]

stanford-II.doc.LC_Call_No string

CONCEPT thesis-ref [SELECTION,stanford-II.doc,[=,stanford-II.doc.Series,"thesis"]]

stanford-II.doc.LC_Call_No string

CONCEPT doctoral-thesis-ref

[SELECTION,stanford-II.doc,[AND , [=,stanford-II.doc.Series,"doctoral"],[=,stanford-II.doc.Series,"thesis"]]]

stanford-II.doc.LC_Call_No string

CONCEPT master-thesis-ref

[SELECTION,stanford-II.doc,[AND, [=,stanford-II.doc.Series,"master"],[=,stanford-II.doc.Series,"thesis"]]]

stanford-II.doc.LC_Call_No string

CONCEPT technical-report-ref [SELECTION,stanford-II.doc,[=,stanford-II.doc.Series,"technical report"]]

stanford-II.doc.LC_Call_No string

CONCEPT technical-manual-ref [SELECTION,stanford-II.doc,[=,stanford-II.doc.Series,"technical manual"]]

stanford-II.doc.LC_Call_No string

CONCEPT computer-program-ref [SELECTION,stanford-II.doc,[=,stanford-II.doc.Series,"computer program"]]

stanford-II.doc.LC_Call_No string

CONCEPT cartographic-map-ref [SELECTION,stanford-II.doc,[=,stanford-II.doc.Series,"map"]]

stanford-II.doc.LC_Call_No string

Mappings for the LSDIS Ontology

CONCEPT publications lsdis.pub lsdis.pub.id string

ROLE title lsdis.pub lsdis.pub.id string lsdis.pub.title string none

ROLE authors lsdis.pub lsdis.pub.id string lsdis.pub.authors string none

ROLE published-in lsdis.pub lsdis.pub.id string lsdis.pub.published-in string none

ROLE subject lsdis.pub lsdis.pub.id string lsdis.pub.subjects string none

ROLE location-document lsdis_html.pub lsdis_html.pub.id string lsdis_html.pub.document string none

CONCEPT workflow-pub [SELECTION, lsdis.pub, [=,lsdis.pub.subjects,"WORKFLOW"]]

lsdis.pub.id string

CONCEPT information-modeling-pub [SELECTION, lsdis.pub, [=,lsdis.pub.subjects,"MODELING"]]

lsdis.pub.id string

CONCEPT metadata-pub [SELECTION, lsdis.pub, [=,lsdis.pub.subjects,"METADATA"]]

lsdis.pub.id string

CONCEPT integration-pub [SELECTION, lsdis.pub, [=,lsdis.pub.subjects,"INTEGRATION"]]

lsdis.pub.id string

CONCEPT consistency-pub [SELECTION, lsdis.pub, [=,lsdis.pub.subjects,"CONSISTENCY"]]

lsdis.pub.id string

APPENDIX 7.E: Algorithm for Lossy Translations

```
BEGIN   /* INITIALIZATION */
  T = (targetOnt, transRoles, transConstr, nontransConstr);
  mergedOnt = integrate(targetOnt, userOnt);
  createDefinedConcept(Q, nontransConstraints); /* Q is  exactly
                                                 non-translated constr. */
  planSet = translate(Q, Anything, Nothing);
  planSetWithLoss = calculateLoss(Term, plans); /* Calculates loss of
                                                 information in each plan */
  plan = leastLoss(planSetWithLoss); /* determines plan with least loss */
  final-plan = composePlan(transConstr, INTERSECTION, plan);
       /* combines with plan for translated constraints to give final answer */
END
/* Given a term, it returns a (simplified) set of plans containing all the
   possible translations for a term */
translate(Term, Top, Bottom): planSet
BEGIN
  IF subsumes(Term, Top) OR subsumes(Bottom, Term) OR Term=Nothing THEN
       RETURN EmptySet;
  IF belongs(Term, targetOnt) THEN
       RETURN Term;
  IF disjoint(Term, Bottom) THEN /* disjointness constraint */
     BEGIN
parentList = immediateParents(Term, mergedOnt)
```

```
RETURN translateList(INTERSECTION, parentList, Top, Term)
     END
  ELSE BEGIN /* Intersection of the immediate parents */
       parentList = immediateParents(Term, mergedOnt);
       planSet1 = translateList(INTERSECTION, parentList, Top, Term);
         /* Union of the immediate children */
       childList = immediateChildren(Term, mergedOnt);
       planSet2 = translateList(UNION, childList, Term, Bottom);
       planSet = union(planSet1, planSet2);
       RETURN planSet;
       END
END
/* Obtaining all the possible plans for the intersection/union (Op) of the
   terms included in TermList  */
translateList(Op, TermList, Top, Bottom): planSet
BEGIN
  IF length(TermList) = 0 THEN
     RETURN EmptySet
  planSet1 = translate(first(TermList), Top, Bottom);
  planSet2 = translateList(Op, restOf(TermList), Top, Bottom);
  IF planSet2 = EmptySet THEN
     RETURN plans1;
  planSet = EmptySet;
  FOR EACH plan1 IN planSet1 DO
       FOR EACH plan2 IN planSet2 DO
           BEGIN
              newPlan = composePlans(plan1, Op, plan2);
              newPlan = simplifyPlan(newPlan); /* performed by DL System */
              planSet = union(planSet, newPlan);
           END
  RETURN (planSet);
END
```

Chapter 8

AN ILLUSTRATIVE EXAMPLE

We now illustrate how information brokering techniques discussed in this book, can be used to obtain information relevant to an example information request.

1. ONTOLOGIES AND CONSTRUCTION OF METADATA

C-contexts or m-contexts corresponding to the query are constructed using terms from the appropriate domain specific ontology. As discussed earlier, c-contexts are constructed in cases where complex relationships between various terms are represented in the ontologies. M-contexts are constructed in all the other cases. The user ontology from which a c-context is constructed takes its terms from the WordNet 1.5 ontology and is illustrated in Figure 8.1. The terms PUBLICATION and PRINT-MEDIA are the same as those in the WN ontology, and the subtrees under these terms can be viewed in Figure 2.3. The metadata corresponding to the information request is as follows.

Query Metadata:

```
[title, author, document, describes.map] for
    (AND USGSPublication
        (ALL describes (AND REGION
            (ALL population (AND INTEGER (MIN 5000)))
            (ALL area (AND REAL (MIN 1000)))
            (FILLS land-cover-type "urban"))))
```

The roles, while not shown in Figure 8.1, are as follows:

- The roles population, area and land-cover-type are used to model properties of the concept REGION.

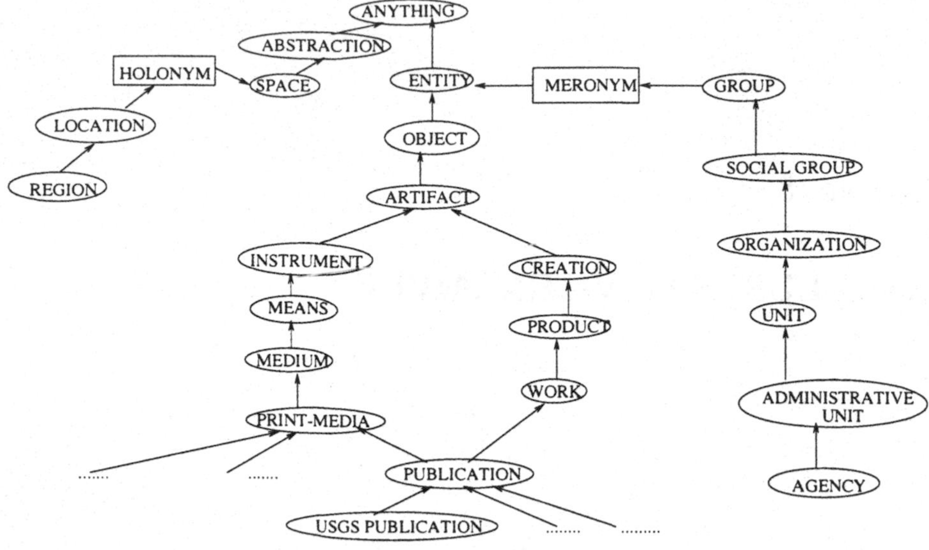

Figure 8.1. User Ontology: A Subset of WordNet 1.5

- The concept USGSPublication models publications distributed by the USGS. USGSPublication ≡ (**AND** PUBLICATION (**FILLS** has-agency "USGS"))
- The roles has-agency and describes are used to model properties of publications.

English Paraphrase:

Get the titles, authors and maps published by the United States Geological Service (USGS) of regions having a population greater than 5000 and area greater than 1000 acres and having an urban land cover.

The other ontologies used in this example are the Stanford-I (Appendix 7.A) and Stanford-II (Appendix 7.A) ontologies. They support ontological inferences based on concept descriptions. One ontology used in the example, however, does not support complex ontological inferences. The fire ontology is simply a collection of entities, attributes and relationships, and is illustrated in Figure 4.1. This is one reason why the MIDAS system only supports computation of m-contexts. The various terms of interest in this ontology are:

- The terms population, area and land-cover-type are defined as metadata attributes that are used to construct m-contexts.
- The concept REGION has as synonym the term Geological-Region. Terms such as Urban, Forest, Water are related to Geological-Region by a generalization hierarchy (Figure 4.13). They are based on the type of land cover obtained from the USGS Land Cover and Land Use Classification.

- Terms such as County, Block are related to Geological-Region by an aggregation hierarchy (Figure 4.13). They are based on the Population and Area classification by the US Census Bureau.

2. VOCABULARY BROKERING

We now illustrate translations of the query metadata into various ontologies along with the inter-ontology relationships used.

Fire ontology Consider the following inter-ontology relationships between terms in the user Fire ontologies:
region ≡ geological-region; population ≡ population; area ≡ area;
land-cover-type ≡ type; map ≡ map
Also, there is a transformer function, f: land-cover-type → type,
such that f("Urban") = "Low Density Urban Area".
Based on these relationships, the query metadata translation is:
<fire-ontology, [self, NULL, NULL, NULL, map],
{geological-region,
(**ALL** population (**AND** INTEGER (**MIN** 5000))),
(**ALL** area (**AND** REAL (**MIN** 1000))),
(**FILLS** type "Low Density Urban Area")},
{USGSPublication, (**ALL** describes **Anything**)}>
It must be noted that the translated part in this ontology is actually an m-context represented as a DL expression for the sake of uniformity. Issues of computing the m-context fall under the purview of **metadata brokering** and shall be discussed later in the section.

Stanford-I ontology The concept USGSPublication in the user ontology cannot be directly translated into this ontology. Hence the concept description is used to perform the translation.
USGSPublication ≡ (**AND** PUBLICATION (**FILLS** has-agency "USGS"))
PUBLICATION ≡ document; has-agency ≡ organization-name;
title ≡ title; author ≡ author; document-copy ≡ document.self
Also, there is a transformer function, f: has-agency → organization-name, s.t. f("USGS") = "United States Geological Service". Based on these relationships, the translation of query metadata is:
<Stanford-I, [describes, title, author, self, NULL],
{document,
(**FILLS** organization-name "United States Geological Service"),
(**ALL** describes **Anything**)},
{geological-region,
(**ALL** population (**AND** INTEGER (**MIN** 5000))),
(**ALL** area (**AND** REAL (**MIN** 1000))),
(**FILLS** type "Urban")} >

Stanford-II ontology The concept USGSPublication in the user ontology cannot be directly translated into this ontology. Hence the concept description is used to perform the translation.
USGSPublication ≡ (**AND** PUBLICATION (**FILLS** has-agency "USGS"))
PUBLICATION ≡ publication-ref; title ≡ title; author ≡ author;
document-copy ≡ document; has-agency ≡ organization
Also, there is a transformer function, f: has-agency → organization-name, s.t. f("USGS") = "United States Geological Service". Based on these relationships the translation of query metadata is:
<Stanford-II, [describes, title, author, document, NULL],
{publication-ref,
(**FILLS** organization "United States Geological Service"),
(**ALL** describes **Anything**)},
{geological-region, (**ALL** population (**AND** INTEGER (**MIN** 5000))),
(**ALL** area (**AND** REAL (**MIN** 1000))),
(**FILLS** type "Urban")}>

The next task of the vocabulary broker is to be able to combine various translations in such a way that all metadata constraints are satisfied. Based on the above translations, we observe that:

- From the Fire ontology, we obtain all regions that satisfy population and area constraints, and are urban areas.

- From the Stanford-I and Stanford-II ontologies, we obtain all documents published by the United States Geological Service that contain some piece of information. Note, it can be any information (without any constraints imposed on it) as long as it is non-empty or non-null information.

- The constraint (**ALL** describes (**AND** REGION ...)) has not been fully translated at either of the above ontologies. In fact, the constraint (**ALL** describes **Anything**) is computed at the Stanford-I and Stanford-II ontologies whereas the constraint (**AND** REGION ...) is computed at the Fire ontology. The complete constraint is then computed by the vocabulary broker which appropriately correlates objects returned by the Stanford-I and Stanford-II ontologies on one hand, and those returned by the Fire ontology on the other. This is an example of *intra-constraint correlation.*

3. METADATA BROKERING

We now discuss how metadata expressions (represented as m-contexts and c-contexts) computed by the vocabulary broker are evaluated by the respective metadata brokers underlying the various ontologies.

MIDAS system As discussed earlier, the metadata expression at this ontology is represented as a m-context. This affects the computation and combination of the various mappings corresponding to the ontological terms. The m-context presented below may be considered a view on base tables which belong to the various data repositories discussed in Chapter 4.

select region, map from Metadata_Table[1] where area > 1000
and population > 5000
and type = "Low Density Urban Area"

Since this is an m-context, mappings corresponding to the various metadata attributes, population, area, and type are not combined into a composite mapping before being evaluated. Thus, each metadata attribute is evaluated independently and the results are correlated by the metadata broker. The metadata computation takes place in two steps:

Join Correlation As discussed earlier, we have stored metadata corresponding to structured data in the Parameterized_Routine table (Table 4.7). These routines encode mappings between the metadata area and population, and the schema of **Census DB**, and are invoked by the MIDAS server. Let Obj_{area} and $\text{Obj}_{population}$ be the objects returned by the parameterized routines compute_area(1000) and compute_population(5000) after evaluation of constraints on the metadata area and population respectively. The final set of objects is then computed as:
$\text{Objects} = \text{Obj}_{area} \cap \text{Obj}_{population}$

Selection Correlation The metadata for image data are stored as procedural fields as illustrated in Figure 4.9. The routine compute_land_cover encodes mapping between the metadata type, and the underlying image data. For each region selected in the join correlation step, this routine computes the land cover. The metadata broker returns only those regions that are low density urban areas.

Stanford-I The metadata expression at this ontology is a c-context represented as a DL expression. As discussed in Chapter 7, mappings corresponding to concepts and roles in the DL expression are combined into a composite mapping which is then translated into the local repository query language for metadata computation. Consider the metadata expression at this ontology:

---

[1]In the MIDAS system we have made the closed world assumption. If we had made the Open World Assumption the corresponding SQL expression would be:

select region, map from Metadata_Table
where region not in (select region
from Metadata_Table
where area ≤ 1000 or population ≤ 5000 and type ≠ "Low Density Urban Area")

This would, however, not change the correlation plan in any manner.

```
[describes, title, author, self, NULL] for
(AND document
    (FILLS organization-name "United States Geological Service"))
```

The composite mapping corresponding to this expression is given by:

```
<[SELECTION, stanford-I.document,
  [=, stanford-I.document.publishing_agency,
    "United States Geological Service"]]
  [stanford-I.document.describes, stanford-I.document.title,
  stanford-I.document.name, stanford-I.document.loc, NULL]
  [string, string, string, string, NULL] >
```

The translation of the mapping into the local repository query language (SQL) is:

```
select describes, title, name, loc, "NULL"
from document
where publishing_agency = "%United States Geological Service%"
```

Stanford-II The metadata expression at this ontology is also a c-context, and is evaluated in a manner similar to that at Stanford-I. Consider the metadata expression at this ontology:

```
[describes, title, author, document, NULL] for
(AND publication-ref (FILLS organization "United States Geological Service"))
```

The composite mapping corresponding to this expression is given by:

```
<[SELECTION, stanford-II.doc,
  [=, stanford-II.doc.corporate_name "United States Geological Service"]]
  [stanford-II.doc.describes, stanford-II.doc.Title,
  stanford-II.doc.Author, stanford-II.doc.document, NULL]
  [string, string, string, postscript, NULL] >
```

The translation of the mapping into the local repository query language (Z39.50 protocol) is :

```
firstrecord = 1 & maxrecords = 1000 & dbname = BOOKS &
term_term_1 = "United States Geological Service" &
term_use_1 = Organization & port = 2210 & esn = F & host = ibm2.loc.gov
& attrset = BIB1 & rtype = USMARC & DisplayRecordSyntax = HTML
```

Correlation of the Extensions

The metadata broker is responsible for evaluating metadata constraints on the data underlying a particular ontology. The metadata broker returns the object instances satisfying the constraints in the metadata expression. The correlation is discussed below.

```
User_Query_Objects
= Objects('[title author document describes.map] for
          (AND USGSPublication
                   (ALL describes (AND REGION
                             (ALL population (AND INTEGER (MIN 5000)))
                             (ALL area (AND REAL (MIN 1000)))
                             (FILLS land-cover-type "urban")))))')
Fire_Objects
= Objects('[self, NULL, NULL, NULL, map] for
          (AND geological-region
                   (ALL population (AND INTEGER (MIN 5000)))
                   (ALL area (AND REAL (MIN 1000)))
                   (FILLS type "Low Density Urban Area"))')
Stanford-I_Objects
= Objects('[describes, title, author, self, NULL] for
          (AND document
                   (FILLS organization-name "United States Geological Service")
                   (ALL describes Anything))')
Stanford-II_Objects
= Objects('[describes, title, author, document, NULL]for
          (AND publication-ref
                   (FILLS organization "United States Geological Service")
                   (ALL describes Anything))')
```

As observed earlier, the fire ontology returns (geological) regions satisfying partial constraints, and the Stanford-I and Stanford-II ontologies return publications that describe some objects. Hence, an initial correlation plan would be:

Region_Objects = Fire_Objects

Publication_Objects = Stanford-I_Objects ∪ **Stanford-II_Objects**

User_Query_Objects = combine(**Region_Objects**, **Publication_Objects**)

The final correlation of the region and publication instances can be performed in the following manner:

```
User_Query_Objects
= select P1.title, P1.author, P1.document, R.map
from Publication_Objects P1
where P1.document NOT IN (select document
                  from Publication_Objects P2
                  where P2.describes NOT IN (select geological-region
                                   from Region_Objects R))
```

4. SUMMARY

In this chapter, we demonstrated with the help of an illustrative example, various techniques for information brokering discussed in this book. We demonstrated how pre-existing, independently defined ontologies can be used to specify information requests independent of representation and media of the underlying data. We demonstrated how our techniques enabled interoperation across different ontologies. The use of metadata to gather and correlate pieces of information stored in multiple data sources, and represented in different ontologies was also demonstrated.

Chapter 9

RELATED WORK

Several research efforts have addressed issues that arise in Information Brokering on the GII. We now present a discussion of some of the efforts and techniques, giving preferences to those efforts that resulted in demonstrable prototypes. A comparison of various systems that perform information brokering is presented at the end of this chapter.

1. THE SIMS PROJECT

The overall goal of the SIMS (Arens et al., 1993) project at ISI is to provide intelligent access to heterogeneous, distributed information sources (databases, knowledge bases, flat files, programs, etc.), while insulating human users and application programs from the need to be aware of the location of the sources, their query languages, organization, size, etc. A model of the application domain is created using a knowledge representation system to establish a fixed vocabulary describing objects in the domain, their attributes, and relationships among them. For each information source, a model is constructed that indicates the data-model used, query language, network location, size estimates, etc., and describes the contents of its fields in relation to the domain model.

Queries to SIMS are written in the high-level uniform language of the domain model, a language independent of the specifics of the information sources. Queries need not contain information describing which sources are relevant, where they are located, or how information obtained from different sources should be combined or manipulated. SIMS uses a planning system to determine how to retrieve and integrate the data necessary to answer a query. The planner selects appropriate information sources and orders sub-queries to appropriate information sources, to determine an optimized plan for distributed execution of the query. The architecture of the SIMS system is illustrated in Figure 9.1 and the functionality of various components are described as follows.

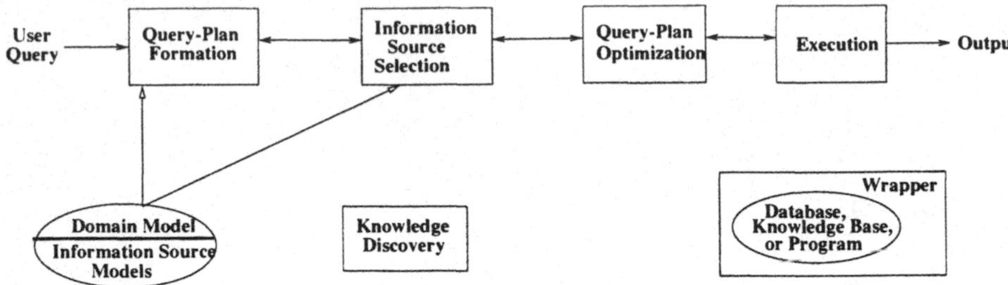

Figure 9.1. The Architecture of the SIMS System

Modeling SIMS provides a uniform way to describe the application domain and information sources to the system. This functionality is found in the *metadata broker* component of the brokering architecture, which is responsible for maintaining the vocabulary of the information domain.

Information Source Selection Given a query, SIMS performs the following actions.

- It determines information sources containing data relevant for answering the query. This functionality is provided by the *mappings composer* and *correlation server* in the *metadata broker* component of the brokering architecture. The components also utilize mapping information stored in the *metadata repository*.
- For those concepts mentioned in the query that have no matching information source, it determines if any knowledge encoded in the domain model (such as relationship to other concepts), can be used to determine relevant information sources. This functionality can be found in the *metadata broker*, which is responsible for retrieving the definition of a term based on other terms in a domain vocabulary.

Query Plan Optimization SIMS constructs a plan for retrieval of information requested by the query (or some equivalent transformation of it). The plan involves steps such as sending a specific query to some information source, and joining results from different information sources. This functionality can be found in the *correlation server*, a component of the *metadata broker*, which is responsible for decomposition of metadata expressions, and correlation of the data retrieved. SIMS also exploits learned knowledge about the contents of databases to perform semantic query optimization.

Execution The fourth component executes the optimized plan. To support execution, SIMS makes use of *wrappers* that mediate between it and the information sources themselves. This functionality is provided by the *translator* and *wrapper* in the *metadata system* component of the brokering architecture.

The SIMS system performs brokering primarily at the level of information content, and partially at the level of vocabulary. The user can query heterogeneous data repositories by using high level expressions in the SIMS knowledge representation language. Since the focus in the SIMS system is within one application domain, it lacks *inter-domain* adaptability. However, it does support *intra-domain adaptability* via query reformulation operations, that use knowledge encoded in the form of interrelationships between concepts for selection of relevant information sources.

2. THE TSIMMIS PROJECT

TSIMMIS (Garcia-Molina et al., 1995) - The Stanford-IBM Manager of Multiple Information Sources - is a system for integrating information. It offers a data model and a common query language, that are designed to support integration of information from many different sources. It also offers tools for generating automatically, components needed to build systems for integrating information. The TSIMMIS system (Figure 9.2) has the mediator (Wiederhold, 1992) architecture, the principle components of which, may be described as follows.

- A "lightweight" object model called Object-Exchange Model (OEM), serves to convey information among components, and is so-called because it does not require strong typing of its objects. It has a rich collection of structures including nested structures, and handles missing and related information gracefully. Meta-information or *metadata*, i.e., information about the structures and meanings of terms used in the data is also supported by the model. This is similar to the object model used to store domain vocabularies in the *metadata repository* component of the brokering architecture.

- A common query language called "Lightweight Objects REpository Language" (LOREL) is used to link components and query substructures in OEM objects. This is similar to the language used by the *metadata broker* to represent metadata query expressions.

- *Translators* ("wrappers") allow LOREL queries to be converted into source-specific queries. The information sources are not necessarily databases, and it is an important goal of the project to cope with radically different information formats in a uniform way. Translators provide the functionality provided by *translators* and *wrappers* in the *metadata system* component of the brokering architecture.

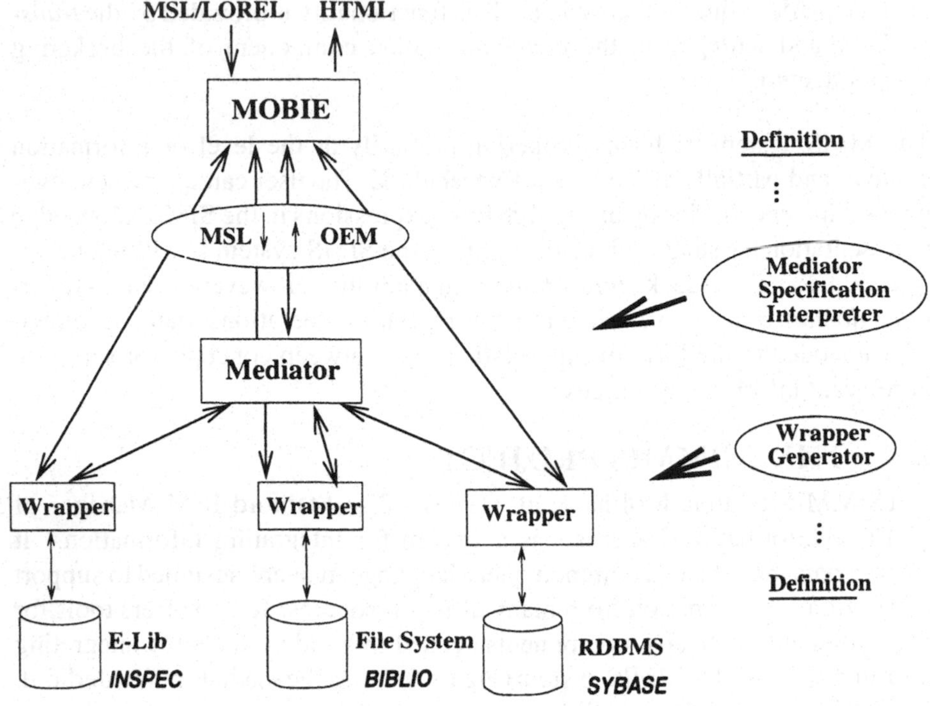

Figure 9.2. The Architecture of the TSIMMIS System

- Mediators talk LOREL, both to ask and answer queries. Some example mediators used in TSIMMIS are:
  - A *union mediator* takes queries and passes them unchanged to two or more sources. It integrates the answers from each source.
  - A *join mediator* creates a view of two or more sources (possibly other mediators). The view contains an object for each pair of objects, one from each of the two sources, that agree in certain values.

  The above functionality is provided by the *correlation server* in the *metadata broker* component of the brokering architecture. The correlation server is responsible for decomposition of metadata expressions and correlation of data after the metadata has been computed.

- Methodologies are being developed for generating classes of translators and mediators automatically from simple descriptions of their functions.

The emphasis in the TSIMMIS system is that of automatic generation of translators and mediators for accessing and combining information in heterogeneous data sources. When these are indeed generated, they constitute a system which performs brokering at the level of information content where a high level data model (OEM) and language (LOREL) may be used to query information in data repositories storing structured or unstructured data. The problem of using different vocabularies to construct LOREL expressions describing similar information is not tackled. Thus, TSIMMIS does not support vocabulary brokering.

3. THE INFORMATION MANIFOLD PROJECT

The Information Manifold (IM) (Levy et al., 1995; Levy et al., 1996) at AT&T Research is a system for retrieval and organization of information from disparate (structured and unstructured) information sources. The architecture of IM is based on a knowledge base containing a rich domain model that describes the properties of information sources. The user can interact with the system by browsing the information space (which includes both the knowledge base and information sources). The presence of information source descriptions enables the user to pose high-level queries based on the content of the information sources. The architecture of the Information Manifold system (Figure 9.3) may be described as follows.

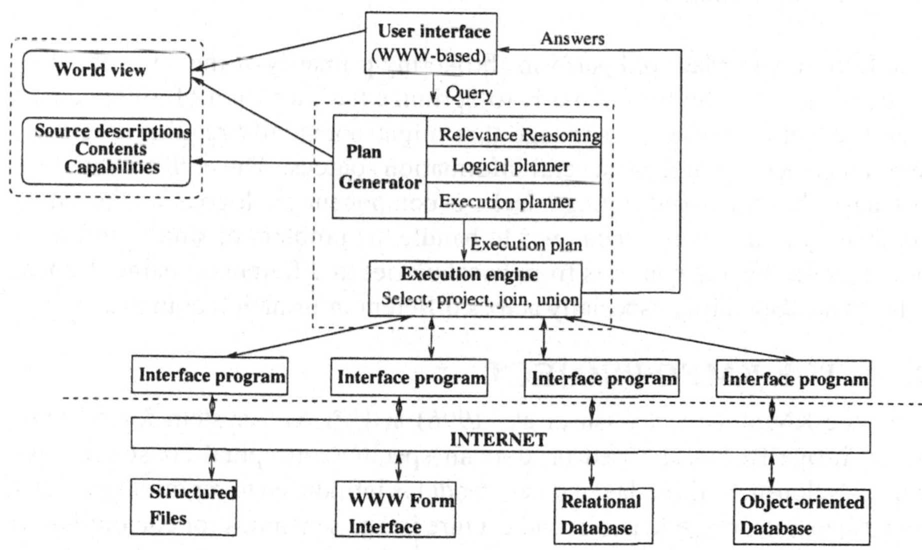

Figure 9.3. Architecture of the Information Manifold System

Domain Model This is a knowledge base describing the domain model. It also contains descriptions of information sources including their contents and capabilities. This corresponds to the vocabulary of a domain, the capability of querying which is provided by the *metadata broker* component of the brokering architecture.

Plan Generator This helps map the user query specified in a high level language using concepts and relations in the domain model, to relations (and views) exported by the information sources. This is the main focus of this system. Algorithms that use descriptions of contents and capabilities to prune the set of information sources required to answer a query, have been developed. This functionality is provided by the *correlation server* and *mappings composer* in the *metadata broker* component of the brokering architecture.

Execution Engine This component is responsible for the actual execution of query plans and talks to the **interface programs** through which there is actual interaction with the information sources. For every information source, there is an interface program that accepts any query executable at that source and returns the appropriate answer. Whereas the interface program provides a functionality similar to that of the *wrapper*, the execution engine may be thought of as responsible for translation and distributed execution of the high-level plan, a functionality similar to that of the *correlation server* and *translator*. These are present in the *metadata system* component of the brokering architecture.

The Information Manifold performs brokering primarily at the level of information content. The focus here is to optimize the execution of a user query expressed in a high-level language that might potentially require access to, and integrate content from several information sources. The architecture does not have the functionality (e.g., lacks a component analogous to the *inter-vocabulary relationships manager*) to handle the problem of similar information expressed using concepts from vocabularies in different domains. Hence, it lacks in adaptability especially across different information domains.

4. THE KMED PROJECT

In the KMed project (Hsu et al., 1996) at UCLA, a system for content-based Image Retrieval based on domain specific conceptual constructs, has been developed. A three-layered data model is introduced to represent physical images, extract image features, and capture image semantics for content-based image retrieval. This model consists of a Representational Layer (RL), a Semantic Layer (SL), and a Knowledge Layer (KL). The architecture of the system based on this data model is illustrated in Figure 9.4, and reflects the two levels of brokering enunciated in the brokering architecture. The KMed architecture may be described as follows.

Representation Layer (RL) The raw images and interesting object contours are captured in the representation layer. Related images are organized

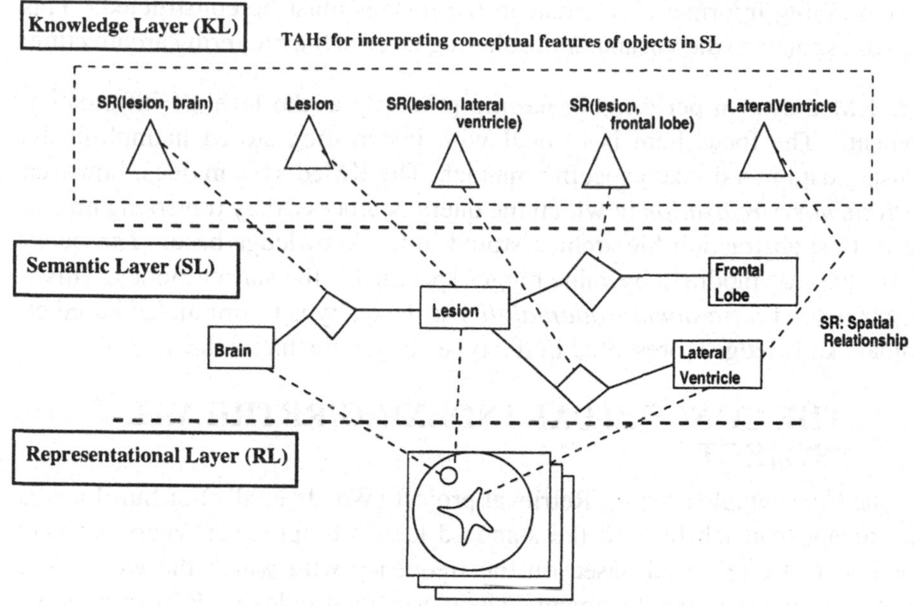

Figure 9.4. Architecture of the KMed System

and stored in various stacks for efficient access. This layer essentially corresponds to repositories available on the GII.

Semantic Layer (SL) This layer mimics the user's conceptual view of the image content, providing the framework and guidelines for extracting image features. Object oriented techniques are used to model image content extracted from image representations in the RL. In the SL, object features and relationships among objects are captured and modeled. Hierarchical, temporal, spatial (e.g., CONTAIN, OVERLAP, etc.), and evolutionary relationships (e.g., EVOLVE, SPLIT, FUSE) among image objects are captured and represented in the SL. The focus here is to abstract from representational details (i.e., details of image representations) in the RL, and capture information content. This corresponds to brokering at the layer of information content in the brokering architecture.

Knowledge Layer (KL) This layer conceptualizes image features and semantics. A knowledge-based Type Abstraction Hierarchy is used to represent domain knowledge for supporting approximate and conceptual query answering, involving similar-to predicates, spatial semantic operators, and conceptual terms. The model allows the expression of spatial, temporal and evolutionary objects captured by a set of snapshots taken over time. The domain model essentially expresses the **vocabulary** from which expressions describing information content in the images must be constructed. This corresponds to the vocabulary brokering layer in the brokering architecture.

The KMed system performs brokering primarily at the level of information content. The focus here is to deal with information stored in multimedia (image) data in a domain specific manner. The KMed system does, however, perform *query relaxation* in which the query is processed by traversing up and down type abstraction hierarchies stored in the knowledge base. The query constraints are modified by value ranges specified at the various nodes. This is an example of *intra-domain adaptability* as the query is reformulated based on domain knowledge represented in the type abstraction hierarchies.

5. THE CONCEPTUAL INDEXING/RETRIEVAL PROJECT

The Conceptual Indexing/Retrieval project (Woods et al.,) at Sun Labs is an attempt to reach beyond the standard keyword approach where relevant documents are retrieved based on the frequency with which the words in a user query occur in the document. The Conceptual Indexing Project uses the knowledge of concepts and their interrelationships to find correspondences between concepts in a query and those appearing in the text of a document. The technology, which is called "Precision Content Retrieval", is composed of two parts and is described next.

Conceptual Indexing This part builds structured conceptual taxonomies of phrases extracted from the indexed retrieval. Using knowledge bases of general semantic facts, structured conceptual taxonomies (a type of semantic network) can be constructed from words and phrases. These words and phrases can be extracted automatically from text and parsed into conceptual structures. The taxonomy can be organized by the most-specific-subsumer (MSS) relationship, where each concept is linked to the most specific concepts that subsume it. The process of extracting phrases from documents may be viewed as a type of *domain and media specific metadata extraction*, as identified in the *metadata system* component of the brokering architecture. The conceptual structured taxonomies and knowledge bases might be considered as *domain specific vocabularies* characterizing a set of documents.

Dynamic Passage Retrieval This part finds specific passages and ranks them according to their relevance to the query. Terms in a query are individually matched with corresponding concepts in the taxonomy together with their subconcepts. For example, given the general semantic facts that "washing" is a kind of "cleaning" and "car" is a kind of "automobile", an algorithmic classification system can classify "car washing" as a kind of "automobile cleaning". A query for "automobile cleaning" will immediately retrieve hits for "car washing".

The notion of an interlingua in NLP was first introduced by Schank (Schank, 1972; Schank, 1975) in his work on conceptual dependencies. This notion has been used in this project, albeit in a limited manner in the form of structured conceptual taxonomies and the most specific subsumer relationship. The brokering being carried out here, is a special case **vocabulary brokering** identified in the brokering system architecture. In essence, there is brokering taking place between two component vocabularies:

- vocabulary of the document collection characterized by extracted phrases and sentences
- vocabulary of the knowledge bases containing semantic facts.

The process of *linguistic morphological analysis* and *lexical taxonomic subsumption* used to organize phrases extracted from the documents, as structured conceptual taxonomies, based on semantic facts in knowledge bases, might be viewed as a special kind of **vocabulary brokering**. This is an example of information brokering based on the *text body* of a document as opposed to an entity attribute schema built on top of a document collection.

6. HERMES: A HETEROGENEOUS REASONING AND MEDIATOR SYSTEM

The HERMES project (Subrahmanian et al.,) is a heterogeneous reasoning and mediator system being developed at the University of Maryland that provides a framework for developing integrated mediated systems. The prime motivation behind the design of HERMES is to modularize the activities involved in creating a mediator. The backbone of the HERMES system is a logic-based language for representing these mediators. The system interoperates between database management systems; implementation of reasoning paradigms developed by third parties; and indexing schemes operating over B-trees, spatial and multimedia data. The architecture of HERMES (Figure 9.5) has the following components.

Heterogeneous User Interface It consists of a framework wherein end-users may pose a conjunctive query A1 & ... & An, using a variety of input forms. Part of the query can be pictorially specified by selection of images displayed on the screen. However, functions for image matching and underlying database schemas based on which the query is constructed, is either known to the end-user, or may be obtained from the *yellow pages server*. In our approach, the concepts used to construct the query are obtained from *domain specific ontologies*.

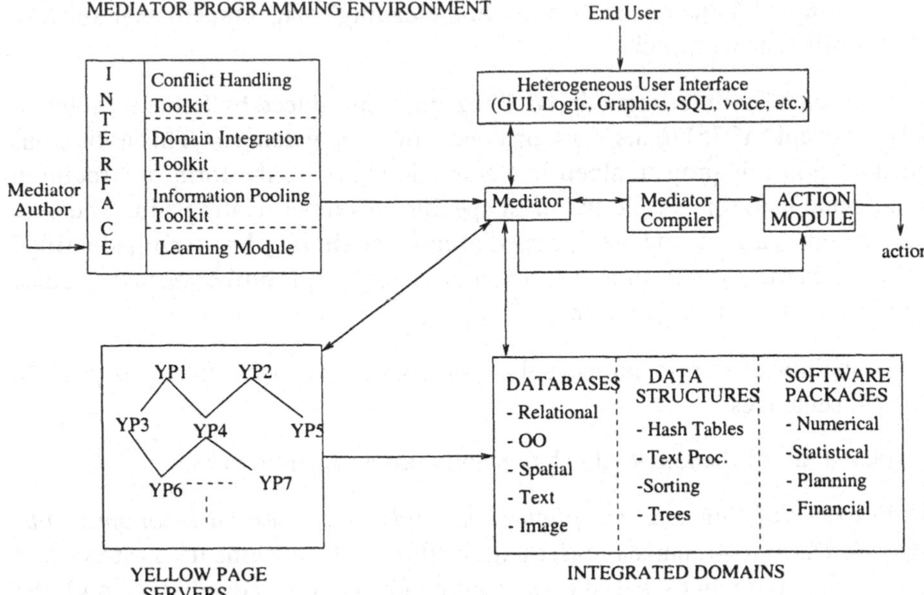

Figure 9.5. The HERMES System Architecture

Mediator Programming Environment The key function of the environment is to enable a mediator author to design and implement a code that integrates data across data resources and reasoning systems. The tools offered by the environment fulfill the following three functions.

Domain Integration This is the process of adding another data source or reasoning system to HERMES so that mediation code may access the information/software contained within. In our architecture, this corresponds to the design of *wrapper* and *translator* sub-components of the *metadata brokering* component.

Conflict Resolution This is the process of resolving conflicts that may exist between information reported from different data sources. In our architecture, *mappings* between concepts in domain specific ontologies and underlying data structures in the data sources are used to abstract out potential conflicts.

Information Pooling There might be multiple ways of coalescing information from multiple data sources to obtain new information that could not be inferred from a single database by itself. In our architecture, this functionality is supported by the *mappings composer* and *correlation server*.

Yellow Page Servers A basic problem that arises when creating a mediator is that often, one may not know which data source contains the information desired or how it can be accessed. A *hierarchy* of yellow pages servers assist the mediator author in accessing the above information. A mediator can invoke a function called *topic* that takes a string representation of the topic, and returns a list of functions and types, that can be used to access information related to a topic in a particular domain.

7. INFOSCOPES: MULTIMEDIA INFORMATION SYSTEMS

InfoScopes (Jain, 1996) are multimedia information systems that allow users to access information independent of locations and types of data sources, and provide a unified picture of information. Due to their ability to represent information at different levels of abstractions, these systems must recover and assimilate information from disparate sources. These systems allow a closer and detailed view of the data to an observer who wants to extract information. The VIMSYS data model (Gupta et al., 1991) described a hierarchical representation of the data (Figure 9.6), using various levels of semantic interpretation that may satisfy needs of InfoScopes.

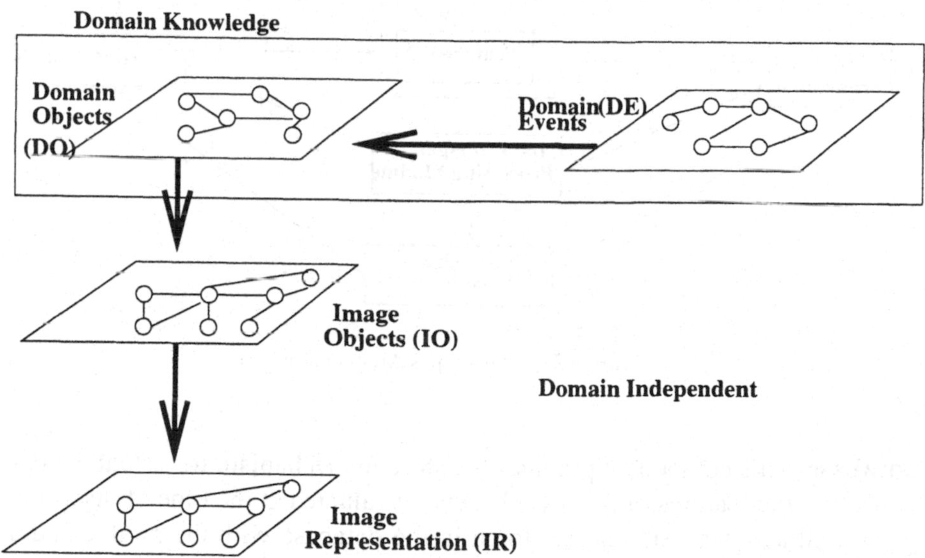

Figure 9.6. A Four Layered Data Model

At the image representation (IR) level, the actual image data is stored. Image objects (such as lines and regions) are extracted from the image and stored in the image object (IO) layer, with no domain interpretation. Each of these objects may be associated with a domain object (DO) in the DO layer. The semantic interpretation is incorporated in these objects. The domain event (DE) layer can then associate objects of the DO layer with each other, providing semantic representation of spatial or temporal relationships. This hierarchy provides a mechanism for translating higher-level semantic concepts into content-based queries using the corresponding image data. In our approach, objects at the IR level correspond to *data*, objects in the IO level correspond to *domain independent metadata*, and objects at the DO and DE levels correspond to *domain specific metadata*, and are similar to concepts obtained from domain specific ontologies. Thus, queries based on object similarity can be generated, without requiring the user to specify low-level image structures and attributes of objects. The architecture of InfoScopes has four basic modules (Figure 9.7):

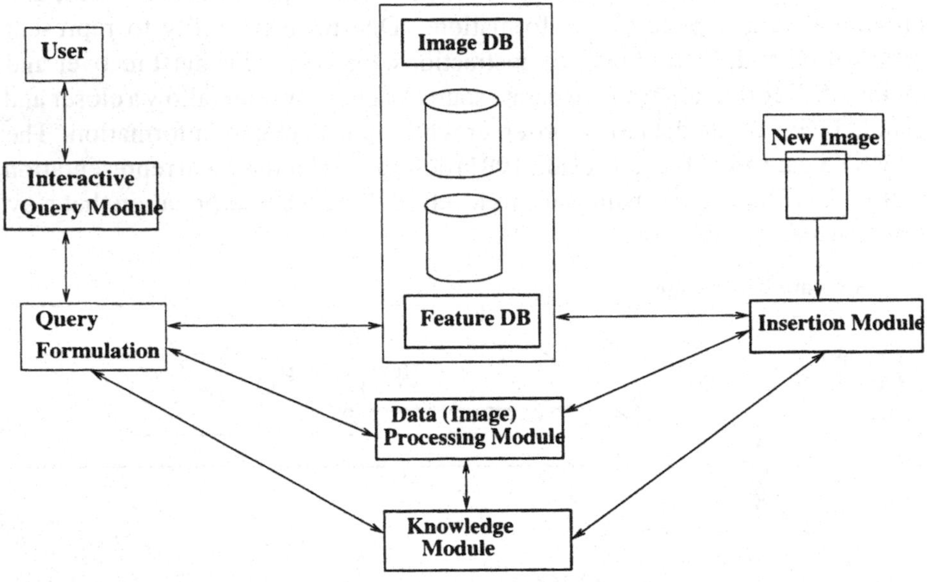

Figure 9.7. Infoscopes Architecture

Database This component provides the storage mechanism for actual data as well as the features of the data. Features evaluated at the time of insertion, as well as meta features are stored in the database with their value and a reference to the image containing it. Similarly, every image in the database references the features which it contains. Data is represented in the database at different levels of the hierarchy. This allows well- defined relationships between the actual images, image objects, and real-world domain objects which they represent. In addition to storing actual image data, segmented regions of the image which pertain to domain objects are also identified and stored.

Insertion Module This component allows insertion and evaluation of images in the database. In Infoscopes, data must be analyzed and appropriate features extracted for insertion into the database. It is during the input process that values will be computed for all important features in the image. Features in the image will be examined to determine which domain object they correspond to (if any). Computer vision techniques are required to analyze data and input it into the system. Unfortunately, computer vision techniques can automatically extract features only in certain limited cases. In many applications, semi-automatic techniques need to be developed for extracting features. Domain knowledge plays a very important role in defining the processes used for automatic feature extraction.

Interface This module is used interactively by the user to retrieve information from the database. A user will articulate his request using symbolic and visual tools provided by the system. Also, the system must decide the best display methods. Queries may either be completely user-specified, or generated based on the results of previous queries. The latter type consists of feature values derived from an actual image that has been retrieved for the user. During the retrieval process, a similarity value is assigned to data which satisfies constraints of the generated query. In our approach, a high level query may be specified using concepts from domain specific ontologies, and computing loss of information corresponding to the answer returned.

Knowledge Base This component maintains domain-specific information for each specific application. This information is used at every step of processing in this system. In our approach, this corresponds to the knowledge encoded in a *domain specific ontology*. Domain object descriptions are used to locate and evaluate important features in the image. These features are then stored in the database, using the specified representational scheme. During query processing, user-specified descriptions must be mapped into relevant feature values and value-ranges. These correspond to *mappings* between concepts and data structures that are stored as metadata in our approach. The knowledge module also maintains data describing how to create and alter these feature values, and how to evaluate the similarity of images and individual features.

8. THE CONTEXT INTERCHANGE NETWORK PROJECT

The overall goal of the Context Interchange (COIN) Project at the Sloan School of Management, MIT (Goh et al., 1995) is to provide intelligent integration of contextually (semantically) heterogeneous data. The context interchange approach defines a strategy for integrating *data sources* and *data receivers* across traditional organizational and functional boundaries. This approach requires that the interoperating component systems describe unambiguously, the assumptions they make in the routine representation and interpretation of data. The collection of assumptions pertaining to a source or receiver forms its *context*. The various components of the architecture (Figure 9.8) are as follows:

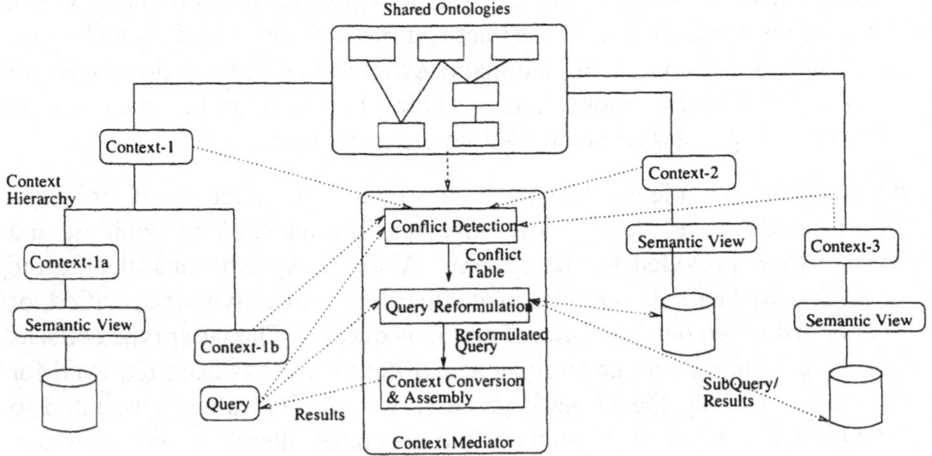

Figure 9.8. The Context Interchange Network Architecture

Context Mediator This is responsible for intercepting queries submitted by a data receiver. It performs the following functions:

Conflict Detection The context mediator compares the contexts of data sources and receivers to determine if semantic conflicts exist and if so, what conversions need to take place to resolve them. This is referred to as conflict detection, and arises after a pair-wise comparison of the contexts involved. In our approach, we would formulate the query based on ontological terms, and conflict detection would boil down to appropriately choosing, combining (*mappings composer*), and decomposing (*correlation server*) contexts.

Query Reformulation The original query is reformulated to form subqueries, which can be directly executed by the selected data sources. This functionality may be found in the *correlation server, translator*, and *wrapper* components of the *metadata system*. The context mediator may also engage in *context-based query optimization*.

Context Conversion and Reassembly Finally, the intermediate answers obtained from the component systems are merged together and converted to the context expected by the receiver who initiated the query.

This functionality is found in the *correlation server*, and in our approach we would transform results in the language of the ontology *wrt* which the query was originally specified.

Shared Ontologies Meaningful comparison of contexts is only possible if they are described with reference to some conceptualization of underlying domains shared among the component systems. These shared domain models are called shared ontologies, and form the basis of context interoperation supported in the project, a perspective shared by us in our approach.

9. A COMPARISON OF BROKERING SYSTEMS

We now discuss various systems viewed from the perspective of information brokering, and compare and contrast the various approaches taken. The brokering architecture presented in Chapter 3 is used as the reference point for this discussion. The level at which (*wrt* the architecture) the systems perform brokering is first identified. The types of metadata used, the models and languages used to represent them, and the approach taken for their computation are discussed (summarized in Table 9.1). We then discuss the "SEA" properties (Chapter 3) satisfied by each of the systems (summarized in Table 9.2).

9.1 LEVEL OF INFORMATION BROKERING

As discussed earlier, we perform brokering at two levels: *information content* and *vocabulary*. Systems that deal with issues of abstracting out representational details of data, into intensional metadata descriptions, or mapping metadata terms/descriptions into underlying data repositories, fall in the first category. On the other hand, systems have been developed, whose main focus is to provide an environment for developing programs (extractors, mediators) that enable brokering. Systems that transform metadata descriptions based on relationships between terms within and across domain ontologies belong to the second category. Of the various systems discussed in earlier sections of this chapter, an informal categorization based on the above criteria may be as follows:

- *Environments for developing Mappings*: The HERMES and TSIMMIS systems are geared towards specification and generation of mediators and mapping programs.
- *Brokering at the level of information content*: Systems such as SIMS, Information Manifold, KMed, Context Interchange, and InfoScopes belong to this category.
- *Brokering at the level of Vocabulary*: Systems such as SIMS, KMed, and Conceptual Indexing Project fall into this category.

The Conceptual Indexing Project is a system that deals with textual documents. It maps phrases to domain specific taxonomies and navigates taxonomies in the process of answering a query. Since navigation of a taxonomy results in replacing a term with other related terms, the above system belongs to the latter category (brokering at the level of vocabulary).

We now discuss systems that belong to the first category. The main focus in these systems is the ability to map domain specific metadata terms/descriptions to underlying data repositories. It may be noted that some of these systems also belong to the second category. An interesting fact to be noted, however, is that they perform brokering at the vocabulary level within an information domain and this is used to enable a better mapping of domain specific metadata terms/descriptions to underlying data repositories.

The Context Interchange Network system performs brokering by comparison of contexts. Contexts are collections of meta-attributes obtained from a shared ontology, and brokering essentially consists of executing "conversion functions" that transforms values of meta-attributes from one context to another. This type of brokering is limited to be at the *attribute level* and is not able to handle cases where the values of the attributes may be objects or entities. The InfoScopes and KMed systems map domain specific metadata terms/descriptions at both, the *entity* and *attribute* levels, to features in images whereas, the other systems map them to structured data.

The Information Manifold system performs reasoning based on the information content of the repositories which are captured as intensional metadata descriptions. It uses constraint matching (satisfiability and disjoint concepts) to prune off irrelevant data repositories and construct optimal plans to retrieve and correlate data across the various repositories. In addition, Information Manifold enhances the optimality of plans generated by modeling capabilities of individual data repositories. A distinct disadvantage of these approaches is that in case there is no data retrieved, the system cannot adapt itself to retrieve related data. For example, if a query about "students" does not return any data, the system could return data about "graduate students".

The above drawback is tackled in the SIMS and KMed systems, which reformulate metadata descriptions/queries based on terminological relationships or type abstraction hierarchies, and process them again. In the SIMS system, the focus is on the generation of more optimal plans, whereas in the KMed system, the emphasis is on getting more but related data from the system.

9.2 METADATA: TYPES, LANGUAGES AND COMPUTATION

The types of metadata used by various systems are influenced by the level at which they support information brokering. Since most systems surveyed supported brokering at the level of information content, they invariably sup-

Brokering System	Level of Brokering	Types of Metadata	Models/ Languages	Metadata Computation
Conceptual Indexing	domain specific content/ vocabulary	domain specific	semantic nets	Bottom-Up
HERMES	information content	content based	logic based language	Top-Down
TSIMMIS	domain specific content, capabilities	domain specific	OEM, LOREL	Top-Down
COIN	domain specific content	domain specific contexts	object model, C-SQL	Top-Down
InfoScopes	domain specific content	domain specific	VIMSYS Query By Example	Bottom-Up
Information Manifold	domain specific content, constraints, capabilities	domain specific site descriptions	rich model high level language	Top-Down
KMed	domain specific content/ vocabulary	domain specific	TAHs, E-R models SQL	Bottom-Up
SIMS	domain specific content/ vocabulary	domain specific	frame/ slot LOOM	Top-Down

Table 9.1. A Comparison of Various Brokering Systems

ported computation of domain specific metadata. An interesting commonality that emerges, is that almost all systems support construction of metadata descriptions based on a domain model or some kind of shared ontologies. In particular, systems that support vocabulary brokering also support some kind of ontological inferences and constraint matching on the metadata descriptions.

The exceptions to the above are the HERMES and TSIMMIS systems. As discussed earlier, the HERMES and TSIMMIS systems are designed to support semi-automatic generation of wrappers and mediators. Hence, the type of metadata supported are those that enable generation of mediators and wrappers, and might be domain specific. However, these metadata are hand-crafted by the application programmer and hence there is no support for domain specific ontologies, as is the case with the other systems.

The type of metadata used, on the other hand, also determines the type of data/meta model used to represent the various metadata. If ontological inferences are performed on metadata descriptions, then the meta model would have a lot of semantically rich constructs. Examples of meta models are E-R models, frame-slot models supporting subsumption, semantic nets, etc. An interesting and more general graph based data model is used in TSIMMIS where the emphasis is on integration of semi-structured data.

Lastly, as the scope of the system is enlarged, a top-down methodology is adopted for metadata computation if the underlying data is stored with a predefined structure and format. As discussed earlier, this enhances extensibility of the system. In cases where the data is relatively less structured (text) or unstructured (image), systems such as KMed, InfoScopes, and Conceptual Indexing, depend on bottom-up computation of metadata.

9.3 ARCHITECTURAL PROPERTIES

We have discussed earlier the "SEA" properties (Chapter 3), which an information brokering architecture should satisfy. In this section, we discuss to what extent systems surveyed earlier in this chapter, have these properties.

Brokering System	Scalability	Extensibility	Adaptability
Conceptual Indexing	depends on most specific subsumer	No	Partial within domain
HERMES	N/A	Yes	No
TSIMMIS	depends on execution plan	Yes, due to mediator generation	No
COIN	depends on execution plan	No, due to O(N(N-1)) mappings	No
InfoScopes	depends on feature indexing	No	No
Information Manifold	depends on execution plan	Yes	No
KMed	depends on TAHs, indexing	No, some TAHs based on data	Partial based on relaxation
SIMS	depends on execution plan	Yes	Partial, query reformulation

Table 9.2. A Comparison of Brokering System Properties

9.3.1 SCALABILITY OF THE VARIOUS SYSTEMS

The key factor determining scalability of the various systems is the approach adopted by each of them for computing various types of metadata. There are systems that adopt a bottom-up approach, which facilitates creation of indexing structures, thus enhancing their scalability. On the other hand, systems that employ a top-down approach and provide access to a large number of data repositories, depend on computation of execution plans for enhancing their scalability.

The KMed, Conceptual Indexing, and InfoScopes systems, essentially extract metadata from the underlying textual and image data. The KMed and InfoScopes Systems support indexing of extracted image features. The KMed system also supports query reformulation. Part of the type abstraction hierarchies also, are constructed based on the underlying data distribution and hence, enhance scalability of the query reformulation process. The scalability in the Conceptual Indexing Project depends on the efficiency of the most specific subsumer operation, as metadata extracted from text documents are mapped to classification taxonomies.

The other category of systems compute metadata in a top-down manner and their scalability depends on how the computation is mapped to an optimized execution plan. The SIMS system depends on approaches based on domain knowledge-based query reformulation to generate an optimal execution plan. The Information Manifold system does content-based constraint matching and reasons about capabilities of underlying data repositories to generate an optimal query execution plan. The TSIMMIS system also reasons about capabilities of repositories to generate an optimal plan.

9.3.2 EXTENSIBILITY OF THE VARIOUS SYSTEMS

The extensibility of various systems is also dependent on the approach adopted for metadata computation. In general, extensibility of systems dependent on bottom-up metadata computation, is limited in comparison with systems that depend on top-down metadata computation. Extensibility can be at different levels of granularity: addition of more data, addition of more data types/schema elements, and addition of more data repositories. We discuss extensibility of various systems *wrt* to the addition/removal of data repositories.

In the SIMS system, models of data repositories, called information source models, are linked to terms in the domain model. In the Information Manifold system, individual site descriptions are those that relate views supported by individual data repositories to relations in a rich domain model. Among all these systems, the Context Interchange Network system is the least extensible, as whenever a new data repository is added, conversion functions need to be defined between its context and contexts of all the other data repositories of the system. In all the above cases, the rest of the system is not affected during the process.

The TSIMMIS and HERMES systems have an interesting approach and seek to automate the development of wrappers, translators, and mediators. The users express mediator functionality in a high level logic based language, and the system locates the relevant code from a pre-stored library and helps generate code for the mediator required by the user. This helps to enhance extensibility of the system.

9.3.3 ADAPTABILITY OF THE VARIOUS SYSTEMS

As discussed earlier, most of the systems surveyed perform brokering at the level of information content. However, some of them support reformulation of query expressions based on domain specific relationships for a variety of purposes. SIMS does reformulation to help compute a more optimal execution plan. KMed performs reformulation to provide some answer to the user. The Conceptual Indexing project on the other hand, transforms keyword-based queries *wrt* a classification taxonomy, in order to increase the precision of results.

10. SUMMARY

In this chapter, we discussed a set of information brokering prototypes. We compared and contrasted these systems to our information brokering approach. The systems' architectural properties, the level of brokering (information content or vocabulary based) supported by them, and types of metadata computation used, provided the basis for comparison.

Chapter 10

CONCLUSION

As information retrieval systems become global in their scope, and as a wide variety of multimedia data is being created and managed, information overload is emerging as the critical issue that threatens to swamp the emerging "information economy". *Information brokering*, defined as the process of arbitration between information consumers and providers, was identified as a key solution to address information overload. Heterogeneity of information and scaling-up of information systems to a global level, were identified as the main factors behind information overload. This led us to identify various levels at which brokering might take place, and define an architecture that reflects the multiple levels.

Our approach identified three levels, *representation, information content*, and *vocabulary*, at which brokering needs to be performed. Brokering at each level results in progressive reduction of the volume of data/information that needs to be handled. Different types of metadata capturing information content to various degrees were identified, and their use for information brokering was discussed in the context of systems presented in this book. An information brokering architecture that supports brokering across the three levels was proposed. A set of "SEA" (scalability, extensibility, and adaptability) properties of an architecture that are desirable in the presence of information overload were defined, and trade-offs between them were discussed. Metadata that captured information content in a *domain* and *application specific* manner was the focus of this book. We demonstrated the advantages of using domain specific metadata for media-independent correlation and vocabulary-based interoperation across different domains. The specific contributions of this work are as follows.

A Metadata-based Architecture We presented an architecture for information brokering, where brokering is supported at the levels of representation, information content, and vocabulary. The architecture is validated by the following prototype systems:

- The *InfoHarness System* (Chapter 4) performs brokering primarily at the level of representation, and partially at the level of information content, and consists only of the metadata brokering component.
- The *MIDAS System* (Chapter 4) performs brokering primarily at the level of information content, and partially at the vocabulary level, both performed by the metadata brokering component.
- The *InfoSleuth System* (Chapter 6) is an agent-based system that implements information brokering techniques at the level of information content, and partially at the vocabulary level within the context of a common domain ontology.
- The *OBSERVER System* (Chapter 7) performs brokering at the vocabulary level, and those forms of brokering at the level of information content necessary to support vocabulary brokering. The system consists of both the metadata and vocabulary brokering components.

Media-Independent Correlation The MIDAS system demonstrated use of *domain specific metadata* to effect correlation of information independent of the medium of representation (e.g., structured and image data). Domain specific metadata is also viewed as a schema on the underlying digital data, which lacks the structuring present in relational, object-relational, and object-oriented databases. This schema is represented in an object-relational model in the MIDAS system.

Characterization of Schematic Heterogeneities One approach to capturing information content in digital data, is by representing domain specific metadata as the schema in a structured database. An important intermediate step is to identify and resolve possible schematic heterogeneities that might arise. Assuming an object-based model, we identify possible schema heterogeneities (Chapter 5). An approach for resolution of these heterogeneities by abstraction of representational details, and mapping schema elements to terms in *domain specific ontologies* was also presented.

Capturing Information Content in Structured Data Once the underlying representational details have been abstracted out, two aspects of this problem are as follows (Chapter 5):

- The ability to *reason* about the information. Our approach maps underlying database schema to terms in domain specific ontologies. Descriptions consisting of these terms (c-contexts) may be used to represent information specific to a particular database. Inference operations on c-contexts (possibly involving certain ontological inferences), were presented to reason about the information content.

- The ability to map these descriptions or c-contexts to the underlying schema of the database. A set of operations and an algebra over those operations were presented. These operations helped map c-contexts to the underlying data. The algebra is based on inference operations on the c-contexts. We illustrated, with the help of examples, how these descriptions capture *extra information* not stored in the database schema.

Vocabulary Brokering Similar information content may be characterized by c-contexts using different but related terms from different domain specific ontologies. We presented algorithms to perform vocabulary brokering in the presence of heterogeneous vocabularies (Chapter 7). These algorithms transform a c-context constructed using terms from one ontology, into c-contexts constructed using terms from other related ontologies:

- The first algorithm uses *synonym* relationships between terms across ontologies and generates translations. It also combines translations in a manner that semantics of the original c-context are preserved.
- The second algorithm uses *hyponym* and *hypernym* relationships between terms across ontologies, to transform a c-context constructed from terms in one ontology into those from another. The resulting loss of information of the candidate translations is measured, and the one with the least loss of information is chosen.

Characterization of Trade-Offs Support for information brokering at various levels leads to trade-offs which we characterize as *infrastructural trade-offs* and *information trade-offs*.

- In the *InfoHarness* system, we identified trade-offs between various schemas used to store the metadata. In the *MIDAS* system, we identified trade-offs between the pre-computation and run-time computation of metadata. These are examples of infrastructural trade-offs.
- In the *OBSERVER* system, we identified the trade-off based on loss of information from using different terms and translations. This is an example of an information trade-off.

The problem of information brokering is a difficult one, and we have identified and characterized various trade-offs in this book. Whereas the current emphasis is on optimization of infrastructural trade-offs, as the information overload on the GII explodes, and processes for abstraction of representational details and capturing information content are better understood, future research shall witness an increasing emphasis on information trade-offs. We have, in this book (via identification of the brokering levels and techniques for optimizing the information trade-offs), presented a road-map for the transition from infrastructure to information oriented issues.

References

Abiteboul, S. (1997). Querying Semi-Structured Data. In *Proceedings of ICDT*.

Anderson, J. and Stonebraker, M. Sequoia 2000 Metadata Schema for Satellite Images, in (Klaus and Sheth, 1994).

Arens, Y., Chee, C., Hsu, C., and Knoblock, C. (1993). Retrieving and Integrating Data from Multiple Information Sources. *International Journal of Intelligent and Cooperative Information Systems*, 2(2).

Baader, F. and Hollunder, B. (1991). KRIS: Knowledge Representation and Inference System. *SIGART Bulletin*, 2(3).

Batini, C., Lenzerini, M., and Navathe, S. (1986). A comparative analysis of methodologies for database schema integration. *ACM Computing Surveys*, 18(4):323–64.

Bayardo, R., Bohrer, W., Brice, R., Cichocki, A., Fowler, G., Helal, A., Kashyap, V., Ksiezyk, T., Martin, G., Nodine, M., Rashid, M., Rusinkiewicz, M., Shea, R., Unnikrishnan, C., Unruh, A., and Woelk, D. (1997). Infosleuth: Semantic Integration of Information in Open and Dynamic Environments. In *Proceedings of the 1997 ACM International Conference on the Management of Data (SIGMOD), Tucson, Arizona.*

Blanco, J., Illarramendi, A., and Goñi, A. (1994a). Building a Federated Database System: An approach using a Knowledge Based System. *International Journal on Intelligent and Cooperative Information Sy stems*, 3(4).

Blanco, J., Illarramendi, A., Goñi, A., and Perez, J. (1994b). Using a terminological system to integrate relational databases. *Information Systems Design and Hypermedia, Cepadues-Editions.*

Bohm, K. and Rakow, T. Metadata for Multimedia Documents, in (Klaus and Sheth, 1994).

Boll, S., Klas, W., and Sheth, A. (1998). Overview on Using Metadata to manage Multimedia Data. In Sheth, A. and Klas, W., editors, *Multimedia Data Management*. McGraw-Hill.

Borgida, A. (1992). From Type Systems to Knowledge Representation. *International Journal of Intelligent and Cooperative Information Systems*, 1(1).

Borgida, A. and Brachman, R. (1993). Loading Data into Description Reasoners. In *Proceedings of 1993 ACM SIGMOD*.

Borgida, A., Brachman, R., McGuinness, D., and Resnick, L. (1989). CLASSIC: A structural data model for objects. In *Proceedings of ACM SIGMOD-89*.

Brachman, R. and Scmolze, J. (1985). An overview of the KL-ONE knowledge representation system. *Cognitive Science*, 9(2).

Bray, T., Paoli, J., and Sperberg-McQueen, C. M. Extensible markup language (xml) 1.0. http://www.w3.org/TR/REC-xml.

Breitbart, Y., Olson, P., and Thompson, G. (1986). Database Integration in a Distributed Heterogeneous Database System. In *Proceedings of the 2nd IEEE Conference on Data Engineering*.

Chen, F., Hearst, M., Kupiec, J., Pederson, J., and Wilcox, L. Metadata for Mixed-Media Access, in (Klaus and Sheth, 1994).

Collet, C., Huhns, M., and Shen, W. (1991). Resource Integration using a Large Knowledge Base in Carnot. *IEEE Computer*.

Czejdo, B., Rusinkiewicz, M., and Embley, D. (1987). An approach to Schema Integration and Query Formulation in Federated Database Systems. In *Proceedings of the 3rd IEEE Conference on Data Engineering*.

Dayal, U. and Hwang, H. (1984). View definition and Generalization for Database Integration of a Multidatabase System. *IEEE Transactions on Software Engineering*, 10(6).

Deen, S., Amin, R., Ofori-Dwumfuo, G., and Taylor, M. (1985). The architecture of a Generalised Distributed Database System PRECI*. *IEEE Computer*, 18(4).

Deerwester, S., Dumais, S., Furnas, G., Landauer, T., and Hashman, R. (1990). Indexing by Latent Semantic Indexing. *Journal of the American Society for Information Science*, 41(6).

Excite. http://www.excite.com.

Garcia-Molina, H., Papakonstantinou, Y., Quass, D., Rajaraman, A., Sagiv, Y., Ullman, J., and Widom, J. (1995). The TSIMMIS Approach to Mediation: Data Models and Languages. In *Proceeding of NGITS (Next Generation Information Technologies and System)*.

Glavitsch, U., Schauble, P., and Wechsler, M. Metadata for Integrating Speech Documents in a Text Retrieval System, in (Klaus and Sheth, 1994).

Goh, C., Madnick, S., and Siegel, M. (1995). Ontologies, contexts and mediation: Representing and reasoning about semantic conflicts in heterogeneous and autonomous systems. Technical Report CISL-95-04, Working paper #3848, Sloan School of Management.

Goñi, A., Blanco, J., and Illarramendi, A. (1995). Connecting Knowledge Bases with Databases: A complete mapping relation. In *Proc. of the 8th ERCIM Workshop. Trondheim, Norway.*

Goñi, A., Illarramendi, A., Blanco, J., and Mena, E. An approach to define an Optimal Cache for a Multidatabase System. unpublished manuscript.

Gruber, T. (1993). A translation approach to portable ontology specifications. *Knowledge Acquisition, An International Journal of Knowledge Acquisition for Knowledge-Based Systems*, 5(2).

Gruber, T. (1994). Theory BIBLIOGRAPHIC-DATA. http://www-ksl.stanford.edu/knowledge-sharing/ontologies/html/bibliographic-data/index.html.

Guarino, N. (1993). The Ontological Level. In *The 16th Wittgenstein Symposium.*

Guha, R. (1991). Contexts: A Formalization and some Applications. Technical Report STAN-CS-91-1399-Thesis, Department of Computer Science, Stanford University.

Guha, R. V. (1990). Micro-theories and Contexts in Cyc Part I: Basic Issues. Technical Report ACT-CYC-129-90, Microelectronics and Computer Technology Corporation, Austin TX.

Gupta, A., Weymouth, T., and Jain, R. (1991). Semantic queries with pictures: The VIMSYS model. In *Proceedings of the 17th VLDB Conference.*

Hammer, J. and McLeod, D. (1993). An approach to resolving Semantic Heterogeneity in a Federation of Autonomous, Heterogeneous, Database Systems. *International Journal of Intelligent and Cooperative Information Systems.*

Hanson, E. (1988). Processing Queries against Database Procedures: A Performance Analysis. In *Proceedings of the ACM SIGMOD 1988 Annual Conference.*

Heimbigner, D. and McLeod, D. (1985). A federated architecture for Information Managment. *ACM Transactions on Office Information Systems*, 3(3).

Hsu, C. C., Chu, W. W., and Taira, R. K. (1996). A Knowledge Base Approach for Retrieving Images by Content. *IEEE Transactions on Knowledge and Data Engineering*, 8(4).

Huhns, M., Jacobs, N., Ksiezyk, T., Shen, W. M., Singh, M., and Cannata, P. (1992). Enterprise information modeling and model integration in carnot. In *Enterprise Modeling: Proceedings of the First International Conference.*

Huhns, M. and Singh, M. (1998). *Readings in Agents*. Morgan Kaufmann.

Inc., V. (1994). Verity developer kit (vdk) api reference guide v1.0.3.

Jain, R. (1996). Infoscopes: Multimedia Information Systems. In Furht, B., editor, *Multimedia Systems and Techniques*, chapter 7, pages 217–254. Kluwer Academic Publishers, Norwell, MA.

Jain, R. and Hampapuram, A. Representations of Video Databases, in (Klaus and Sheth, 1994).

Jhingran, A. (1988). A Performance Study of Query Optimization Algorithms on a Database System Supporting Procedures. In *Proceedings of the 14th VLDB Conference.*

Kahle, B. and Medlar, A. (1991). An Information System for Corporate Users: Wide Area Information Servers. *Connexions - The Interoperability Report*, 5(11).

Kahng, J. and McLeod, D. (1997). Dynamic classificational ontologies: Mediators for sharing in cooperative federated database systems. In Papazoglou, M. and Schlageter, G., editors, *Cooperative Information Systems: Current Trends and Directions.*

Kashyap, V. (1997). *Information Brokering over Heterogeneous Digital Data: A Metadata-based Approach.* PhD thesis, Rutgers University, New Brunswick, USA.

Kashyap, V. and Sheth, A. (1994). Semantics-based Information Brokering. In *Proceedings of the Third International Conference on Information and Knowledge Management (CIKM).*

Kashyap, V. and Sheth, A. (1995). Schematic and Semantic Similarities between Database Objects: A Context-based Approach. Technical Report TR-CS-95-001, LSDIS Lab, University of Georgia. Available at http://lsdis.cs.uga.edu/˜amit/66-context-algebra.ps; An abridged version (Kashyap and Sheth, 1996) appears in the VLDB Journal.

Kashyap, V. and Sheth, A. (1996). Semantic and Schematic Similarities between Databases Objects: A Context-based approach. *The VLDB Journal*, 5(4):276–304.

Kim, W., Choi, I., Gala, S., and Scheevel, M. (1993). On resolving schematic heterogeneity in multidatabase systems. *Distributed and Parallel Databases - An International Journal*, 1:251–279.

Kim, W. and Seo, J. (1991). Classifying Schematic and Data Heterogeneity in Multidatabase Systems. *IEEE Computer*, 24(12).

Kiyoki, Y., Kitagawa, T., and Hayama, T. A meta-database System for Semantic Image Search by a Mathematical Model of Meaning, in (Klaus and Sheth, 1994).

Klaus, W. and Sheth, A. (1994). Metadata for digital media. *SIGMOD Record, special issue on Metadata for Digital Media*, W. Klaus, A. Sheth, eds., 23(4).

Klusch, M. (1999). *Intelligent Information Agents.* Springer.

Krishnamurthy, R., Litwin, W., and Kent, W. (1991). Language features for Interoperability of Databases with Schematic Discrepancies. In *Proceedings of 1991 ACM SIGMOD.*

Larson, J., Navathe, S., and Elmasri, R. (1989). A Theory of Attribute Equivalence in Databases with Application to Schema Integration. *IEEE Transactions on Software Engineering*, 15(4).

Lassila, O. and Swick, R. R. Resource description framework (rdf) model and syntax specification. http://www.w3.org/TR/REC-rdf-syntax/.

Lenat, D. and Guha, R. V. (1990). *Building Large Knowledge Based Systems : Representation and Inference in the Cyc Project*. Addison-Wesley Publishing Company Inc.

Levy, A., Rajaraman, A., and Ordille, J. (1996). Querying Heterogeneous Information Sources Using Source Descriptions. In *Proceedings of the 22nd VLDB Conference*.

Levy, A., Srivastava, D., and Kirk, T. (1995). Data Model and Query Evaluation in Global Information Systems. *Intelligent Information Systems*, 5(2).

Litwin, W. and Abdellatif, A. (1986). Multidatabase Interoperability. *IEEE Computer*, 19(12).

MacGregor, R. (1987). A deductive pattern matcher. In *Proceedings AAAI-87*.

McCarthy, J. (1993). Notes on formalizing Context. In *Proceedings of the International Joint Conference on Artificial Intelligence*.

Mena, E., Illarramendi, A., and Blanco, J. M. (1994). MAGIC: An Interface for generating mapping information between object-based and relational systems. In *Information Systems Design and Hypermedia*. Cepadues-Editions.

Mena, E., Kashyap, V., Illarramendi, A., and Sheth, A. (1996a). Managing Multiple Information Sources through Ontologies: Relationship between Vocabulary Heterogeneity and Loss of Information. In *Proceedings of the workshop on Knowledge Representation meets Databases in conjunction with European Conference on Artificial Intelligence*.

Mena, E., Kashyap, V., Illarramendi, A., and Sheth, A. (1998). Domain specific ontologies for semantic information brokering on the global information infrastructure. In *Proceedings, International Conference on Formal Ontology in Information Systems (FOIS)*.

Mena, E., Kashyap, V., Sheth, A., and Illarramendi, A. (1996b). OBSERVER: An approach for query processing in global information systems based on interoperation across pre-existing ontologies. In *Proceedings of the First IFCIS International Conference on Cooperative Information Systems (CoopIS '96)*.

Michalski, R. (1993). Inferential Theory of Learning as a Conceptual Basis for Multistrategy Learning. *Machine Learning*, 11(2/3).

Miller, G. (1995a). WordNet: A Lexical Database for English. *Communications of the ACM*, 38(11).

Miller, G. (1995b). World Wide Web interface to WordNet 1.5. http://www.cogsci.princeton.edu/~wn/w3wn.html.

of Congress, T. L. (1995). Library of Congress WWW Z39.50 gateway. http://lcweb.loc.gov/z3950/.

Ordille, J. and Miller, B. (1993). Distributed Active Catalogs and Meta-Data Caching in Descriptive Name Services. In *Proceedings of the 13th International Conference on Distributed Computing Systems*.

Ouksel, A. and Naiman, C. (1993). Coordinating Context Building in Heterogeneous Information Systems. *Journal of Intelligent Information Systems*.

Ouksel, A. and Sheth, A. (1999). Semantic interoperability in global information systems. *SIGMOD Record, special issue*, A. Ouksel, A. Sheth, eds., 28(1).

Ouksel, M. A. and Ahmed, I. (1999). Ontologies are not the Panacea for Data Integration: A Flexible Coordinator to mediate Context Construction. *Distributed and Parallel Databases - An International Journal*, 7(1):7–35.

Paepcke, A., Chang, C., Garcia-Molina, H., and Winograd, T. (1998). Interoperability for Digital Libraries Worldwide. *Communications of the ACM*, 41(4).

Piepenburg, S. (1994). Easy MARC: A simplified guide to creating catalog records for library automation systems: Pre-format integration.

Rusinkiewicz, M., Sheth, A., and Karabatis, G. (1991). Specifying Interdatabase Dependencies in a Multidatabase Environment. *IEEE Computer*, 24(12).

Salton, G. (1989). *Automatic text processing*. Addison-Wesley.

Schank, R. (1972). Conceptual Dependency: A theory of natural language understanding. *Cognitive Psychology*, 3.

Schank, R. (1975). The primitive ACTs of Conceptual Dependency. In *TINLAP-1*.

Sciore, E., Siegel, M., and Rosenthal, A. (1992). Context Interchange using Meta-Attributes. In *Proceedings of the CIKM*.

Sellis, T. (1987). Efficiently supporting Procedures in Relational Database Systems. In *Proceedings of the ACM SIGMOD 1987 Annual Conference*.

Shah, K. and Sheth, A. (1999). *IEEE Internet Computing*.

Sheth, A. (1999). Changing focus on Interoperability: From System, Syntax, Structure to Semantics. In Goodchild, M., Egenhofer, M., Fegeas, R., and Kottman, C., editors, *Interoperating Geographic Information Systems*. Kluwer Academic Publishers.

Sheth, A. and Kashyap, V. (1992). So Far (Schematically), yet So Near (Semantically). *Invited paper in Proceedings of the IFIP TC2/WG2.6 Conference on Semantics of Interoperable Database Systems, DS-5*. In IFIP Transactions A-25, North Holland, 1993.

Sheth, A. and Kashyap, V. (1996). Media-independent Correlation of Information. What? How? In *Proceedings of the First IEEE Metadata Conference*. http://lsdis.cs.uga.edu/~kashyap/IEEEpaper.

Sheth, A., Kashyap, V., and LeBlanc, W. (1995). Attribute-based access of Heterogeneous Digital Data. In *Proceedings of the Workshop on Web Access to Legacy Data, Fourth International WWW Conference.*

Sheth, A., Kashyap, V., and Lima, T. (1999). Semantic Information Brokering: How can a Multi-Agent approach help ? In *Proceedings of the Third International Workshop (CIA-99) on Cooperative Information Agents.*

Sheth, A. and Larson, J. (1990). Federated Database Systems for managing Distributed, Heterogeneous and Autonomous Databases. *ACM Computing Surveys*, 22(3).

Sheth, A., Rusinkiewicz, M., and Karabatis, G. (1992). Using Polytransactions to manage Independent Data. In *Database Transaction Models.*

Shklar, L., Shah, K., and Basu, C. (1995a). The InfoHarness Repository Definition Language. In *Proceedings of the Third International WWW Conference.*

Shklar, L., Shah, K., Basu, C., and Kashyap, V. (1995b). Modelling Heterogeneous Information. In *Proceedings of the Second International Workshop on Next Generation Information Technologies (NGITS '95).*

Shklar, L., Sheth, A., Kashyap, V., and Shah, K. (1995c). Infoharness: Use of Automatically Generated Metadata for Search and Retrieval of Heterogeneous Information. In *Proceedings of CAiSE '95*. Lecture Notes in Computer Science, #932.

Shoens, K., Luniewski, A., Schwartz, P., Stamos, J., and Thomas, J. (1993). The Rufus System: Information Organization for Semi-Structured Data. In *Proceedings of the 19th VLDB Conference.*

Speel, P. (1995). *Selecting Knowledge Representation Systems.* PhD thesis, University of Twente, Enschede, the Netherlands.

Stonebraker, M. et al. (1985). Extending a Data Base System with Procedures. Technical Report UCB/ERL/M85/59, University of California, Berkeley.

Stonebraker, M., Jhingran, A., Goh, J., and Potamianos, S. (1990). On Rules, Procedures, Caching and Views in Database Systems. In *Proceedings of the 1990 ACM SIGMOD International Conference on Management of Data.*

Stonebraker, M. and Rowe, L. (1986). The Design of POSTGRES. In *Proceedings of the ACM SIGMOD 1986 Annual Conference.*

Subrahmanian, V. et al. HERMES: Heterogeneous Reasoning and Mediated System. http://www.cs.umd.edu/projects/hermes/overview/paper/index.html.

van Rijsbergen, C. J. (1979). *Information Retrieval.* Butterworths and Co. Ltd.

von Luck, K., Nebel, B., Peltason, C., and Schmiedel, A. (1987). The anatomy of the BACK system. Technical Report KIT Report 41, Technical University of Berlin, Berlin, F.R.G.

Wiederhold, G. (1992). Mediators in the architecture of future information systems. *IEEE Computer*, 25(3).

Wiederhold, G. (1996). *Intelligent Integration of Information*. Kluwer Academic Publishers.

Woods, W. A. et al. Conceptual Indexing for Precision Content Retrieval. http://www.sunlabs.com/research/knowledge/index.html.

Yu, C., Sun, W., Dao, S., and Keirsey, D. (1991). Determining relationships among attributes for Interoperability of Multidatabase Systems. In *Proceedings of the 1st International Workshop on Interoperability in Multidatabase Systems*.

Index